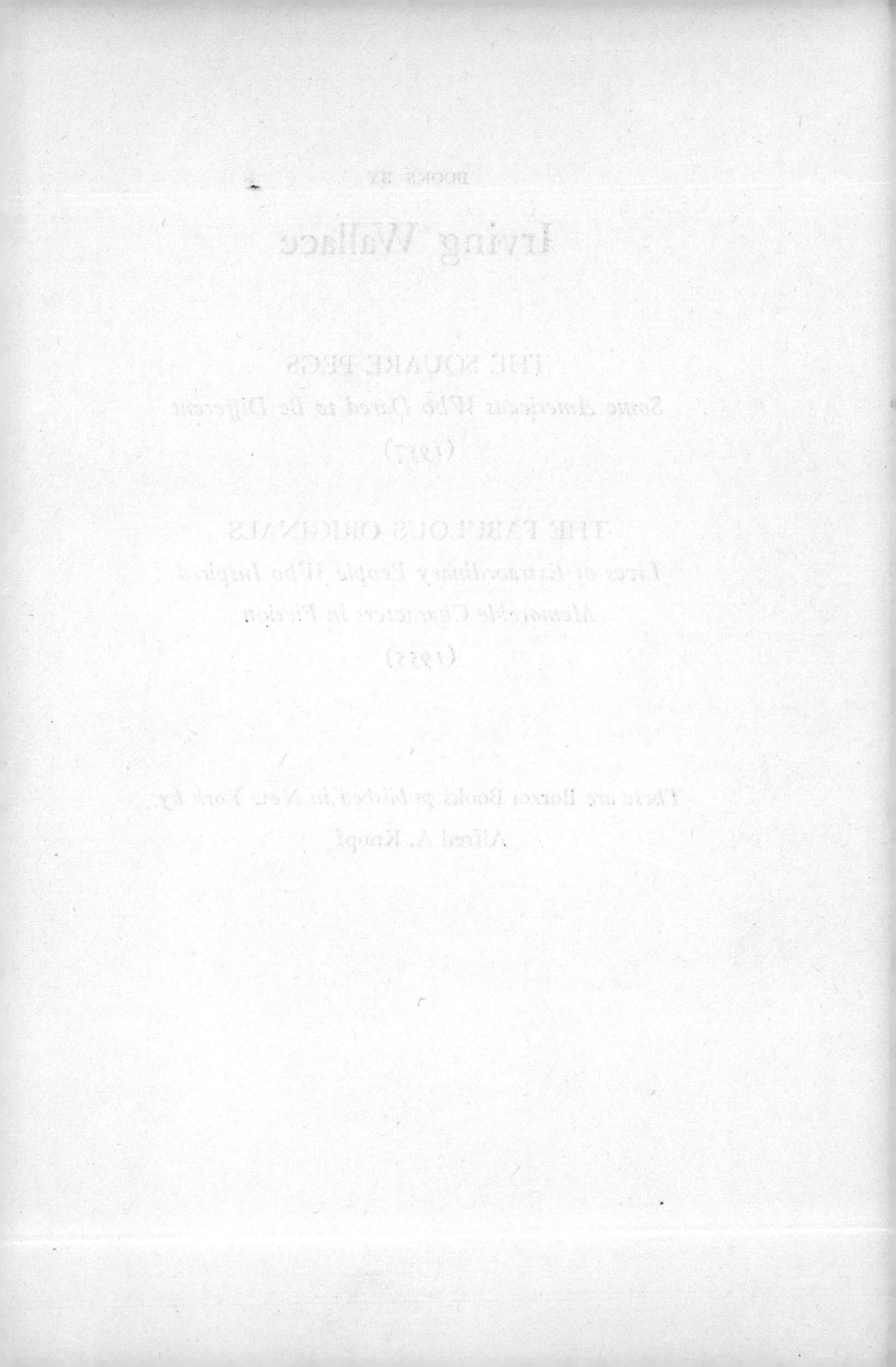

BOOKS BY

Irving Wallace

THE SQUARE PEGS

Some Americans Who Dared to Be Different

(1957)

THE FABULOUS ORIGINALS

Lives of Extraordinary People Who Inspired Memorable Characters in Fiction

(1955)

These are Borzoi Books *published in New York by* Alfred A. Knopf

The Square Pegs

THE SQUARE PEGS

Some Americans Who Dared to Be Different

by Irving Wallace

NEW YORK

Alfred · A · Knopf

1 9 5 7

L. C. CATALOG CARD NUMBER: 57-7552

THIS IS A BORZOI BOOK,
PUBLISHED BY ALFRED A. KNOPF, INC.

FIRST EDITION

FOR

MY MOTHER AND FATHER

"They were learning to draw," the Dormouse went on, "and they drew all manner of things—everything that began with an M—"

"Why with an M?" said Alice.

"Why not?" said the March Hare.

LEWIS CARROLL

Contents

I· In Defense of the Square Peg . . . *Wherein we meet Wilbur Glenn Voliva, who believed the earth was flat, and wherein we learn the need for encouraging individualism and nonconformity.* 3

II· The King of Thirty-Sixth Street . . . *Wherein we meet Baron James A. Harden-Hickey, American ruler of Trinidad, who became an authority on the art of suicide.* 25

III· The Man Who Was Phileas Fogg . . . *Wherein we meet George Francis Train, millionaire member of the Commune, who was the first man to travel around the world in eighty days.* 61

IV· The Free Lover Who Ran for President . . . *Wherein we meet Victoria Woodhull, stockbroker, spiritualist, and prostitute, who competed with Ulysses S. Grant for tenancy of the White House.* 100

V· The Forty-Niner Who Abolished Congress . . . *Wherein we meet Joshua Norton, self-appointed Emperor of the United States and Protector of Mexico, who issued orders to Abraham Lincoln.* 148

VI· The Lady Who Moved Shakespeare's Bones . . . *Wherein we meet Delia Bacon, schoolteacher frustrated in love, who became the implacable enemy of the Bard of Avon.* 168

VII · THE EXPLORER OF THE HOLLOW EARTH . . . *Wherein we meet John Cleves Symmes, hero of the War of 1812, who planned an expedition into the interior world through holes in the North and South poles.* 223

VIII · THE EDITOR WHO WAS A COMMON SCOLD . . . *Wherein we meet Anne Royall, widow and author, who interviewed a Chief Executive while he was in the nude.* 243

IX · THE FIRST IN THE EAST . . . *Wherein we meet Timothy Dexter, merchant prince and foe of grammar, who sent coals to Newcastle and published a book without punctuation.* 267

A NOTE ON *Principal Sources* 313

Index FOLLOWS PAGE 315

Illustrations

Baron James A. Harden-Hickey *facing page* 48
(Brown Brothers)

George Francis Train 49
(Brown Brothers, from original negative in the Meserve Collection)

Victoria Woodhull 112
(Bettmann Archive)

Emperor Norton I 113
(California State Library)

Delia Bacon 208
(New York Public Library)

Captain John Cleves Symmes 209
(Library of the Ohio Historical Society)

Lord Timothy Dexter 272
(Newburyport [Massachusetts] Public Library)

The Square Pegs

I

In Defense of the Square Peg

". . . a square person has squeezed himself into the round hole."

SYDNEY SMITH

On an autumn afternoon in 1932, when I was sixteen years old and filled with wonder, I sat in an office in the medieval American community of Zion City, Illinois, and heard a strange and wealthy man named Wilbur Glenn Voliva tell me that the world was not round. "The world is flat like a saucer," Voliva said. "The North Pole is in the center of the flat earth, and the South Pole is a great ice barrier around the rim. The sky is a solid dome above, like an inverted blue basin, and the sun, the moon, the stars hang from it like a chandelier from a ceiling."

This theory, with which I was already familiar, made a deep impression on me, not so much for its scientific stimulation as for its oddity. It was to this incredible interview that I like to attribute my first interest in the role played by the extreme individualist and nonconformist in our society. Furthermore, it was to this interview, I suppose, that I must trace the beginnings of this biography of American eccentricity.

Of course, I had always known about Wilbur Glenn Voliva. I had been raised to maturity in the shadow of his singular personality. During the first eighteen years of my life I dwelt with my parents in the small, pleasant, half-rural, half-industrial town of Kenosha, Wisconsin, which lay several miles over the state boundary from Zion City, Illinois. As a child I nibbled chocolate-covered cookies—"Filled with vitamins, a modern, luscious tidbit"—that were produced in Voliva's factories and that contributed to the $10,000,000 fortune he was to accumulate. As a youngster I patiently manipulated the complexity of dials on our first radio set to listen to station WCBD, then one of the five most powerful in the nation, which was owned by Voliva, and I regularly devoured the columns of print in the Milwaukee and Chicago newspapers that gave space to Voliva's annual offer of $5,000 to anyone who could prove to him that the world was not flat.

But most memorable of all were my frequent glimpses of Zion City itself. For years it was a ritual in our family that twice a month we must visit our large brood of relatives in Chicago. On every second Sunday my father would seat himself behind the wheel of his lumbering touring car, with my mother beside him, and my younger sister and myself in the rear, and we would start the two-hour journey south. To reach Chicago, the intrepid traveler had, of necessity, to pass through the main street of Zion City, and it was this necessity that always made the trip an exciting adventure. For, within the precincts of Zion City, even the transient visitor was not permitted to whistle, sing, or smoke, and the speed limit was five miles an hour. Offenders were quickly arrested by members of Voliva's Prætorian Guard, who wore the word *Patience* on their helmets, the outline of doves on their sleeves, and Bibles and clubs on their belts. The penalties for frivolity or haste were a stiff fine, and, even more barbaric, an enforced one-hour lecture.

It was not until later that I learned that Voliva controlled the entire community, that he never leased property for less than 1,000 years, that he would not permit more than two persons to congregate at once in public, that he made it unlawful for women to wear ordinary bathing suits, short dresses, high heels, or lipstick, that he banned all sales of ham, bacon, oysters, liquor, and tobacco, that he would allow no drugstore, medical building, or movie theater inside the City, and that he rigidly enforced a ten o'clock evening curfew.

When my father, without cigarette but humming defiantly, drove us slowly through Zion City, past the immense white frame hotel known as Shiloh House, past the police station, past the streets marked with Biblical names, I would crouch tensely in the rear seat, casting tentative glances to the right and to the left, forever seeking, with mingled fear and curiosity, a glimpse of Voliva himself.

By 1932, though Voliva's fascination for me had not decreased, it had been somewhat diverted to Franklin D. Roosevelt and Sinclair Lewis. In that year I was an extremely vocal member of a debating society in Kenosha Central High School. Once a month we staged a formal debate on a topic usually more humorous or bizarre than serious. In preparation for one such debate there was disagreement as to a suitable subject. Suddenly I remembered Voliva, and I put forward his name and his theory. I proposed a debate on the resolution that Voliva was right and Columbus was wrong—in short, that the earth was flat. While the quaintness of the proposal had immediate appeal, there was some opposition to it on the grounds that proponents of a saucer world might not be able to make a strong enough case. Somewhat recklessly—for my curiosity to see Voliva in person had never abated—I promised that if I was permitted to represent Voliva's point of view, I would certainly make a strong enough case. The opposition snickered but agreed, and the subject was scheduled for debate. At once I wrote to Voliva, stating my need to interview him. There was an immediate response from his male secretary. I was informed that the General Overseer would be delighted to receive me within the week.

I made feverish preparations for the interview. I ransacked the libraries of three cities to brief myself on Voliva's background. I learned that his predecessor, and the actual founder of Zion City, had been one John Alexander Dowie, a Scot who studied for the ministry at Edinburgh University and then went on to establish a pastorate near Sydney, Australia. In 1888 Dowie brought his theories of faith healing to America. At the Columbian Exposition in Chicago he pitched a tent, and there, as Prophet Elijah III, competed with John Philip Sousa and Sandow for customers. He soon had 50,000 followers and sufficient funds to purchase ten square miles of land on the shores of Lake Michigan north of Chicago and establish his private religious settlement, Zion City. From the pulpit of his enormous Christian Apostolic Church he thundered forth against the sins of sex, oysters, and life insurance. He built huge lace, candy, and furniture factories, and he made $20,000,000.

When he tried to spread his gospel Dowie met his first reverses. He failed in New York, in London, and finally in Mexico. In desperation, he sent to Australia for one of his most successful assistant prophets, a thirty-seven-year-old Indiana-born preacher named Wilbur Glenn Voliva. By the time Voliva reached Zion City, old Dowie had suffered a paralytic stroke. In a moment of weakness, he gave Voliva power of attorney, and Voliva savagely turned upon him. In 1905 Voliva ordered his superior suspended from the church and exiled from Zion City on the charges that he had appropriated $2,000,000 of community funds for private luxuries and that he had engaged in polygamy. Dowie was driven to insanity and finally to his death two years later. Thereafter, Voliva was dictator, and the 6,000 persons who depended upon his tabernacle for spiritual comfort and upon his industries for physical sustenance were entirely in his grip.

Yet, when I was led into his presence in an expansive office of Shiloh House on the day of our appointment, I was agreeably surprised. In his record I had read only ruthlessness, and I had been apprehensive. But seated in the straight chair behind his walnut desk, he had the look of a benevolent businessman. His head was massive, partially bald, and his eyes were quick. He closely resembled portraits I had seen of President William McKinley, but when he grasped his black satin robe and began to speak, it was not McKinley but Savonarola.

Voliva made it plain at once that the Bible was his entire scientific library. Astronomers were "ignorant fools." The Scriptures suggested a flat world, and Voliva was a fundamentalist. The earth was as "flat as a saucer, a pancake, a stove lid." It was surrounded by an enormous wall of ice that was the South Pole. "That barrier exists," he said. "If you doubt me, then go read the testimony of Sir James Ross, the only explorer who ever went all the way around the world near the inside of the ice wall, sailing some sixty thousand miles and taking nearly four years to make the trip. The Byrd expedition was only further proof of that wall. They found an unconquerable barrier—what I call the falling-off place, the end of the world."

Voliva's conception of the universe, with its blue, solid roof, was equally bizarre. "Books tell you the sun is ninety-three million miles away," he said. "That's nonsense. The sun is only three thousand miles away, and is only thirty-two miles in diameter. It circles above the plane earth, spirally, and makes one circuit every twenty-four hours, always at the same height. All that talk about the rising and setting sun is an optical illusion." On another occasion, when asked to explain why he thought the sun so near the earth, he remarked: "God made the sun to light the earth, and therefore must have placed it close to the task it was designed to do. What would you think of a man who built a house in Zion and put a lamp to light it in Kenosha, Wisconsin?"

During our hour meeting, I timorously suggested that I had prepared a scientific list of proofs usually given in support of a globular earth. These proofs were, indeed, sophomoric, but they were the best I knew at that time, and I thought they would serve to draw Voliva out. With great forbearance, he asked for my proofs. I presented them in the form of a series of questions. Why does a vessel disappear in the distance when it steams away? How can astronomers predict eclipses? Why is the earth's shadow on the moon round? How was Magellan able to circumnavigate the earth?

Obviously, Voliva had been through all this before, and he recited his answers as if by rote. "Ships don't disappear in the distance, at all. You can see a ship twenty-five miles out at sea if you look through field glasses. According to scientists, the curvature of the earth for those twenty-five miles, allowing for refraction, should be three hundred and fifty-eight feet. If the earth is round, how can you see your ship over a hump of water three hundred and fifty-eight feet high? . . . Modern astronomers weren't the first to predict eclipses. Before Columbus, when sensible people knew the world was flat, they were constantly predicting eclipses with accuracy. One old-time scientist, who knew the earth was flat, predicted fifteen thousand eclipses and they all turned out exactly right. As for that round shadow on the moon, the flat earth would still cast a round shadow. A saucer is round, isn't it? . . . Of course Magellan sailed around the world and came back to where he started. He went around the flat earth exactly as a Victrola needle goes around a phonograph record. Millions of men have sailed around the world from east to west, and west to east. It can be done on a saucer, too. But do you know of anyone who has ever sailed around the world from north to south? Of course not. Those who tried fell off. That's why so many explorers have disappeared."

Well, that all took place in 1932, and now it seems very long ago. The depression years ruined Voliva's industries, rival churches moved their missionaries in to destroy his religious control, and finally a newly enlightened generation rejected his candidates at the polls. His grip was broken. By the time he died, in October 1942, Zion City had cigarettes, pork, lipstick, and a physician at last.

Wilbur Glenn Voliva was wrong, of course. He was a

throwback to a darker era of ignorance and superstition. He was a bigot. He was a tyrant. Perhaps he was even a fool. He stood for nothing I then believed or now believe. But occasionally, still, I remember him with grateful affection. For, by his existence, he taught me two lessons: first, that I must never forget Voltaire's promise to Rousseau: "I do not believe in a word that you say, but I will defend with my life, if need be, your right to say it"; and second, that I must never forget that the nonconformist, no matter how eccentric, no matter if pathetically wrong or divinely right, deserves tolerance, respect, and the human freedom to be different.

The high school debate?

My colleagues and I won it easily. The judges, you see, were also no more than aged sixteen—and they, too, in those shining years, had not yet become the fainthearted captives of conformity.

If it was Voliva who stimulated my first interest in nonconformity, it was certainly the venerable Sydney Smith, English preacher, editor, and wit, who inadvertently suggested the framework for this biographical examination of eccentricity. During the course of a lecture delivered before the Royal Institution in 1824, Smith stated:

"If you choose to represent the various parts in life by holes upon a table, of different shapes,—some circular, some triangular, some square, some oblong,—and the persons acting these parts by bits of wood of similar shapes, we shall generally find that the triangular person has got into the square hole, the oblong into the triangular, and a square person has squeezed himself into the round hole. The officer and the office, the doer and the thing done, seldom fit so exactly that we can say they were almost made for each other."

While Smith's graphic analogy was meant to illustrate the variance between most people and the roles assigned to them in life, it was corrupted by a passage of time to mean something quite different. For from this speech evolved the familiar expression "like a square peg in a round hole," indicating the unusual individualist who could not fit into a niche of his society. When I determined to investigate, and recount, in terms of human beings, the drama of Americans in history at odds with the mores of their times, I decided I would limit my search to Smith's "square person" or square peg who was trying to fit himself "into the round hole." To my mind, the square peg represented the eccentric personality, and the round hole represented the pattern of conformity demanded by the society in which he lived.

The usual dictionary definition of conformity is "correspondence in form, manner, or character; a point of resemblance, as of tastes . . . Harmony; agreement; congruity . . . Action, or an act, of conforming to something established, as law or fashion; compliance; acquiescence." In short, the conformist moves in step with his fellows, following the social standards, established and supported by law, religion, and custom, generally practiced by the majority in his time. Various psychological tests, given through the years, have indicated that from ninety to ninety-eight persons out of every hundred conform to the dictates of their law, religion, and custom. They conform for many reasons: because it is easier and less exhausting; because it is simpler and less confusing; because it is safe and less dangerous; because it enhances the ego and invites less disapproval; because it is more relaxing and less lonely; and because it is a habit of long training, and less radical. No doubt, many of these very reasons for conformity had great appeal to Mary Shelley, who had lived with a total nonconformist for eight years. Shortly after the drowning of her poet-husband she was urged to send her son to an advanced school, where the boy might be encouraged to think for himself. "To think for himself!" she exclaimed. "Oh, my God, teach him to think like other people!"

The most spectacular type of nonconformist is, of course, the eccentric. The word itself derives from the Greek "out of the center." The historical and literary definition of eccentricity is "deviation from customary conduct; oddity . . . divergence from the usual." Psychiatric sources are even more explicit. According to one, eccentricity means "off center or unsymmetrical with reference to a center; hence odd in behavior." According to another, eccentricity denotes "unusual freedom from conventional types of response."

While psychiatrists, in their exploration of eccentricity, have found that causes vary widely in individual cases, they have emerged with a few basic generalities. Most full-time eccentrics are regarded as psychopathic personalities who, in the words of a British psychiatric dictionary, "have been from childhood or early youth abnormal in their emotional reactions and in their general behavior, but who do not reach, except perhaps episodically, a degree of abnormality amounting to certifiable insanity, and who show no intellectual defect. They exhibit lack of perseverance, persistent failure to profit by experience, and habitual lack of ordinary prudence."

Dr. Eugen Kahn, who was Sterling Professor of Psychiatry at Yale University, finds that most eccentrics, emerging from an insecure childhood, grow up in opposition to their environment, intent on making their way alone. Usually they become obsessed by some "overvalued idea," and their personalities are clouded by dementia præcox, excessive fanaticism, paranoia, and schizophrenia. They may be more imaginative and even more intelligent than the so-called average person, but at the same time they are likely to be more immature and impractical.

Above all, most psychiatrists seem to agree that the lot of the eccentric is unhappier than that of the conforming "average personality." If the eccentric is sufficiently integrated to succeed in some field, to gain wealth or power, he is admired and respected and his oddity is overlooked. But if the eccentric fails, he is pitied or ridiculed and shunned as something strange. Most often, the penalties for deviation from the norm are harsh. The eccentric is alone, suspected, and often hurt. Constantly he is hounded by society's watchdogs—the government, the church, the social organization, the community—and he suffers physical punishments such as arrest, exile, personal violence, or spiritual punishments in the form of social boycott and disapproval.

Yet, despite these unhappy prospects, men have continued to indulge in eccentricity—sometimes because they could not do otherwise, but as often because they preferred the freer air of nonconformity. And all through history these few individualists, though often persecuted by the many, have had encouragement from the best minds of their day. Ralph Waldo Emerson dared, as we shall see, to flaunt public opinion in assisting the eccentric Delia Bacon. "The virtue in most request is conformity," wrote Emerson. "Self-reliance is its aversion. It loves not realities and creators, but names and customs . . . Whoso would be a man must be a non-conformist."

In all ages the eccentric—perhaps because of, and not in spite of, his nonconformity—has furthered the cause of science, built great empires, improved the public welfare, and created memorable works of art. In their own time such men as Kant, Thoreau, Paganini, Pascal, Disraeli, Poe, Whitman, Heine, and Goldsmith were considered eccentric. History has recorded countless other names of rare individualists—ranging from the poet Charles Baudelaire, with his green hair and his confessions of cannibalism, to the millionaire businessman Russell Sage, with his pride in eight-dollar suits and formal lunches at which he served only apples—all of whom contributed to their contemporary society and to civilization. Yet, the major bequest of most eccentrics has been something less tangible. In subtle ways, they have helped their fellows profit by their original example. "Eccentrics do a lot of good," Henry Morton Robinson once wrote. "They point out what the rest of us forget—the delightfully erratic possibilities of human life. They get far away from the good, the true, and the beautiful, substituting for this dour trinity the rarer qualities of the rare, the cuckoo, and the courageous."

Intolerance for the eccentric has known no geographical limits. Yet, possibly, in the West, Europe has been more appreciative of its irregular personalities than has America. Europe, with an older civilization and character, with sharper variety in its landscape and nationalities, with more differences in its systems of government and teachings and social life, has quite naturally bred a greater proportion of eccentrics and has learned to tolerate and even to encourage them. Especially is this true in Great Britain.

England has always had its eccentrics—the French like to say that "the British prefer to walk in the road, although there are pavements laid down for their convenience"—and, generally, the English have been proud of their most outrageous nonconformists. Edith Sitwell tried to account for this happy condition in the security that Englishmen have always found in their superiority and tradition. "Eccentricity exists particularly in the English . . . because of that peculiar and satisfactory knowledge of infallibility that is the hallmark and birthright of the British nation."

In discussing the Whig aristocracy of the eighteenth century in *Melbourne*, Lord David Cecil also examined this English phenomenon of nonconformity: "The conventions which bounded their lives were conventions of form only. Since they had been kings of their world from birth, they were free from the tiresome inhibitions that are induced by a sense of inferiority. Within the locked garden of their society, individuality flowered riotous and rampant. Their typical figures show up beside the muted introverts of to-day as clear-cut and idiosyncratic as characters in Dickens. They took for granted that you spoke your mind and followed your impulses. If these were odd, they were amused but not disapproving. They enjoyed eccentrics: George Selwyn, who never missed an execution, Beau Brummell, who took three hours to tie his cravat. The firm English soil in which they were rooted, the spacious freedom afforded by their place in the world, allowed personality to flourish in as many bold and fantastic shapes as it pleased."

In England, utopia of the individualist, eccentricity has indeed taken on many bold and fantastic shapes. The nation's vast and continuing literature of oddity points with pride to unusual men and women who would have been quickly stunted or stoned in less amiable lands. While the English quality of eccentricity has been matched elsewhere—as I shall attempt to demonstrate in this book—nowhere else has as much sheer quantity of eccentricity been achieved. "Clearly, it is in the individualist phases of society," said Richard Aldington, "that the eccentric flourishes. In other epochs he becomes a heretic and goes up in flames, or is marked down as politically undesirable and is liquidated." In England the eighteenth century was particularly amenable to the unrestricted growth of the individualist. During sixty-nine years of that century there were born four classical examples of Sydney Smith's "square human."

In 1713 occurred the birth of Edward Wortley Montagu. His father was a millionaire member of Parliament renowned for his miserliness. His mother was the clever and eccentric "female traveler," Lady Mary Wortley Montagu, who attained notoriety for her journeys in the Near East and fame for her remarkable letters. But, by a dint of perseverance, Edward Montagu exceeded his mother in eccentricity. As a boy he could curse in Greek and Turkish. At Oxford, when he was thirteen, he took his landlady for his mistress. He was an officer at the battle of Fontenoy, he was a member of Parliament for one month, and he was an outstanding Arabic scholar. He assumed, and discarded, almost as many religions as wives. He was a Protestant, then a convert to Catholicism, and at last a Mohammedan. At seventeen he married a washerwoman, and then, neglecting to divorce her, he was wedded successively to a Miss Elizabeth Ashe, to a Catholic widow named Caroline Feroe, and to an Egyptian serving-girl known as Ayesha.

At the age of sixty-three Montagu advertised for one more wife, demanding only that she be of "genteel birth, polished manners and five, six, seven or eight months gone in her pregnancy." This startled no one since, only three years before, at sixty, he had asked to be circumcised—arguing that Abraham had been circumcised at ninety-nine—so that he might make a pilgrimage to Mecca. His gaudy attire forever attracted crowds. He wore a turban and an embroidered coat with diamonds for buttons, but that was not all. "The most curious part of his dress," said Horace Walpole, "is an iron wig; you literally would not know it from hair." He was aware of his oddity, and no less proud. "I have never committed a *small* folly," he once remarked. He died in 1776.

William Beckford was sixteen years old when Montagu, whose Oriental manuscripts he would collect and translate, expired in Italy. Beckford followed in the capricious footsteps of his idol. When Beckford was still a child he inherited his father's West Indies plantations, one million pounds, and the family estate near the village of Fonthill in Wiltshire. His education was acquired through private tutors. He learned Arabic and Persian from an Orientalist, and he learned to play the piano from Wolfgang Mozart. He traveled to France, Portugal, and Italy. In Venice he supported an elderly mistress who had earlier entertained Casanova. Though he had married a lady of title, and had had four children, he was publicly accused of homosexuality. Scandalous rumor, which he never legally denied, revealed to the world that he had been seen committing perversion in Powderham with a young man named Courtenay.

Beckford wrote ten or eleven books, two under women's names. His masterpiece, admired by Lord Byron, was an Oriental romance entitled *Vathek*. He composed it in French, and then had a clergyman translate it back into his native English. He collected books both rare and popular, scribbled brilliant criticisms in their margins, and then offered these jottings for sale to the publisher Richard Bentley under the title of *Fruits of Conceit and Flowers of Nonsense*, but they were rejected as too controversial. He was certainly, as Richard Garnett remarked, "the most brilliant amateur in English literature." As such, he decided to build a monument to himself. In 1790 he told Lady Craven: "I grow rich and mean to build towers." He determined to abandon Fonthill and nearby erect the tallest private residence in all Europe.

Beckford hired the leading architect of the day, James Wyatt, and had him construct a wall twelve feet high and seven miles in circumference to keep out sight-seers. This done, work was promptly started on the Great Tower. Because of Beckford's impatience to see his monstrosity completed, 500 laborers were employed to work in two shifts—half by sunlight and half by torchlight. In 1800 the flimsy timber-and-cement structure, set on a narrow base, was done. It rose 300 feet into the air—and the very first mild wind broke it in two and sent it crashing to the ground.

Undeterred, Beckford ordered another Great Tower built on the rubble of the old. At an expenditure of 273,000 pounds, stone was added to the timber and cement, and the new 300-foot structure was finished in less than seven years. Beckford moved into one of its eighteen cramped, unventilated bedrooms. Here, with a Spanish dwarf in livery receiving guests, he entertained his friends, among them Lady Emma Hamilton, but refused to invite the curious Prince Regent. After fifteen years, having lost his income and his fortune, Beckford sold the tower for 330,000 pounds to a munitions dealer named John Farquhar. He was not surprised to learn that, shortly after his own removal to Bath, the tower again collapsed in a gale. On a hillside near Bath, Beckford built a third tower, this one a mere 130 feet in height, and peopled it with dwarfs. His aversions were mirrors and women (special niches were built in the corridors for his maids to hide in when he passed). Aged eighty-four, he died in 1844.

As Beckford was a devotee of the arts, he may at some time have been witness to the dogged eccentricity of a contemporary named Robert Coates, who had been born in the West Indies in 1772. Coates, nicknamed Romeo for his passionate desire to act, and Diamond for his originality in attire, became stage-struck in his puberty. In 1809 he invaded —perhaps assaulted would be the more accurate word—the London theater. Often referred to as the Gifted Amateur, Coates devoted a long and riotous life to proving he was another Garrick. He was not, but he was certainly as entertaining. He liked to play Shakespeare, and he designed his own costumes for Hamlet and Macbeth—as Romeo he appeared in white feather hat, spangled cloak, and pantaloons. He wore these same costumes in public. Before appearing in a Shakespearean play, he would rewrite it to suit his talents. "I think I have improved upon it," he told his shocked friends. In *Romeo and Juliet* he improved the ending by trying to pry open Juliet's tomb with a crowbar. If he particularly enjoyed playing a scene, he would repeat the same scene three times in one evening as his audiences sat stupefied. He was probably the worst actor in the history of the legitimate theater. Yet he tirelessly tramped up and down the British Isles declaiming from the boards. Year after year he was met with derision and catcalls and hilarity, but he persisted. At a performance in Richmond, several spectators were so shaken by laughter that a physician had to be summoned to attend them.

When theater managers, fearing violence, barred him from their stages, he bribed them to let him appear. When fellow thespians, fearing bodily injury, refused to act beside him, he provided police guards to reassure them. Eventually, by sheer persistence and by the audacity of his mediocrity, he became a legendary figure decked out in furs, jewels, and Hessian boots. He starred in London's leading theaters and responded to command performances before royalty. Nothing, it seemed, not criticism, not ridicule, not threats of lynching, could remove him from the footlights. Only death, it was agreed, might silence him and save the English stage. But he would not die. In his seventy-fourth year, reduced in circumstances, but spouting and gesturing still, he was as active as ever. But the year following, on an afternoon in 1848, a carriage ran him down, and he died. Though English drama survived his passing, its comedy would never be the same again.

While perhaps no English eccentric would ever exceed Coates in audacity, it is possible that Charles Waterton, in his own field, was his match. Waterton was born of wealthy parents in Yorkshire during 1782. At the Jesuit College of Stonyhurst he demonstrated a talent for natural history. Sent to British Guiana to supervise the family plantations, he displayed the first evidences of his originality during a four-month sojourn in the Brazilian jungles. During this exploration Waterton sought the poison Indians used in their blowguns, which he called wourali and which we know as curare. He hoped to employ this poison as a cure for hydrophobia. In the course of this and three other trips, Waterton performed incredible feats of oddity. Moving through the bush on bare feet, he captured a python by binding its head with his suspenders. On another occasion he was having some difficulty pulling a crocodile from the river. "I saw he was in a state of fear and perturbation. I instantly dropped the mast, sprang up, and jumped on his back." After riding the crocodile forty yards to the bank, Waterton relaxed only briefly. He became enchanted with the idea of having a vampire bat suck blood from his big toe. He took one into his sleeping quarters, and dozed with a foot nakedly exposed, but the reluctant bat preferred the less formidable toe of a neighbor.

Upon his father's death Waterton returned to England to become the twenty-seventh squire of Walton Hall. He decided to convert the family property into a bird sanctuary. He constructed an eight-foot barrier three miles around his grounds to keep out beasts of prey and hunters. He brought in an ex-poacher to serve as game warden, and he set up a telescope for use in bird-watching. His greatest pleasure was in clambering up trees and observing his creatures at close hand. When he had guests he would invite them to climb with him. At the age of eighty—like "an adolescent gorilla," Norman Douglas observed—he was still ascending trees. Occasionally, as when he visited Vatican City, he would climb something else. In 1817 he scaled St. Peter's to its summit, and then went thirteen feet higher to plant his gloves at the top of a lightning conductor. Pope Pius VII was unamused, and made him climb back up again to remove the gloves.

At Walton Hall, where no gunfire was permitted and where all dogs were confined, he dwelt as naturally as the first man on earth. He went about barefooted, prayed in a private chapel, slept on the floor of his bedroom with a block of oak for his pillow, and rose at four o'clock in the morning. He occupied himself by building a stable so arranged that his horses might converse, by playing practical jokes on friends (often pretending to be a dog and biting them), and by attempting to fly with the use of homemade wings. His hobby was taxidermy. Every nook of his house was filled with some strange, preserved specimen. Sometimes, like Frankenstein, he created composite creatures made of the parts of four animals. Because he was a Catholic he named many of these monsters after prominent Protestants. His favorite, with the head of a red howler monkey, was called The Nondescript and looked startlingly human.

On the rare occasions when Waterton left Walton Hall he was no less eccentric. He visited the London zoo to interview a savage orangutan recently imported from Borneo. Though warned that he would be torn apart, he insisted upon entering the cage. "The meeting of those two celebrities," said his friend Dr. Richard Hobson, "was clearly a case of love at first sight, as the strangers not only embraced each other most affectionately, but positively hugged each other and . . . kissed one another many times." Waterton visited Italy accompanied by a retinue of owls. And finally, excited by an American book on ornithology, he traveled to the United States in 1824. He saw New York and adored its women. He saw Charles Willson Peale, who had painted Washington, and who had four sons named Rembrandt, Raphael, Titian, and Rubens. He saw Niagara Falls, and having sprained his ankle and been advised that it should be immersed in water, held his ankle beneath the great Falls. The year after returning from America he published a successful account of his travels and explorations. In 1829, in Belgium, he met a convent girl who was the granddaughter of a Guiana Indian princess and thirty years his junior. He married her at four o'clock one May morning, and for their honeymoon took her to Paris to study stuffed birds. In his eighty-third year, on his estate, he tripped, fell against a log, and was seriously injured. He died in May 1865.

In the English atmosphere of conformity, mellowed by centuries of individualism, such extreme nonconformists as Waterton, Coates, Beckford, and Montagu met with little resistance. In the United States, with its deep-rooted and rigid Calvinistic beginnings, similar nonconformists grew and survived, but with far more difficulty and with far less tolerance. Many reasons have been put forward by sociologists, historians, and psychologists to explain the undeviating worship of group living and group thinking in America. James Bryce credited American conformity to uniform stretches of landscape, to uniform cities, to uniform political institutions in federal, state, and municipal government. Everywhere schools, libraries, clubs, amusements, and customs were similar. "Travel where you will," he wrote, "you feel that what you have found in one place that you will find in another."

Above all, there was the rapid advance of industrial science. In America an all-powerful technology, with its standardized techniques and methods of mass production, reached its zenith. As technology attracted larger numbers of people to urban centers, and compressed them into smaller areas, community living became a necessity. This, in turn, encouraged people to co-operate, and created relationships that invited similar activities and opinions.

Gradually there emerged on the American scene, against all natural development of culture and against all individual traits inherent in every man, two striking attitudes that made American conformity broader, more unyielding, and more dangerous. The first attitude, assumed by the majority, was that the act of becoming average, of being normal, was more important than that of being distinct or superior. The second attitude, also assumed by the majority, was that the state of being well adjusted to the crowd and the community was more important than that of being a unique and original human being.

Today this growing affection for the safety of the similar, the usual, and the accepted, and the consequent fear of any challenging ideas or personalities, presents a serious threat to the development of American society. But how then to allay this threat? What practical course is open? In his book *Must You Conform?* Dr. Robert Lindner supplied an answer:

"The first requisite for a teacher or parent who wishes to assist the evolutionary process by rearing our young toward genuine maturity is that he root out from himself every last vestige of the myth of adjustment. He must exorcise from his heart and mind, and from his behavior, adulation of the fiction of conformity that has brought society within sight of doomsday and that threatens to engulf the world in another long night of medievalism. He must deny that passivity, surrender, conformism and domestication pave the road to human happiness and salvation. Instead he must affirm the rights of protest and individuality, encourage uniqueness, and be unshaken in an abiding faith that only in these ways will he discover himself and the true vocation of his life."

To be one's self, and unafraid whether right or wrong, is more admirable than the easy cowardice of surrender to conformity. That is the contention and that is the theme of this book. Sociologists and psychologists have, in the past, propagated this point of view in their own specialized terms. While my own interest, like theirs, is the human animal, I have preferred to dramatize the subject as storyteller and biographer.

Since 1932, when I met Wilbur Glenn Voliva, and since 1945, when I began to make notes on the gyrations of individualists who had swung away from the safety of society's center, I have been rather constantly in the company of the American eccentric. I have met him in the pages of yellowed newspapers, periodicals, and books. I have visited the arenas where once he performed, and have often seen his autograph on cracked documents and creased letters. For all of this, I may not have loved him, but I have known him well and respected him.

To be sure, I have not attempted to include every American eccentric in this modest examination. There were more of these unfettered souls than the reader may imagine, though, indeed, altogether too few for the nation's need. I have made hard choices. My formula has been simple: I would write not about celebrated men and women who were possessed of eccentricity, but rather about men and women who were celebrated *for* their eccentricity.

It was with genuine reluctance that I was forced to discard Edward Hyde, Lord Cornbury, Governor of New York in 1702, who charged admissions to his private dinners, wore his wife's dresses, and taxed all male colonists who used wigs; William Miller, the Massachusetts prophet of doom, who delivered 3,200 speeches predicting the end of the world in 1843 and sold muslin ascension robes at a profit; Hetty Green, the miser of Wall Street, who wore newspapers for undergarments, subsisted on onions and eggs, dwelt in a fireless tenement, permitted only the lower half of her petticoats to be laundered, and was worth eighty million dollars; and Joseph Palmer, a New Englander, who persisted in wearing a beard in a clean-shaven society and was jeered, beaten, and finally sentenced to jail for one year.

These eccentrics were good, but I feel I have settled upon

eight who were better. The nonconformists in this book represent the complete saga of American eccentricity from the days of the founding of the republic to modern times. Their stories are not success stories in the familiar language of accumulated wealth, power, fame, or contributions to their time. True, some, like George Francis Train, were rich, and some, like Victoria Woodhull, were politically renowned, and some, like Anne Royall, were pioneers in free speech. But such tangible accomplishments are not the point. For, what these eccentrics offer, beyond diversion, is the example of uninhibited personality in America, a trait so lacking in this highly organized age. By their presence in these pages it is my hope that some small boundaries of sympathy, understanding, and tolerance may be broadened.

Though these eccentrics contributed little to science, government, or the arts, it is my belief that they gave something of more value to their contemporaries—and, as a consequence, to us, their heirs. A James Harden-Hickey can still remind us that the age of the plebiscite and the machine need not be an age without dreams and romance. A Delia Bacon can remind us that the libraries of scholarship, even if tidy and already filled, must always allow room for one more investigation, no matter how disorderly. A Timothy Dexter can remind us that public hearing and attention need not be the private prerogative of the formally educated and the well bred. A John Cleves Symmes can remind us that the frontiers of science and imagination must know no limits and no dogma, but that they may be crossed by anyone—in the hope that once in a century, by a miracle of freedom and genius, a trespasser may contribute to the welfare of all humanity.

These are the square pegs who would not fit into round holes. They went backward when everyone went forward, and they went forward when everyone stood still. They said nay when others said aye, and they saw black when others saw white. Despite suffering, economic and spiritual, they refused to be garmented in the strait jacket of conformity.

This, and no other, is their achievement—and it is enough. For when our society no longer has a single square peg, when it no longer has a recalcitrant individual out of step, when it no longer has a voice that will rise to dissent and disagree and persist in an unorthodoxy, then, and only then, will man have lost his last battle and his last chance.

In 1859 John Stuart Mill, the brilliant and sensitive English political economist and philosopher, published *On Liberty*. In it he defended the square peg, and he wrote a warning to generations yet unborn:

"Eccentricity has always abounded when and where strength of character has abounded; and the amount of eccentricity in a society has been proportional to the amount of genius, mental vigor, and moral courage it contained."

II

The King of Thirty-Sixth Street

"We, James, Prince of Trinidad, have resolved to commemorate our accession to the throne of Trinidad by the institution of an Order of Chivalry. . . ."

JAMES A. HARDEN-HICKEY

Surprise was an emotion few subscribers to the *New York Tribune* felt by the year 1893. During the previous half decade, most had been stunned into silent acceptance of every new human hydra-head. Through the medium of their favorite front-page, readers had absorbed cruel and unusual punishment at the hands of Ignatius Donnelly, who ran for vice-president and published a book resurrecting the lost continent of Atlantis from the sea; Anthony Comstock, who disapproved of Little Egypt and was well on his way to destroying 160 tons of obscene literature; and Dr. Mary Walker, who served as a physician during the Civil War and frightened a Medal of Honor out of Congress with her daily attire of frocked coat and striped trousers.

Yet, despite their resistance to bizarre individualists, even the oldest and most calloused Constant Readers blinked on the morning of November 5, 1893, when they picked up their twenty-four-page Sunday *Tribune* and read the exclusive lead story on page one.

The column-long story, which spilled over into the next

column, was headlined "To Be Prince of Trinidad." The subheadline explained: "He Is Baron Harden-Hickey." Beneath that, in slightly smaller type, one more bit of exposition: "His Ambition Is To Found A Nation On A Little Island In The Sea."

The opening paragraph of the news story, which would have been considered somewhat lackadaisical by latter-day *Tribune* editors and stockholders, stated:

"If the plans of Baron James A. Harden-Hickey are carried out there will be a brand new nation brought into existence on the face of the earth next spring. That sounds like a remarkable undertaking, but Baron Harden-Hickey is confident that it can be carried through successfully and as easily as many other remarkable and apparently impossible achievements. He does not propose to overthrow any established government or split any twain. He is not going to encroach upon anybody's territory or interfere with anybody's rights. He has found a place where nobody lives, which, he says, nobody owns, and which is not claimed among the possessions of any existing nation. The place is the Island of Trinidad, situated in the South Atlantic Ocean, in latitude 20 degrees 30 minutes south and longitude 29 degrees 22 minutes west. It is 700 miles from the coast of Brazil, which is the point of land nearest to it. It contains about sixty square miles of territory. There Baron Harden-Hickey proposes to found an independent state, the head of which shall be sovereign and treat on equal terms with the mighty rulers of the earth."

Five paragraphs later, the *Tribune* took time out to remind its subscribers that this was an authentic scoop. "A *Tribune* reporter found Baron Harden-Hickey at his home last evening, and asked him about his extraordinary undertaking. Baron Harden-Hickey expressed surprise that the *Tribune* should have learned of his scheme, but added good-naturedly, 'I know that great newspapers have wonderful means of getting information. I used to be a newspaperman myself. As for my plans, they are not yet mature, but I will tell you as much about them as I can.' "

What Harden-Hickey did not tell the *Tribune*, in the twelve quotes that followed, and what the *Tribune* did not tell its readers, was that Harden-Hickey planned not only to found a new island-nation, but also to crown himself King James I of that nation.

In subsequent months most of New York, as well as the rest of America, became more fully acquainted with Baron Harden-Hickey's project. At first, much to the consternation of his wife, a Standard Oil and iron heiress, Harden-Hickey worked out of his residence at 18 West Fifty-second Street in Manhattan. Later he established the more formal Chancellerie de la Principauté de Trinidad in a brownstone house at 217 West Thirty-sixth Street. While he toured the country to arrange for serfs he left an old Parisian friend and onetime wine merchant, Count de la Boissière, behind as his Secrétaire d'État pour les Affaires Étrangères.

In San Francisco, Harden-Hickey purchased a schooner to transport colonists to Trinidad and to ferry supplies and mail between Trinidad and Brazil. He hired an agent to bargain for construction of docks, wharves, a lighthouse, and homes. As he planned an idle aristocracy, with four orders of chivalry, and as his island-empire had nothing native to subjugate beyond turtles, Harden-Hickey decided to buy himself a ready-made proletariat. After months of dickering in California, he contracted for five hundred Chinese coolies to do all the manual labor on the island. Back in New York, he ordered a quantity of postage stamps bearing pictures of the island, several red flags imprinted with yellow triangles, and one sparkling royal crown.

Constant Readers scratched their heads. Nine days had elapsed, and then nine months, and the cuckoo was still with them. But between November 5, 1893, when the *Tribune* first broke the story of Harden-Hickey, and August 1,

1895, when his island-kingdom became an international *cause célèbre*, some New Yorkers slowly began to realize that what they had on hand was not a madman, but simply a human born out of time. It was like having King Arthur in—well—Bridgeport, Connecticut.

James Aloysius Harden-Hickey was born in San Francisco on December 8, 1854. His father, E. C. Hickey, was a well-to-do Irish miner. His mother was French. Thirty-three years after his birth, in a book called *Our Writers*, an encyclopedia of famous French authors which he wrote in French and had published in Paris, Harden-Hickey included a full page of material on himself and his antecedents alongside biographies of such other writers as Guy de Maupassant, Alphonse Daudet, Victor Hugo and *their* families.

"My old Irish family traces its origin to Milesius, King of Spain," he wrote. "Several members of the Hickey family have served the French kings as officers in the Irish Brigade. One of them was wounded at Fontenoy. The Hardens were from Normandy. Their nobility was acknowledged by a charter given Antoine de Harden by Henry II in 1556. Jacques de Harden, the last offspring from this family, took a ship with James II for Kinsale, settled in Ireland, and allied himself to the Hickey family." When King James II, a converted Catholic, tried to fight the Established Church of England, he met strong resistance from clergy and gentry alike. By November 1688 William of Orange had landed at Tor Bay, and James II was on his way into French exile, dutifully followed by the Hickeys, ardent Catholic Royalists.

Harden-Hickey's parents were among San Francisco's earliest settlers. As he was born only five years after the gold rush, the San Francisco of his youth was one vast brawling beerhall. His French-born mother, remembering the amenities of the Old World, remembering perhaps that not so long before, other Hickeys had known courtlier days at Saint-Germain, suggested that the boy be educated in a more cultured climate.

Harden-Hickey was taken to Paris. It was the Paris of Alexandre Dumas, Gustave Flaubert, Jean Troppmann, Cora Pearl, the Goncourts, and the young Sarah Bernhardt, "Paris at her maddest, baddest and best," a New York correspondent reported. Above all, Paris was again part of a storybook monarchy, gay and garish in the old tradition. Sober historians spoke of "the French Court's glitter and intrigue." J. M. Thompson wrote that "the Court had never been so formal or magnificent since the time of Louis XV, or so frivolous since that of Marie Antoinette."

Napoleon III, though he appeared ill-cast for his glamorous role and though he too often resembled a figure misplaced by Madame Tussaud, proved himself a true grandson of the earlier Napoleon's Josephine. He instituted the Médaille Militaire for courage in the field of combat. He resumed the stag hunts, in eighteenth-century costume, at Fontainebleau. He constructed the great Paris Opéra, and he completed the Louvre. He introduced footmen in knee breeches and Cent-Gardes in steel helmets to the Tuileries. He again made the institution of mistress fashionable: Elizabeth Howard, the onetime English barmaid, who saved 20,000 pounds from the generosity of her patrons and backed Napoleon's *coup d'état;* Marguerite Bellanger, the circus rider and acrobat, whose remarkable energies gave the Emperor a child and a physical collapse, thereby provoking the Empress to rage at her: "Mademoiselle, you have got to go! You are killing the Emperor!"; and the Contessa Nicchia de Castiglione, the Florentine beauty who counted the Pope her friend and the King of Sardinia her lover, whose mission by order of her King was to win Napoleon's affection for herself—and for her homeland—and whose mission was, at least partially, accomplished.

This dazzling, dreamlike environment was James Harden-Hickey's childhood playground. It made a lasting imprint on his memory. For while impressionable youngsters in the New World were being prepared for the American Century by Ragged Dick and Mark The Match Boy, Harden-Hickey was becoming convinced that Napoleon III, who had won the Crimean War, restored the Pope to Rome, and sent Maximilian and Carlotta to Mexico, could defeat and dominate anyone on earth. The Emperor could not, of course, as the Germans proved a few years later at Sedan, but Harden-Hickey always thought so. He would never quite forget Napoleon's waxed mustache, the giant Zouave guards, the Empress Eugénie in her carriage, the jingling of medals and the rattling of swords in the Tuileries and about the Elysées, the prefect Baron Haussmann's sweeping grand boulevards (widened so that mobs could no longer impede troop movements by throwing furniture into the streets), and, as he would later write, "the Parisian crowds gaily leaving the theatres to fill the brilliantly lit cafés with their windows sparkling as from a thousand fires."

He was soon taken from Paris and enrolled in the Jesuit College at Namur, Belgium, near Liège. The change seems to have distressed him. The only record Harden-Hickey left of that experience was in an autobiographical novel, *Souvenirs of a Gommeux*, published in Paris during 1877. *Gommeux* was slang of that period for dandy. In this novel Harden-Hickey sends his hero, Henri, "son of wealthy though honest people," to a Jesuit College in Belgium. "Lock up the youth, as is the habit nowadays," wrote Harden-Hickey, "and they become sullen, unhealthy; their sap dries up."

After the Jesuit College, Harden-Hickey was sent to the University of Leipzig for two years to study law. When he was nineteen it was agreed that he would make the French Army his career. He passed the competitive examinations for the Military College established by Napoleon I in 1808 at Saint-Cyr-L'École, three miles west of Versailles. This, apparently, was more like it. In Saint-Cyr, where students wore uniforms, swords, and monarchist manners, Harden-Hickey had little difficulty in conjuring up a very real picture of the imperial court.

In 1875 Harden-Hickey was graduated, with honors, from Saint-Cyr, and shortly thereafter his father died in San Francisco. There was a small inheritance. Reluctantly, Harden-Hickey decided to abandon his military career and to spend the money on a new profession in France. For two years he dabbled in sculpture, and, under the pseudonym of Saint-Patrice, wrote and sold his first novel. Angered by the attacks of Parisian Republicans on the Catholic Church, he turned his full attention to writing. By 1878 he had been made a Baron of the Catholic Church for his numerous pamphlets defending the Faith and had married the Countess de Saint-Pery, by whom he later had a boy and a girl. He was twenty-four years old, powerfully built, a tall, square-faced young man with a crew haircut, drooping mustache, clean-shaven chin, and thick neck. Though he wore a low collar, and affected to dress like the late Baudelaire, he was proper, conservative, Catholic, and a little dull. If he possessed the qualifications for royal rule, no one, not even his wife, yet suspected it.

Between 1876 and 1880, Baron Harden-Hickey poured forth eleven full-length novels. All were written in French under the name Saint-Patrice. Recently when I visited the Bibliothèque Nationale I found all but three of Harden-Hickey's novels still on the shelves. His first, *A Love in Society*, moves its cosmopolitan characters from Paris to Interlaken to Lourdes to Moscow. In the climax of the book, the young Scottish-born, French-bred hero, Robert, pursues his Polish love, Sophie, who is being forced to marry rich old Barewski, to the wintry (twenty-two degrees below zero) steppes of Russia. Robert kidnaps Sophie and flees with her in a sleigh while hungry wolves and Barewski give chase. Robert fights them off with a hatchet. The wolves, discouraged, give up and settle for Barewski.

Four years later, Harden-Hickey's eleventh and final novel, *Fierpepin's Metamorphosis*, written in Belgium during September 1880, appeared. Fierpepin is a bony, haughty nobleman, a dim carbon-copy of Don Quixote, whose ancestors were all failures (one, notably, left his wife in a chastity belt, forgetting that her lover was a locksmith). Fierpepin determines to run for the Chamber of Deputies against a common Republican, Dr. Theodore Globule, the town doctor and mayor. As Dr. Globule hypnotizes the masses with magnificent oratory, Fierpepin knows he must muffle the man. Fierpepin employs an air pump to extract the bark from a large dog, and with this goes to call upon his opponent. When the doctor stands openmouthed at some audacious remark made by his visitor, Fierpepin promptly stuffs the dog's bark into his rival's mouth. After that, instead of speaking, Dr. Globule can only woof at political meetings. Fierpepin wins the election easily.

While all of Harden-Hickey's novels contain a certain amount of muttering against democracy, his most socially significant effort, presented in the form of twelve satirical letters exchanged between an underpaid American correspondent in Europe, Jonathan Smith, and his editor on the *Boston Daily News*, Samuel Jones, was called *Letters from a Yank*. Editor Jones assigns his correspondent to seek out an amazing new French invention—"a power capable of replacing water, steam, horses, windmills, velocipedes and all known engines"—a bottle of human perspiration, extracted from "the toil of others." In Paris, while hunting down the concoction, Reporter Smith is chased by the police, hides in a stuffed ostrich, is given away as first prize in the National Lottery, and is won by James Gordon Bennett of the *New York Herald*.

Many who read these novels must have been confused by their unevenness. On the one hand, the plots were naïve and the characters stereotyped, and the French was fluent but flat. On the other, there was an occasional flash of wit, and sometimes an idea or situation so extravagant as to take the breath away. To some readers, the novels must have appeared to have been written by a two-headed man: one head conventional, the other eccentric; one head mediocre, the other utterly mad. "You begin to wonder," a librarian at the Bibliothèque Nationale remarked recently, "what manner of a person did all this."

Among the people who wondered about Harden-Hickey at the time was a small group of French Royalists. They were less interested in the literary style of Harden-Hickey's novels than in their political content. They delighted in his thrusts at the new Republic, as in *A Love in Vendée*, when he accused the "noble propagandists of Liberty, Equality, Fraternity" of having written "a blood-stained page in the annals of this country, so quiet and peaceful before."

The Royalists, followers of Henri, Count de Chambord, grandson of Charles X of France, approached Harden-Hickey. The Third Republic was eight years old. Among other things, it had turned financial surpluses into deficits and conscripted the educated classes, accomplishments which particularly offended the good taste of the Royalists. The Royalists wanted to place the fifty-eight-year-old Count de Chambord on the throne. The Count stood for parliamentary government and universal suffrage, though he had remarked: "Either I am King by Right Divine or a lame old man with no business in politics." Would Harden-Hickey lend his flair, his invective, to the Count's cause? The Royalists had in mind an illustrated weekly, with a scepter to grind, something along the lines of *Punch*. The Count de Chambord would put up the money; a dozen Royalist writers would help contribute the copy. The project needed only an editor.

Under Napoleon III there were nine hundred daily newspapers, weeklies, and monthly magazines in Paris alone. These were filled with the screened produce of journalists like Villemessant, who founded *Figaro*, Taine, and Edmond About, and with the cartoons of Nadar, Daumier, Cham, and André Gill (whose name, punned, became the Montmartre tavern, Lapin Agile). The opposition press, Republicans, was handcuffed by the severest censorship.

By 1872, with the Emperor in his English exile at Chislehurst (where he joined Eugénie, who had earlier escaped France by yacht with the help of her American dentist, a millionaire Philadelphian in Paris named Thomas W. Evans), and with France for the third time undergoing the preliminary spasms that attend the birth of representative government, the press found itself liberated from censorship. Editors, determined to take full advantage of the new democracy, went berserk. "To write of ministers," complained one Minister, "editors comb the slang of convicts for their most shocking expressions." The scandalous gossip, the mounting insults and lies, forced the government to apply its libel laws vigorously. In a single year, writers and editors were sentenced to 2,319 days' imprisonment for the offense of pornography alone.

It was in this free but highly combative climate of the common man that Baron Harden-Hickey undertook to edit, on behalf of a pretender to an unpopular throne, a satirical weekly called *Le Triboulet*, named after the favorite jester of Louis XII. The first issue appeared on November 10, 1878. The masthead promised an issue every Sunday at fifty centimes and listed Saint-Patrice as editor. The cartoon cover depicted Triboulet, club in hand, representing royalty, belaboring Marianne and other puppets, symbolizing the young republic.

Harden-Hickey left the "Chronicles of High Life" to Gramadock, the "Fashions" to Stella, the "Chronicle of the Boulevards" to Trick, the "Sports" to Count de Mirabel, and himself concentrated on the invective. When he accused the Minister of the Interior of consorting with a syndicate of Spanish swindlers, the Minister's attorney railed at Harden-Hickey and his staff: "You are working for money only. You are journalists deprived of ideas, talent, wit; living from scandal, and acting the same—though in another direction—as the pornographic papers, addressing yourselves to unhealthy and overexcited passions."

Harden-Hickey's editorial policy was endorsed at the kiosks. Buying was brisk; circulation zoomed to 25,000. But, within twelve months, overenthusiasm landed the manager, M. Lampre, in Sainte-Pelagie Prison, and forced the periodical to attempt to fend off eleven lawsuits that cost the staff a total of six months' confinement and 3,000 francs in fines. Despite persistent legal ambushes, *Le Triboulet* continued to expand. By the end of its second year it had grown from a weekly to a daily publication. Harden-Hickey heralded the promise of more prose with a signed editorial: "Our readers must know today that *Triboulet* stands for courage, loyalty; they will therefore understand that our sole aim in starting this new paper is simply the desire to continue with more strength the campaign for royalty and religion. Instead of beating Marianne once a week, Triboulet's club will caress the back of the shrew every day."

For the greater part of nine years, Harden-Hickey edited *Le Triboulet* from headquarters at 35 Boulevard Haussmann. His office was "painted azure-blue, strewn with gold fleurs-de-lys, each panel trimmed with the weapons of France." His exuberance over his task never diminished; he was king-struck. And those radicals who believed in such outrageous lunacy as plebiscites had nothing but his very vocal contempt. When Republican journalists and politicians protested against his insults, Harden-Hickey would usually offer his choice of weapons: "Would you prefer to meet me upon the editorial page or in the Bois de Boulogne?" At least twelve met him with swords in the Bois, among them H. Lavertujon, a member of the Chamber of Deputies, Aurelien Scholl, a celebrated wit, and M. De Cyon, a journalist. Others sought less physical means to repair their honor. Harden-Hickey was sued forty-two times, fined 300,000 francs, and once expelled from France (for cruelly caricaturing the Presidents of the Republic, the Senate, and the Chamber dancing a jig while attired in bathing suits).

In 1884 the sponsor of all the fuss and fury, the Count de Chambord, inconsiderately expired in Austria. Harden-Hickey remained at his desk and in the Bois three more years, valiantly trying to rally the Royalist movement, until, as he later informed the New York press, "he finally grew weary of the long fight against heavy odds and the inaction of the Royalists, and he withdrew from his connection with the paper in 1887." Within a year, *Le Triboulet* had ceased pummeling Marianne. In London, Harden-Hickey announced that the paper had been suppressed by the government and he himself exiled. More likely, with Count de Chambord's death, Saint-Patrice had lost his angel.

At the age of thirty-four, Baron Harden-Hickey had divorced himself from the French Royalists and from his French wife. Now he proceeded to divorce himself from the Catholic Church, though he could not resist retaining the title of nobility that the church had conferred upon him. It is not clear if Harden-Hickey became an undiluted Buddhist, or a Theosophist, or precisely in what manner and on what date this conversion occurred. But occur it most certainly did.

At the time, Madame Helena P. Blavatsky, the Russian-born spiritualist, founder of a new mystic faith called Theosophy, was the lioness of London. In 1873 Madame Blavatsky had made her way from Cairo to New York, where she swiftly graduated from producing artificial flowers in a sweatshop to reigning as High Priestess over an apartment-salon at 302 West Forth-seventh Street (called by the press, somewhat irreverently, The Lamasery). During this period she acquired a sponsor in Colonel Henry Olcott, a Manhattan lawyer who composed occasional feature stories on spiritualism and farming for the *New York Tribune*. The Colonel left his wife and three sons to follow the Madame on a holy pilgrimage to India. After becoming a Buddhist in Ceylon, she founded the Theosophical Society, which borrowed heavily from Hinduism and Buddhism and advocated the doctrine of reincarnation.

When Harden-Hickey arrived in London, Madame Blavatsky, a great pudding of a woman who cursed like a trooper and rolled her own, was installed at 18 Lansdowne Road, Notting Hill, W. "Peers and belted earls and their ladies, scientists, savants, and explorers thronged her drawing room," reported Gertrude Marvin Williams in *Priestess of the Occult*. "Even the Church of England, thundering against her on Sunday, peeked at her on Monday. Leaning back against the cushions at one of her soirees, Madame watched the wife of the Archbishop of Canterbury sitting primly on a front row chair. . . ." Alfred Russel Wallace became a member of the Madame's Theosophical Society, Gladstone penned an essay about her, and Lord Tennyson perused her poetry. In America, Colonel Abner Doubleday, sometimes said to have invented baseball, and Thomas A. Edison, inventor of almost everything else, led the list of her followers.

Baron Harden-Hickey seems to have been equally enamored. After meeting her, he threw off Catholicism, and after traveling halfway around the earth to visit the land of her Masters ("During a fairly long stay I made in India, I have been able to personally ascertain the occult power of the Tibetan adepts"), he returned to France to put his new ideas on religion to paper. In 1890 L. Sauvaitre of Paris published *Theosophy*, by Saint-Patrice. Harden-Hickey's soul-searching foreword, addressed to his French Catholic public, advises readers to emulate him in forsaking the Church of Rome. "You were born in France, from an aristocratic or bourgeois family, and you were most certainly Catholic. The influences that presided over your education have no doubt been created by this double origin. So far, you have perhaps been right in following your faith. But now it is your duty to educate yourself and submit to a cold-blooded analysis, free of foregone conclusions, of the creed which composes your intellectual baggage. I believe, to start with, that the highest aim in life should not be possession of faith, but comprehension of truth."

In the first six chapters of *Theosophy*, Harden-Hickey lashes Christianity with the new Darwinism. "The considerable amount of good achieved in the Occident by Christianity has been offset by its evil and by the infamous doctrine that claims that honest disbelief in dogmas is a moral offense, a deadly sin." From this, Harden-Hickey goes into his last six chapters, explaining Buddhism and Theosophy and examining them also in the light of Evolution. He concludes by quoting heavily from a house organ called *The Theosophist*, and enthusiastically praising Madame Blavatsky and the Theosophical Society.

Less than one year later, a volume called *Bible Plagiarisms*, by Saint-Patrice, appeared in the Paris book-stalls. In its pages Harden-Hickey argues: "As to being a historical work, the Bible is inferior to Perrault's fairy tales; as a literary work, it is inferior to Ohnet; as to obscenity, it is worse than the Marquis de Sade." He adds that Genesis is a plagiarism of the Indian Vedas, the Old Testament a steal from Brahmanism, and Christianity a weak copy of Buddhism.

This conversion, however, was not the main product of Harden-Hickey's twenty-four-month journey around the world. Early during this trip occurred the accident that was to provide him with his *raison d'être*. Before departing he arranged that his young son and daughter, both of whom he controlled under the antiquated French divorce laws, be placed under the guardianship of his closest Parisian friend, Count de la Boissière, who had supported himself as a clerk in the Colonial Office, as a curbstone broker, and as a wine merchant, and who had in common with him a love for *affaires d'honneur* and the Bourbon way of life.

Harden-Hickey sailed on a British merchant ship, the *Astoria*, commanded by a Captain Jackson, which was bound west for Cape Horn en route to India. About seven hundred miles off Brazil a storm drove the *Astoria* into refuge behind a small mountainous island called Trinidad. This was not the larger British West Indian island of Trinidad, six miles off Venezuela, populated by a half-million, and renowned for its asphalt lake. What Harden-Hickey saw from his rolling merchantman was a coral-ridged, barren, uninhabited thumb of land isolated from and almost forgotten by the rest of the world. "One of the most uncanny and dispiriting spots on earth," E. F. Knight of the London *Times* had remarked in 1881, after observing the heavy vapors and mists that hung shroudlike over Trinidad's ravines, cliffs, and lava deposits.

Harden-Hickey requested permission of Captain Jackson to go ashore. From the Captain and crew he had heard the standard romantic stories of burried treasure on the island. In 1821, when General San Martín was liberating Peru, the wealthy Spanish families of Lima had fled to sea with their gold and jewels, estimated to be worth several millions. Some of the Spanish vessels were intercepted by Benito de Soto, a merciless pirate leader, and his crew of ex-slavers. The Spanish were deprived of their lives and their wealth. It is thought that de Soto, hard pressed, secreted his loot on bleak Trinidad before his final capture and execution in Gibraltar. His colleagues in crime were also brought to justice and the rope—that is, all except one. The lone fugitive escaped to serve on a British merchantman. When he died in Bombay, his trunk disclosed his former occupation as well as a canvas map of Trinidad. The merchantman Captain did not take the map seriously until years later when, in retirement at Newcastle, he realized that it might hold the secret to Lima's missing treasure. The map indicated that de Soto had hidden his gold and jewels in a cave near the top of a ravine on Trinidad. In 1880 the Captain's son visited the island, located the treasure site, but found that landslides had covered the cave under tons of earth. Lacking equipment, the heir could do little. He retired from the hunt. But the fascinating map survived to inspire four more treasure expeditions to Trinidad before Baron James Harden-Hickey himself waded ashore.

In his lonely hike across the island, Harden-Hickey found no signs of human life except for some stone huts left by the Brazilian Portuguese who had discovered Trinidad around 1700, and debris of earlier treasure-hunting expeditions. Though the island was desolate and wind-swept, and though there was no evidence of the treasure site, Harden-Hickey was, nevertheless, strangely stimulated. "I explored the island thoroughly," he told a New York reporter five years later, when the passage of time had cast a romantic aura over the visit. "It is about twenty-three miles long and two or three miles wide. It is on a rock foundation, but has a plateau on which there is abundant vegetation. A river of pure, fresh water runs through it. It has all the essential qualifications for supporting several hundred people. Great quantities of wild fowl make it their breeding place, and it is visited periodically by thousands of turtles, which deposit their eggs there."

Before the storm abated and the *Astoria* was able to continue on its way, Harden-Hickey apparently revisited the island, solemnly claimed it in his own name, and "planted a flag of his own design." As he did nothing more about the island at once, this seemed to be merely a momentary romantic gesture. He spent the entire following year in India, listening to holy men and learning Sanskrit, after which he went for brief visits to China and Japan. At last, in 1890, he returned to Republican France, where his earlier offenses seem to have been forgotten.

In Paris, which was just then becoming a shopping center for American heiresses who did their sight-seeing from the *Almanach de Gotha* instead of *Baedeker*, Baron Harden-Hickey met Anna H. Flagler, daughter of John Haldane Flagler, a man whom newspapers referred to as "the Standard Oil magnate," but who had actually made his fortune in the manufacture of iron (some of which was used to construct the $275,000 ironclad *Monitor* in 1861). In 1891, at the Fifth Avenue Presbyterian Church, New York City, Harden-Hickey and Miss Flagler were married by the Reverend John Hall.

During the next few years, while residing in the Flagler home in New York, Harden-Hickey unnerved his family by devoting his energies to several highly original projects, among them translating a book on Buddhism, completing his volume *Bible Plagiarisms*, perfecting a plan for missionary work to convert Americans to Buddha, and developing means of extracting money from his disapproving father-in-law.

Flagler had powerfully opposed the marriage. He regarded Harden-Hickey as a foreign fortune-seeker. In a temper, Harden-Hickey married Anna Flagler "without settlements" and supported her out of his own dwindling savings. When his money was gone, Harden-Hickey tried to obtain his wife's money, left her by her mother, with her father as executor. Flagler, not unexpectedly, refused to turn over the money. He said he had it soundly invested, whereas Harden-Hickey might do something foolish with it. Harden-Hickey was soon reduced to seeking funds from Flagler, whom he hated with mounting intensity, through his friend, Count de la Boissière, who, as a former stockbroker, got on well with Flagler, and who himself was now an American citizen after having married a Virginia heiress.

With this painfully acquired cash, Harden-Hickey not only supported his wife, but also purchased ranches and mines in Texas, California, and Mexico. This involvement in commercialism seemed to have a discouraging effect on the Baron. He was a nonentity without a future, and his mind was filled with the delights of self-extinction. "While he was in New York, I was a reporter on the Evening Sun," wrote Richard Harding Davis in 1912, "but I cannot recall ever having read his name in the newspapers of that day, and I heard of him only twice; once as giving an exhibition of his water-colors at the American Art Galleries, and again as the author of a book I found in a store in Twenty-second Street, just east of Broadway, then the home of the Truth Seeker Publishing Company."

This slender, 167-page volume, entitled *Euthanasia; the Aesthetics of Suicide*, by Baron Harden-Hickey, published by the Truth Seeker Company in 1894, is perhaps one of the most depressing documents in the history of literary eccentricity. Copies have become extremely rare. I was able to find one in the New York Public Library and one in the Library of Congress. Recently I visited the Truth Seeker bookstore, at 38 Park Row, New York, on the chance that they might still stock one of their old authors. The store was on the tenth floor of an office building, and the glazed-glass entrance bore the names of three organizations: "Truth Seeker Company . . . National Liberal League . . . American Association For The Advancement of Atheism, Inc." The Truth Seeker people were somewhat suspicious of my request for a volume on self-destruction by an American Buddhist. Their latest catalogue, while listing such titles as *What Would Christ Do About Syphilis?* and *Bible Myths* and recent volumes on free thought, made no mention of *Euthanasia; the Aesthetics of Suicide*. One of the clerks in the office telephoned his father, Dr. Charles F. Potter, who had been the first president of the Euthanasia Society. I repeated the title and the name of the author to Dr. Potter, and he thought he remembered it. "If I remember correctly," he said, "there was a brief flurry of sales, and then the authorities suppressed it. They never seem to like books condoning suicide."

In this book, the only one he wrote wholly in English, Harden-Hickey discusses suicide and justifies it with four hundred quotations ranging from the Bible to Shakespeare. While he claims to have written only the preface, it seems certain that many of the quotations "by the greatest thinkers the world has ever produced" are of doubtful parentage.

Harden-Hickey does not credit the sources of his quotations, and many may have had their origin in the study of the Flagler residence.

At any rate, the preface is the author's own handiwork. On page 4, after a wordy attack on "avaricious and knavish priests . . . vain philosophers . . . cranky scientists" who would obscure the Truth, Harden-Hickey finally gets to the point.

"Suicide has become such a common occurrence in our time—the average being one every three minutes—that it merits to attract more attention than the morbid curiosity of the readers of daily papers. To the Christian, suicide appears as a heinous crime; the followers of Christ seem to have forgotten that if the legend on which their religion was founded were true, Christ would occupy a very prominent place in the annals of suicide—plenty of men have cut the thread of their own life, but we have no authentic record of any God having done so; it may also be added that we have no authentic record of a God performing any act whatsoever."

But Harden-Hickey is just warming to his subject. On pages 6 and 7 he continues with more vigor: "One can readily understand that priests who live off men should object to their dying without paying toll, under the form of sacraments and indulgencies, for crossing over the fatal bridge; but in the name of Reason why should free-thinkers indulge in snickering and bickering at the man independent and brave enough to throw off the burden of life when it has become cumbersome. In so doing they place themselves on the same level as the most blatant churchman.

"To return to suicide, it has been universally approved of by all philosophical religions, and has been practiced by some of the most noted men of antiquity.

"In the following pages will be found the pith of what has been written on the subject by the greatest thinkers the world has ever produced: Zeno, Epictetus, Diogenes, Seneca,

Cicero, Marcus Aurelius, Montaigne, Rousseau, Donne, Hume, Gibbon, Montesquieu, etc.

"May this little work contribute to the overthrow of the reign of fear! May it nerve the faltering arm of the poor wretch to whom life is loathsome, but death full of terrors; let him say with the noble Cato:

> *'Thus I am doubly armed; my death and life,*
> *My bane and antidote, are both before me:*
> *This in a moment brings me to an end;*
> *But this informs me I shall never die.*
> *The soul, secured in her existence, smiles*
> *At the drawn dagger, and defies its point.'*

And let him calmly, without anger or joy, but with the utmost indifference, cast off the burden of existence."

The text and illustrations that follow are for adults only—those with the thickest of skins and the strongest of stomachs. In collaboration with the "greatest thinkers," Harden-Hickey suggests the best means of self-annihilation, mentioning fifty-one instruments (among them scissors) and eighty-eight poisons. The content of the book is further enlivened by a half dozen black-and-white drawings of men and women in various postures of suicide. Few, however, appear to be proper examples of Harden-Hickey's theory that suicide is a privilege. Most seem distressed or downright miserable. The first picture exhibits a man in full attire seated on his bed with a revolver against his right temple. Another picture displays a woman slumped before a coal stove, expiring from the fumes. A third shows a fop writhing on the floor, his glass of poison overturned nearby.

The quotations, whatever their sources, are more convincing and cheerful. On page 43 the intelligent are advised: "The wise man lives as long as he ought, not as long as he can." On page 128 the hedonists are courted: "We must shake off this fond desire of life and learn that it is of little consequence when we suffer; that it is of greater moment to live well than to live long, and that oftentimes it is living well not to live long."

The very year this book appeared, Baron Harden-Hickey seemed suddenly to have found a reason for *not* committing suicide. Hemmed in, as he was, by Flagler's New York—Wall Street, J. Pierpont Morgan, Sr., Procter and Gamble's first $40,000 advertising campaign, the Plaza, the horseless carriage—Harden-Hickey began to retreat more and more into the world of Napoleon III. Retreating, he remembered Trinidad. Or perhaps he had never forgotten it. At once the raucous new civilization of the stock exchange and the sky-scraper seemed less real than the barren isle off Brazil. Harden-Hickey decided to claim the isle off Brazil for his very own.

By the time the *New York Tribune* reporter came calling, in November 1893, Harden-Hickey had managed to endow his fantasy with a certain amount of legality. "I propose to take possession of the Island of Trinidad under a maxim of international law which declares that anybody may seize and hold waste land that is not claimed by anybody else," he explained. "The island is uninhabited and has been so for more than a hundred years. Two or three centuries ago the Portuguese attempted to colonize it, probably by a penal colony. They soon gave up the attempt, however. The English also once made a feeble effort to plant a colony upon it, but the project was abandoned after a short settlement. The remains of these early settlements may still be seen upon the island."

The *Tribune* representative, still skeptical, then inquired: "How will other nations regard the fact of your possession? Does Portugal or England or any other nation lay claim on the island?"

"No nation lays any claim on it," Harden-Hickey insisted. "It has been abandoned for over a century. I do not expect any difficulty. I have already informed several governments of my purpose, and have received favorable replies from some of them. I am assured that at least one nation will formally recognize my government as soon as I get it established."

In succeeding months, after crowning himself King James I of Trinidad, and appointing Count de la Boissière his Foreign Minister, Harden-Hickey opened his chancellery at 217 West Thirty-six Street, New York City, to treat with potential subjects as well as with other powers. "Trinidad's Chancellery is not a palace," reported *The New York Times*. "It is in one of the rooms of a dwelling house built on the block system." A *Tribune* man, going to visit de la Boissière, found it "a surprisingly humble place for so high a dignitary." Richard Harding Davis, calling for an interview, reported: "The chancellery was not exactly in its proper setting. On its doorstep children of the tenements were playing dolls with clothes-pins; in the street a huckster in raucous tones was offering wilted cabbages to women in wrappers leaning from the fire-escapes; the smells and the heat of New York in midsummer rose from the asphalt. It was a far cry to the wave-swept island off the coast of Brazil."

Almost two decades later, Richard Harding Davis returned to Thirty-sixth Street, and then recorded: "Three weeks ago I revisited it and found it unchanged." The neighborhood was the same except that the York Hotel had replaced the brownstone.

Four decades after Davis's last visit, I went to 217 West Thirty-sixth Street. The chancellery had undergone one more metamorphosis. It was now a narrow barbershop, with a watch-repair concession in the front of the shop near the window. This was located in what was called the Garment Center Building, and it looked out upon a street thick with trucks, vans, and taxis, and upon a sidewalk filled with workmen who were pushing racks of dresses. I did not go inside.

In 1894 the interior of the chancellery, while it gave more promise of adventure than a barbershop, also invariably disappointed those who had been educated to expect a certain lushness in connection with the purple. On the door to the chancellery was pasted a strip of paper which, in the handwriting of de la Boissière, announced: Chancellerie de la Principauté de Trinidad. The austerity of the interior made a Trappist monastery, by comparison, seem positively frivolous. "There is an oilcloth covering on the floor of the room," reported the *Tribune*, "and the furniture of the room consists of a small wooden table, much the worse for wear and having a covering of wrapping paper; three chairs, which bear the marks of age; a bookcase such as might be bought in a second-hand store for one dollar, and some shelves with pigeonholes. Some rubberstamps on the table take the place of State seals." Richard Harding Davis recalled that on the chancellery table were also copies of a recent royal proclamation, newly printed Trinidad postage stamps, and several pasteboard boxes filled with gold-and-red enameled crosses of the Order of Trinidad. On the wall hung a large announcement: Sailings To Trinidad—March 1 and October 1.

When the press asked the sorely tried John H. Flagler if he recognized King James I, he, busy as he was with his National Tube Company and his banking, insurance, and mining investments, replied seriously: "My son-in-law is a very determined man. He will carry out any scheme in which he is interested. Had he consulted me about this, I would have been glad to have aided him with money or advice. My son-in-law is an extremely well-read, refined, well-bred man. He does not court publicity. While he was staying in my house, he spent nearly all the time in the library translating an Indian book on Buddhism. My daughter has no ambition to be a queen or anything else than what she is—an American girl. But my son-in-law means to carry on this Trinidad scheme and—he will."

To carry out this scheme, Harden-Hickey produced a four-page prospectus of his kingdom, written in French. He began by stating that, having married the only daughter of an American millionaire, he had become a person of unlimited means—this to prove his seriousness and solvency. He had stumbled upon and taken possession of Trinidad, he went on to explain, and on it he had decided to establish a new state. The government would be a military dictatorship. The officers would all sport mustaches "*à la Louis Napoleon.*" The first white colonists who settled on Trinidad would form the aristocracy. To become eligible as colonists, they must give evidence that their social standing in the United States was high, and that they could afford to buy twenty 1,000-franc government bonds. This investment assured each colonist of free passage from San Francisco to Trinidad on Harden-Hickey's newly acquired schooner, and free passage back to the States after one year, if desired.

Harden-Hickey carefully described the wonders of his empire in the prospectus. "In spite of its rugged and uninviting appearance, the inland plateaus are rich with luxuriant vegetation. Prominent among these is a peculiar species of bean, which is not only edible, but extremely palatable. The surrounding sea swarms with fish, which as yet are wholly unsuspicious of the hook. Dolphins, rock-cod, pigfish, and blackfish may be caught as quickly as they can be hauled out.

"I look to the sea birds and the turtles to afford our principal source of revenue. Trinidad is the breeding place of almost the entire feathery population of the South Atlantic Ocean. The exportation of guano alone should make my little country prosperous. Turtles visit the island to deposit eggs and at certain seasons the beach is literally alive with them. The only drawback to my projected kingdom is the fact that it has no good harbor and can be approached only when the sea is calm."

Harden-Hickey went on to explain that, while the state would retain a monopoly on guano and turtle, the buried pirate treasure would be divided between those who discovered it and the government. All other delights were free —the "*vegetation luxuriante de fougères, d'acacias et de haricots sauvages, propres a la nourriture de l'homme,*" and the

BARON JAMES A. HARDEN-HICKEY

GEORGE FRANCIS TRAIN
about 1860

"vie d'un genre tout nouveau, et la récherche de sensations nouvelles."

Harden-Hickey elaborated on certain points in his prospectus with a series of official royal proclamations. One of the earliest read:

We, James, Prince of Trinidad, have resolved to commemorate our accession to the throne of Trinidad by the institution of an Order of Chivalry, destined to reward literature, industry, science, and the human virtues, and by these presents have established and do institute, with cross and crown, the Order of the Insignia of the Cross of Trinidad, of which we and our heirs and successors shall be the sovereigns.

Given in our Chancellery the 8th of the month of December, 1893, and of our reign, the First Year.

JAMES.

All through 1894 the chancellery on Thirty-sixth Street hummed with activity. Sometimes King James I himself was there to greet the press or the curious. *The Saturday Review* found him "a big, handsome, overdressed fellow, apparently an Irishman by birth." The *Tribune* described him as "a tall man, with a decided French manner. He wears a moustache and imperial, and has light brown hair. He speaks excellent English, emphasizing his remarks frequently with French gestures." Often Harden-Hickey was out of town, and then the jovial Count de la Boissière, working for a salary, fenced with the press. The *Tribune* in an unkindly mood reported him as "a stout Frenchman of thirty in a loosely fitting summer suit of light straw color, flannel shirt and tan shoes . . . so much like an ordinary man that he could go anywhere without attracting suspicion." *The New York Times*, on the other hand, was charmed by "his incandescent eyes under glasses, his hair, which is cut in the French military fashion, short and pointed at the forehead, his ample gestures and the optimisms evident in the enthusiastic, loving colors of his dress engrave."

By 1895 it appeared that King James's Trinidad was here to stay. Harden-Hickey spoke of sending the first shipload of colonists to the island in the spring or early summer. There was every reason for optimism. The great powers were aware of his existence. "Several Central American Republics, for reasons known only to themselves, did recognize him," admitted *The Saturday Review*, "and allowed their representatives in Europe, notably in Austria and at the Vatican, to inscribe Trinidad on their official cards." As to colonists, it was never officially known how many agreed to settle on Trinidad. Harden-Hickey once remarked that he had a colony of 50 whites, and 300 of his 500 Chinese coolies, ready to leave in May 1895, though when that date came there was no such departure. De la Boissière intimated there were forty persons working for Harden-Hickey on Trinidad, presumably doing preliminary labor in laying out the lighthouse, wharves, and coaling station (for ships headed toward Cape Horn).

Though Harden-Hickey left no accounting of sales of his 1,000-franc bonds, he did indicate that he was obtaining a small amount of revenue from sales of postage stamps to philatelists throughout the world. In November 1894 he offered the public seven varieties of postage stamps ranging in price from five centimes to five francs each. All of these stamps, in imitation of a North Borneo stamp issued the same year, showed a view of Trinidad from the south, with a sailing vessel in the foreground, and the inscription: "*Principauté de Trinidad—Timbre Poste et Fiscal.*" These stamps, explained de la Boissière, "have not been introduced to satisfy the curiosity of collectors, but for use. . . ." Few of these survived Harden-Hickey's time. Recently H. E. Harris and Company of Boston, one of the world's largest stamp firms, informed me that they did not "have any of the stamps available or know where they could be obtained." These stamps were not Harden-Hickey's only means of income.

Several Crosses of Trinidad, the medal for chivalry and artistic accomplishment, were also sold. This was the high-water mark in the reign of King James I. He was everywhere, traveling constantly, too busy to see his wife, too busy to argue with his father-in-law. The homemade crown sat firmly on his head. He was a happy man.

On January 3, 1895, a British warship, *Barracouta*, cast anchor off Trinidad, and proceeded to disembark troops and engineers. The British quietly garrisoned the island and began construction of a cable station for a new line stretching from Great Britain to Brazil. When word of this seizure reached South America there was "excitement" in Rio de Janeiro and angry crowds stoned the British Consulate in Baía. Brazil formally demanded that Britain withdraw its troops from Trinidad. Britain refused. The Latin press muttered about security and provocation. The British Foreign Office coolly suggested arbitration; the Brazilian Foreign Office heatedly refused. No one consulted James I. It was not until July that Harden-Hickey learned that he was a king without a country.

There is no record of the thoughts that passed through his mind in those first moments of crisis. We know only that he dictated, and Count de la Boissière transcribed and signed, a stern and detailed protest to the United States Department of State:

New York, July 30, 1895

Excellency:

I have the honor to recall to your memory:

First, That in the course of the month of September, 1893, Baron Harden-Hickey has officially notified all the powers of his taking of possession of the uninhabited island of Trinidad; and,

Second, That in the course of January, 1894, he has renewed to all these powers the official notification of the said taking of possession, and has informed them at the same time from that date the land would be known as Principality of

Trinidad; that he took the title of Prince of Trinidad, and would reign under the name of James I.

In consequence of these official notifications, several powers have recognized the new Principality and its Prince, and at all events none has thought it necessary at that epoch to raise objections or formulate opposition.

The press of the entire world has, on the other hand, often acquainted readers with these facts, thus giving to them all possible publicity. In consequence of the accomplishment of these formalities, and as the law of nations prescribes that "derelict" territories belong to whoever will take possession of them, and as the Island of Trinidad, which has been abandoned for years, certainly belongs to the aforesaid category, his Serene Highness Prince James I was authorized to regard his rights on the said island as perfectly valid and indisputable.

Nevertheless, your Excellency knows that recently, in spite of all the legitimate rights of my august sovereign, an English warship has disembarked at Trinidad a detachment of armed troops and taken possession of the island in the name of England.

Following this assumption of territory, the Brazilian Government, invoking a right of ancient Portuguese occupation, (long ago outlawed), has notified the English Government to surrender the island to Brazil.

I beg of your Excellency to ask of the Government of the United States of North America to recognize the Principality of Trinidad as an independent State, and to come to an understanding with the other American powers in order to guarantee its neutrality.

Thus, the Government of the United States of North America will once more accord its powerful assistance to the cause of right and of justice, misunderstood by England and Brazil, put an end to a situation which threatens to disturb the peace, reestablish concord between two great States ready to appeal to arms, and affirm itself, moreover, as the faithful interpreter of the Monroe Doctrine.

In the expectation of your reply, please accept, Excellency, the expression of my elevated consideration.
The Grand Chancellor,
Secretary of State for Foreign Affairs,
COMTE DE LA BOISSIÈRE.

When Secretary of State Richard Olney received the document, he complained to the Washington correspondents that he could not read the handwriting. He was able to make out, he said, only that it was a formal protest, "signed by somebody, whose name could not be deciphered, as Chancellor," on behalf of somebody else called "James I." Since he could not read it, the Secretary of State could not act upon it. Cruelly, either he or his Second Assistant gave the document to the press.

The chancellery was never more crowded than the next morning. Baron Harden-Hickey, stunned by the annexation, had already left for California, but Count de la Boissière was cheerfully on hand to meet the reporters. Most teased him unmercifully. The *Tribune*, which gave the story a full column, including cuts of both Harden-Hickey and de la Boissière, set the tone:

"The Grand Chancellor said yesterday that he intended to go to Washington today and make an official call upon the Secretary of State. It was understood that the English wanted the island as a coaling station and as a place for landing a cable, he said, and there would be no objections to the cable and shipping wharves if only the rights of the principality were recognized.

" 'In fact,' said the Grand Chancellor, in broken English, 'we would be glad to have them lay a cable to the island, because just now the island is not a good place in which to hear the news of the world.' "

The *Tribune* concluded on a note that would have provoked de la Boissière, or his sovereign, in more fiery days, to suggest a rendezvous in the Bois. Said the *Tribune:*

"The Grand Chancellor seemed to be disinclined to talk about himself. He was a wine agent some time ago, but his only job at present is that of Grand Chancellor. . . . The expenses of the Grand Chancellery have to be kept down to the lowest possible notch, while the Powers are considering whether they will recognize James I as an independent sovereign. If their decision should be adverse to the principality, it is harrowing to think what might happen to the Grand Chancellor. He might have to go back to the wine business."

Only two newspapermen in New York were sympathetic. The managing editor of *The New York Times* sent a reporter, who later became a prominent art and music critic, Henri Pene du Bois, to the chancellery. When du Bois returned to his office the editor asked him what he found. Du Bois shook his head. "There is nothing funny in that story," he said. "It's pathetic. Both those men are earnest. They are convinced they are being robbed of their rights. Their only fault is that they have imagination, and that the rest of us lack it. That's the way it struck me, and that's the way the story should be written." The editor nodded. "Write it that way."

The New York Times published the story on page one, column one, of its August 1 edition. The top headline read: "Trinidad's Prince Awake." The second head read: "An Appeal To Washington Against Brazil And Great Britain." The *Times* played it straight. It reprinted de la Boissière's entire protest to the Secretary of State. It quoted de la Boissière gently and at length:

"M. le Comte de la Boissière is luxuriously dressed. In white wool, and in white silk striped with pale blue, he bowed affably to the reporter for The New-York Times.

"'Do you like my appeal to Washington?' he asked. 'I have sent it to all the Ministers Plenipotentiary, Ambassadors, Envoys, and diplomatic agents. Oh, everybody knows about the Principality now. Everybody knew before, for all the newspapers had made its fame resound. They were not all friendly newspapers; some of them treated us in deplorably frivolous manner, but all served to make ignorance of our claim inexcusable. It would be childish for Brazil or for England to plead ignorance of our authority now. Our claim has been admitted by some powers, since they have sent answers to our notifications.'

" 'Of course,' said the reporter. 'Then there are your subjects to be considered. Nobody believes that they will indifferently let themselves become Britons or Brazilians.'

" 'Our subjects!' exclaimed M. de la Boissière. 'Well, we need not talk about them. The question of population has no bearing in such affairs. There would have been a stock of subjects at Trinidad now, if the English had not seized the land.' "

The very next day *The New York Times* ran a half-column follow-up interview with de la Boissière. The story led off with: "In the State Department at Washington the clerks could not read the signature of Trinidad's Grand Chancellor. One wonders if they could have read that of Talleyrand. He signed 'Ch. Mau. Tal.' with a flourish of flies' legs on a window pane. He used no capital letters. Those of M. le Comte de la Boissière are fantastic and delicate."

When at the end of the second interview the *Times* man asked de la Boissière if he'd ever visited Trinidad, he replied: "No, thank you. I have other tigers to comb. We may take an indemnity from Great Britain, you know. It will be millions. You shall have a commission on the amount."

When these stories reached Harden-Hickey, he proclaimed that *The New York Times* would thereafter be his official news-organ. He awarded Managing Editor Henry Cary and Reporter Henri Pene du Bois each the Cross of Trinidad ("destined to reward literature . . . and the human virtues"), and appointed each a Chevalier of the Court of Trinidad, which entitled them to wear uniforms identical with those of the chamberlains of the court and to receive pensions of 1,000 francs a year once the kingdom again became a going concern.

Richard Harding Davis was the other newspaperman to handle the tottering principality with sympathy. Davis, who had been the model for Charles Dana Gibson's handsome males, earned $100,000 a year writing first-person foreign news stories, plays, and novels. Many considered him a conceited, prudish clotheshorse. They may have been right. But beneath the chill exterior beat the warm heart of a romantic. To play king when there were no more kingdoms? To have one's own toy island? Why not? Richard Harding Davis was an admiring vassal long before he reached the brownstone building on Thirty-sixth Street.

"De la Boissière talked to me frankly and fondly of Prince James," Davis wrote shortly afterwards. "Indeed, I never met any man who knew Harden-Hickey well, who did not speak of him with aggressive loyalty. If at his eccentricities they smiled, it was with the smile of affection. It was easy to see De la Boissière regarded him not only with the affection of a friend, but with the devotion of a true subject. In his manner he himself was courteous, gentle, and so distinguished that I felt as though I were enjoying, on intimate terms, an audience with one of the prime-ministers of Europe. And he, on his part, after the ridicule of the morning papers, to have anyone with outward seriousness accept his high office and his king, was, I believe, not ungrateful."

In San Francisco, Baron Harden-Hickey began to show signs of discouragement. His Foreign Minister's formal protests and the tremendous publicity given these protests brought no response. Great Britain and Brazil continued their diplomatic dispute over Trinidad, and ignored King James I completely. If he read *The Saturday Review* for August 3, as most likely he did, he probably detected there the obituary of his reign. "The guano, the buried treasure, the innocent turtles basking on the sands under the watchful eye of the Zouave with the moustache and imperial, all have been swept abruptly into the rapacious maw of the British Empire."

In January 1896 the tug of war between Great Britain and Brazil was still raging when suddenly the British garrison withdrew, surrendering its cable station and Trinidad itself to Brazil. The Brazilians, of course, had no use for the island; they just had not wanted English troops in the vicinity. Now they did not dare, after months of sound and fury, to hand the island over to an American adventurer. They agreed to retain possession of it on paper. It is unlikely that any Brazilian in his right mind was ever induced to spend a night on the island. As in the beginning, Trinidad again belonged to the turtles.

Harden-Hickey had lost. In the past he had always been able to bounce back into some new project. But Trinidad had become an obsession. Letters of solace poured in, crackpot and legitimate, offering him partnership in various schemes. One of the more tempting came in an envelope postmarked San Francisco, from an army veteran named Ralston J. Markowe, who had undertaken to restore Queen Liliuokalani to the Hawaiian throne and failed. Markowe, still representing the Hawaiian royalist party, offered Harden-Hickey a place to hang his crown. "It is the island of Kauai on which I propose to establish you as an independent sovereign," the letter read. Markowe had a 146-ton vessel and 276 men ready to land in the first and only wave. Harden-Hickey was not interested, though he carried Markowe's letter around with him for two years.

While he knew he could not recover Trinidad, his obsession now took the form of revenging himself upon Great Britain. His head swam with fantasies, until he clung to one. He would keep his honor unsullied by launching an invasion of England through Ireland. The plan seemed eminently logical, but required vast sums of money. He swallowed his pride and approached John H. Flagler. His father-in-law, holding no grudge against England, thought that he had taken leave of his senses.

He wanted funds desperately now, less for Harden-Hickey than for King James I, deposed. Several money-raising efforts failed. His ace in the hole was a large ranch he owned in Mexico. He wrote his wife, who had leased a home in Riverside, California, that he was on his way to Mexico to dispose of the property to the highest bidder. Early in February 1898 the last prospect backed down. The ranch could not be sold.

Weary and heartsick, he decided to return to his wife and children in California. He crossed over into Texas and rode as far as El Paso. There he went to the Pierson Hotel and signed the register "Harden-Hickey, Paris." He remained in the hotel a week, avoiding the other guests. He seemed to be waiting for something. Later, someone thought he had heard him remark that he was waiting for money from friends.

On February 9, at 7:30 in the evening, Harden-Hickey retired to his bedroom. He was not seen that evening. At twelve o'clock noon, the day following, February 10, the chambermaids entering to clean discovered him lying rigidly across his bed. It was at once apparent that he was not sleeping. A doctor was summoned. Harden-Hickey had committed suicide by taking an overdose of morphine. Pinned to the chair beside his bed was a letter addressed to his wife:

My Dearest. No news from you, although you have had plenty of time to answer. Hardes has written me that he has no one in view for buying my land at present. Well, I shall have drained the cup of bitterness to the very dregs, but I do not complain. I prefer to be a dead gentleman to a living blackguard like your father. Goodby. I forgive your conduct toward me and trust you will be able to forgive yourself.

In his hand trunk, among his personal effects, were found Markowe's letter offering him a throne in Hawaii, and the crown he had never worn as King James I of Trinidad.

He was on the front pages again. The *New York Tribune* and *New York Times* gave the news prominence, with identical headlines: "Harden-Hickey A Suicide." John H. Flagler left New York immediately by train for California. The press trapped him in St. Louis. He made a statement to one and all. "Personally I do not believe that he meant to take his life. He was a man of highly wrought nervous organization, and for years had sought relief from insomnia in the use of sedatives and narcotics. He was an habitual user of chloral in various forms. It appears from statements made to me that he took some of the drug without effect, and later took another dose. Neither dose would have killed him, but the combination was fatal. He had been troubled with a heart affliction for years and could not live in high altitudes. His heart weakness may have aided the drug in causing his death. He was a man of cheerful nature, had all any man can desire—plenty of money and a happy home. I never heard of any financial reverses which might have caused despondency." When Flagler finished his statement a St. Louis reporter asked what he thought of Harden-Hickey's reference to him as a "blackguard" in the farewell note. Flagler did his best, "with dignity," the press reported. "I have no personal knowledge that the Baron left any such communication," said Flagler. "I was a good friend to the Baron, and was ready to go to his assistance. If he left a letter tending to show that he was depressed, that in itself would be no sign that he took his life. Among other eccentricities of his genius he had a tendency to melancholy, which sometimes made him say strange things."

On February 12 the El Paso police physician reaffirmed that Harden-Hickey's death came "from drugs taken with suicidal intent." The same day his personal effects, including the royal crown, were forwarded to his wife in Riverside, California. His remains were shipped at his wife's request to his mother, Mrs. E. C. Hickey, in San Francisco.

The New York press, in the three days following his death, gave considerable space to his Parisian and Trinidad adventures. But in all the columns of copy, no New York paper was enterprising or sentimental enough to refer to the foreword of Harden-Hickey's last book, *Euthanasia; the Aesthetics of Suicide:*

"Away with darkness where ignorance creeps in slimy filth, let Truth show herself in her splendid nudity, in her ideal beauty. I now see thy face, it illumines my way. I sought for thee during many weary years and under many bitter difficulties; and when thou knewest that I would never renounce the hope of finding thee and that I would pursue thee, not only in this life, but through a thousand incarnations, thou camest to me saying:

" 'Here am I, what wilt thou?'

" 'Disclose to me the enigma, the remedy to the evils of life?' was my prayer; and thine answer was:

" 'Death.' "

III

The Man Who Was Phileas Fogg

"Remember Jules Verne's 'Around The World In Eighty Days'? He stole my thunder. I'm Phileas Fogg."

GEORGE FRANCIS TRAIN

The inspiration for the most popular novel Jules Verne was to write came to him one day late in 1871 while he sat in his favorite café in Amiens absently leafing through a French periodical.

For months the press had been filled with the disaster of the Franco-Prussian War. Verne had followed the short, bitter conflict closely. He had read about Wörth and Metz, about the capture of Napoleon III at Sedan, about the besieged citizens of Paris forced to partake of their beloved elephants in the Zoological Gardens for sustenance, about the Prussians encamped two days on the shuttered Champs-Elysées. Verne sighed with relief when Adolphe Thiers put his pen to the peace, even though it meant conceding much of Alsace-Lorraine and a one-billion-dollar indemnity to Bismarck.

But though the war was over, the press promised no relief from violence. A savage civil strife was under way. Léon Gambetta, the one-eyed French-Italian deputy from Marseilles who had fled Paris in a balloon, rallied the new republic to suppress the Communards, a fanatical uprising of ordinary laborers, National Guardsmen, and communists who had the blessings of Karl Marx from his headquarters in the British Museum.

For Jules Verne, whose growing reputation at forty-three was based on novels of the future inspired by events of the moment, the periodical he held in his hands, with its painful political reportage, held little hope of either inspiration or escape.

And then, suddenly, as he remembered years later, his gaze fell upon a curious account from abroad.

An eccentric American millionaire had circled the globe in eighty days, an incredible accomplishment in that era of carriages, sailing vessels, and erratic iron horses. It was this new record for speed against countless obstacles that struck Verne at once, this "new possibility of making the circuit in eighty days."

Hastily Verne read on, devouring every detail of the American traveler's difficulties and adventures. The American, a Bostonian named George Francis Train, had sped from New York to San Francisco through red-Indian country in seven days aboard the new Union Pacific train. He had left California on August 1, 1870, and arrived in Japan a mere twenty-five days later. In Tokyo he had astonished the Mikado's subjects by joining them, in the nude, in a public bath. After putting Hong Kong, Saigon, and Singapore behind him, Train passed through the recently opened Suez Canal in the Mediterranean, and thence to Marseilles. In Marseilles he became a leader of the Commune, was jailed for two weeks in Lyons, met Gambetta in Tours, then hired a private *wagons-lits* coach and raced across France to the Channel. From Liverpool he caught a ship for America, and returned to his destination after eighty days of almost perpetual motion.

Jules Verne was fascinated. In 1871 the idea of circling the world at great speed was almost as dramatic as the science fiction he had created earlier about an underwater boat that could travel fifty miles an hour on an exploration beneath the oceans and beneath the Isthmus of Suez (by use of a tunnel). Inspired by George Francis Train's adventures, as well as by the postwar advertisements of Cook's Tours in shopwindows, Verne began to draft his hero, Phileas Fogg, and his story, *Around the World in Eighty Days.*

He finished writing the novel in November 1872. But before permitting his friend Pierre Jule Hetzel to publish it as one of the "*Voyages Extraordinaires*," he agreed to its serialization in the popular press. It appeared in *Le Temps*, a chapter a day in *feuilleton*—that is, in the literary supplement—during the early part of 1873.

It was not literature, but it was high adventure of the most thrilling sort, and it delighted Verne fans then, even as it continues to delight them to this day. By the alchemy of fiction Verne transformed the emotional and erratic American, George Francis Train, into the emotionless and precise Englishman, Phileas Fogg, Esq., enigmatic and respected member of the London Reform Club. Using Train's actual escapades as the basis of his story, Verne had Phileas Fogg wager 40,000 pounds that he could circle the globe in eighty days, and then forced Fogg to traverse a portion of India on an elephant, rescue a Parsi girl named Aouda from a flaming pyre, outwit a detective in China who thought him a thief, reach Omaha on a sledge bearing sails, cross the Atlantic by burning the superstructure of his steamer for fuel, and finally arrive in London one day late—only to learn, at the last moment, that he had gained a day by traveling eastward around the world.

The sensation created by the publication of this story was enormous. No Gallic armchair adventurer was without his *Temps*. English and American foreign correspondents cabled entire chapters daily to their papers in England and the United States, treating Phileas Fogg's progress as straight news. The citizenry of three nations breathlessly, and simultaneously, followed each installment, and many wagered on the success or failure of Phileas Fogg's race against time.

"Seldom has any piece of fiction excited such a furor," wrote Charles F. Horne, who edited an American edition of Verne's collected works. "Liberal offers were made to the author by various transportation companies, if he would advertise their routes by having his hero travel by them. And when the final passage of the Atlantic from America to England was to be accomplished, the bids for notice by the various transatlantic lines are said to have reached fabulous sums."

Verne did not have to compromise or commercialize his story to obtain "fabulous sums." With the publication of *Around the World in Eighty Days* as a novel, and its adaptation into a play which ran in Paris for three years, and after that in Vienna, Brussels, London, and New York, Verne's fortune was made. It is known that he bought a yacht, and it is said that he acquired a mistress. Until his death in 1905 his villa in Amiens was a Mecca for travelers.

Inspired by Fogg, a Hungarian army officer named Lubowitz rode from Vienna to Paris in fifteen days to win a bet, and was received as a guest by Verne for two days. In 1889 an aggressive brunette from the *New York World*, Nellie Bly, carrying gripsack and shoulder bag, paused on her journey into fame to burst upon the surprised Verne in his tower room at Amiens and inform him that she would beat Phileas Fogg's record. Verne was politely doubtful, but wished her luck. Miss Bly lowered Fogg's record by eight days.

In 1901 a journalist representing the *Echo de Paris*, Stiegler by name, interrupted his sixty-three-day tour of the world to shake hands with Verne in the Amiens depot. In the best of humor, Verne glanced over his visitor's shoulder and said: "But I don't see Miss Aouda." Stiegler smiled. "Reality is inferior to the imagination, Monsieur Verne. I didn't even meet her."

They all paid homage to Verne, except the one who was really Phileas Fogg. George Francis Train and Verne never met. And Train would not condescend to visit the man he felt owed him so much.

Around the World in Eighty Days was filled with incidents and activities that closely paralleled the life and travels of George Francis Train. There were differences, of course: Verne had Fogg travel east around the world, whereas Train had actually traveled west. Verne made Fogg a mechanical man, whereas Train was an impulsive, explosive human being. But the handsome, bewhiskered Fogg had in common with the handsome, mustached Train a reputation for eccentricity, a compulsion to read newspapers excessively, a lack of interest in sight-seeing when on the road, a predilection for squalls and typhoons, and an utter disregard for the extravagances involved in chartering special transportation.

In his 100,000-word autobiography, dictated in thirty-five working hours and published the year before his death, Train made constant claim to being the prototype for Phileas Fogg. In recording his account of the trip, he stated: "I went around the world in eighty days in the year 1870, two years before Jules Verne wrote his famous romance, *Le Tour du monde en quatre-vingts jours*, which was founded upon my voyage." Speaking again of the eighty days, he wrote: "Jules Verne, two years later, wrote fiction of my fact." And in summarizing his four trips around the world, Train said: "One of these voyages, the one in which I put a girdle round the earth in eighty days, has the honor of having given the suggestion for one of the most interesting romances in literature."

Once, in London, on a second and faster journey around the globe, shortly after he had been declared insane by a Boston judge (though, actually, few ever seriously thought him insane), Train exploded to English reporters: "Remember Jules Verne's 'Around The World In Eighty Days'? He stole my thunder. I'm Phileas Fogg. But I have beaten Fogg out of sight. What put the notion into my head? Well, I'm possessed of great psychic force."

As a matter of fact, the author Verne and the merchant Train had much in common. Both were interested in the growing technology, in mechanical progress, in speed. Both ranged far ahead of their time. It was only their methods that differed. Verne confined his dreams of progress to paper, where they were acceptable; Train tried to make his real, and was often rebuffed.

Train was Phileas Fogg for eighty days, but he was much more for almost eighty years. Beside him, the fictional Fogg was a one-dimensional dullard. For no author could have invented Train or transferred all of him to manuscript, and made him half believable.

George Francis Train was born in Boston on March 24, 1829. As an infant he was taken by his family to New Orleans, where his father opened a general store. In 1833, when Train was four, the great yellow-fever epidemic hit New Orleans. Families hammered together their own pine coffins, and deposited them on passing "dead wagons." Train lost his mother and three sisters in the dreadful plague. At last a letter came from his maternal grandmother in Waltham, Massachusetts, begging his father to "send on some one of the family, before they are all dead. Send George."

Train's father, before meeting his own death by the fever, sent the boy aboard the ship *Henry* with an identity card pinned to his coat. After twenty-three days at sea without a change of clothes, the four-year-old boy reached Waltham. From the day he entered the Pickering farm, he was in revolt. The members of his family were strict Methodists. Their only topical reading was a weekly periodical called *Zion's Herald*. When his great-grandfather, who wore a fez and tippled, and his grandmother, who smoked a pipe, insisted that he learn to pray, Train complied—but he would not kneel. "I could not see the necessity of God, and no one could ever explain to me the reason why there should be, or is, a God," he said later. "Morality and ethics I could see the necessity of, and the high and authoritative reason for; but religion never appealed to my intelligence or to my emotions."

He helped to sell the family's farm produce. He attended school. But when there was talk of preparing him for the clergy, or at least for the profession of blacksmith, he walked out. He was fourteen when he left the farm for a job in a Cambridgeport grocery. It was hard work. He labored from four o'clock daybreak until ten in the evening for fifty dollars a year. This went on for two years, and might have gone on longer but for the fact that one day he had a visitor who changed his entire life.

His father's cousin, a wealthy, conservative gentleman, Colonel Enoch Train, came calling in a splendid carriage. He made polite inquiries, then returned to the granite building at 37 Lewis Wharf, Boston, which housed the shipping enterprises of Train and Company.

The following day, Train quit the grocery and appeared in Colonel Enoch's office. "Where do I come in?" he bluntly asked. The Colonel was shocked. "Come in? Why, people don't come into a big shipping house like this in that way. You are too young." Train stood his ground. "I am growing older every day. That is the reason I am here. I want to make my way in the world." It was a day when audacity was still respected. Train was put to work with the bookkeeper.

The Colonel's shipping house was never quite the same after that. In two years the tall, darkly attractive Train had become manager of the firm, and within four years he was receiving $10,000 annually as a partner. Completely uninhibited, Train modernized the business. The Colonel's aged clippers were receiving stiff competition from the Black Ball Line and from Cunard's new steamships. When the gold rush began in California, Train made his employer divert forty packets from the English run to the race around the Cape. Dismayed that their largest vessel was only 800 tons, Train prodded the dazed old man into contracting for larger, faster ships. As a result, Donald McKay was commissioned to build a radically new kind of boat, one with a sharp bow that sliced through or clipped the water. His most spectacular product for Train and Company was the 2,000-ton *Flying Cloud,* whose canvas soared ninety feet into the air and carried her around Cape Horn to California in a record-smashing eighty-nine days. She was followed by the 2,200-ton *Monarch Of The Seas.* The former was sold to the Swallow-Tail Line for $90,000, twice her cost, and the latter to a company in Germany for $110,000.

But though he helped the Colonel, Train did not ignore himself. He decided to try a little exporting and importing on his own. He inveigled a company captain into smuggling three tins of opium into China in return for silks and curios. His share of the subsequent profits was an eye opener.

Besides filling his pockets, Train also fed his ego. He liked to meet renowned personalities. One of his first contacts with celebrity occurred quite by accident. In October 1847, Train remembered later, "a gentleman, looking like a farmer, came into the office" and requested passage to England on a boat sailing in an hour. Train told him there was one seventy-five-dollar stateroom left, and then asked his name. " 'Ralph Waldo Emerson,' he replied. Then he took out of his pocket an old wallet, with twine wrapped around it four or five times, opened it carefully, and counted out seventy-five dollars. . . . Mr. Emerson was then starting on his famous visit to England, during which he was to visit Carlyle."

In line of duty, Train met Nathaniel Hawthorne in the Boston customhouse. "He seemed very unassuming, and not in very affluent circumstances. I suppose his salary from the Government at the time was not more than $1,000 a year." When a company ship sank off Boston Light, and it was thought that the captain had sunk it for the insurance, Train hurried to the office of Daniel Webster, the hard-drinking, hard-eating future secretary of State. "I remember now the roar of his great deep voice as he responded to my knock. . . . He sat at his flat desk, a magnificent example of manhood, his massive head set squarely and solidly upon his shoulders."

Webster was grateful for a $1,000 retainer, and later repaid Train by getting him into the White House to meet President Zachary Taylor. Train, then twenty-one, spent an awed half hour with "Old Rough and Ready," a man who had never cast a vote in his life. "He wore a shirt that was formerly white, but which then looked like the map of Mexico after the battle of Buena Vista. It was spotted and spattered with tobacco juice. Directly behind me, as I was soon made aware, was a cuspidor, toward which the President turned the flow of tobacco juice. I was in mortal terror, but I soon saw there was no danger . . . he never missed the cuspidor once, or put my person in jeopardy."

In the years that followed, Train met Napoleon III and the Empress Eugénie and was impressed, saw the elderly Duke of Wellington at a party in London and was not impressed, guided Secretary of State William H. Seward about Paris and decided he knew little "of European thought and power," and paid the stranded Edwin Booth's passage home from Australia, though he "never received a word of thanks or appreciation from Booth."

By 1850 Train's value to the Colonel was so great that he was awarded a one-sixth partnership in the firm and promoted to the position of European manager. In Liverpool he had twenty-five clerks working under him and four ships ferrying steel, crockery, and dry goods across the Atlantic.

Back in the United States on a visit, Train was waiting for transportation on the Syracuse railroad platform, when his gaze fell upon an attractive, brown-eyed Southern girl. It was love at first sight. Impulsively, he sat opposite her and the family doctor who was chaperoning her. He struck up a conversation, learned that she was Wilhelmina Wilkinson Davis, a relation of Jefferson Davis and the daughter of a former Army Colonel who was editor of the *Louisville Courier*. Doggedly, Train followed her on a sight-seeing excursion to Niagara Falls, and there, he said, "our love was mutually discovered and confessed amid the roaring accompaniment of the great cataract." Though a Northerner, he was acceptable to Wilhelmina's family. They were married in the Louisville Episcopal Church in October 1851. She was seventeen; he was twenty-two.

Returning to Liverpool in stormy seas, Train was responsible for ordering the rescue of two hundred persons on a floundering ship carrying railroad iron. After another year in Liverpool dabbling in phrenology, visiting the mansions of the titled, suggesting decorations for Prince Albert's Crystal Palace, Train became restless. The Colonel, he felt, was holding him down. He was destined for bigger things.

He hastened back to Boston and demanded a full partnership. Colonel Enoch's reaction was one of mild apoplexy. After a terrible scene the Colonel offered him a larger share of the business, a share amounting to $15,000 a year. Train waited for the contract and then, instead of signing it, tore it up. He had decided to go off on his own. He would go to Melbourne, Australia, which had been founded less than twenty years before and was in the midst of a gold rush. The Colonel, it must be said, accepted the decision with good grace.

The journey from New York to Australia took ninety-two days. Train occupied himself, on the clipper *Bavaria*, by hooking a shark, harpooning a porpoise, and catching an albatross. He traveled not only with his wife, but also with clerks hired in Boston, crates of business forms and books, and contracts to purchase Australian gold for one firm and to export South Seas goods for another. Despite the gold rush, he expected to find a desolate, isolated Australia, and was speechless when he counted six hundred ships in Sandridge Harbor, the port of Melbourne.

Train wasted no time. His activity was as feverish during his first week Down Under as it would be every week of his two-year stay. He needed a warehouse in Sandridge. He ordered one built in Boston and shipped in sections, thus anticipating prefabricated building by almost a century. The six-story warehouse cost him $25,000. Then, dissatisfied with the crude buildings of Melbourne, he constructed his own corner offices in the heart of the city for $60,000. The city's population had doubled to forty thousand persons almost overnight. Train made a spectacular bid for their business, installing marble trading-counters in his headquarters and lavishing free champagne lunches on impressed customers. He sold gold, sold a 120-day transportation service to Boston, imported Concord stagecoaches, imported canned foods. In a year his profit in commissions was $95,000.

Train was fascinated by Australia. He introduced not only Yankee vehicles, but also American bowling and the Fourth of July to Melbourne. But when his wife became pregnant a second time—their first child, a girl, had died in her fifth month—Train packed her off to the United States. Not only did he want more civilized conditions for her, but he wanted the boy born on American soil so that he might be eligible for the American presidency. The boy turned out to be a girl, named Susan, and she was born in Liverpool, en route to Boston. Later, indeed, there were two boys, George and Elsey, who grew up to become bankers in Omaha. But Susan was Train's favorite. She married a man named Gulager, who worked in the New York Subtreasury, and lived in Stamford, Connecticut, where Train often visited her.

His wife's departure from Melbourne was actually well timed. For shortly after, twenty thousand miners in the Ballarat and Bendigo fields revolted against new government restrictions. The government had saddled the gold miners with increased license fees and banned them from participation in the provincial government. With a roar of protest, the armed, unruly miners marched on Melbourne, killing forty-one soldiers in the process, burning down the Bentley's Hotel, and erecting a stockade in the ruins.

They made plans to establish a democratic Five Star Republic. But first they needed more weapons. One of their number, an American citizen, James McGill, offered to lead a raid on a government shipment. No sooner had McGill left for the raid than government troops swarmed over the miners' stockade and crushed it.

Posters appeared throughout Melbourne offering 1,000 pounds for McGill, dead or alive. Still he did not surrender. Unable to execute his raid, unable to return to his base, he determined to find the vital arms inside Melbourne. In his desperation, he turned to George Francis Train.

Train had been sympathetic toward the miners. And they, in turn, admired him. They felt kinship toward an individualist who came from a nation that had once upended British authority. They proffered him the presidency of their projected Five Star Republic. Train declined. "I neither wanted it, nor could I have obtained it," he remarked years after.

Train was in his office one morning, working at his desk, when the fugitive McGill slipped into the room, locked the door, and stood before him. "I hear that you have some eighty thousand dollars' worth of Colt's revolvers in stock," McGill began. "I have been sent down here to get them."

Train stared at him. "Do you know that there is a reward for your head of one thousand pounds?"

"That does not mean anything."

Train became angry. "This will not do. You have no right to compromise me in this way."

"We have elected you president of our republic."

"Damn the republic . . . I am not here to lead or encourage revolutions, but to carry on my business."

In that tense moment, there was a knock on the door. It was the Melbourne Chief of Police. Hastily, Train hid McGill, admitted the Chief, learned that he merely wanted to requisition some Concord wagons. Train got rid of him, then returned to the fugitive. "Now, McGill, I am not going to betray you, but am going to save your life. You must do as I tell you."

Train found a barber and had him shave off McGill's mustache and cut his hair. Then Train had McGill change into laborers' clothes. In this guise McGill was led to the safety of one of Train's clippers, where he was put to work as a stevedore. Three days later he was safe at sea—and with him went Train's prospects for the Australian presidency.

Actually, Train had more ambitious plans. He felt that his Australian commission business was too limited and that the New Englanders he dealt with were too conservative. He decided to pull up roots and move north. A year before, Commodore Matthew Perry and his seven black ships had sailed into Yedo Bay and opened Japan to world trade. Train set his sights on a new business in Yokohama.

Though he started out for Japan, he never quite reached it. When he arrived in Shanghai, he learned that all sailings for Yokohama had been canceled and would not be resumed until the Crimean War peace treaty had been settled. But neither the journey toward Japan nor the long voyage home after was wasted. The sights Train saw and the adventures he met stimulated a lifelong odyssey that took him four times around the world and across the Atlantic on twenty-seven different occasions.

From the moment Train left Australia he peppered the pages of the *New York Herald* with a provocative running commentary on his travels. Sailing through the Strait of Sunda, he saw the volcanic island of Krakatau threaten eruption. And erupt it finally did, exactly twenty-eight years later, in the loudest blast in all history (heard as far away as Australia), an explosion that sent waves halfway around the earth to the English Channel. He halted in Singapore to visit a Chinese millionaire and his two pet tigers, rode from Hong Kong to Canton with H. E. Green, the future husband of

Hetty Green, and strolled about Manchu-ruled Shanghai shuddering at the "gory heads of rebels hanging from the walls."

Continuing his travels, he visited the Black Hole of Calcutta and felt that "there have been many worse catastrophes." He approved of the cremation pyres on the Ganges because they were economical, costing only one-half cent per body. He found nine flying fish dead in his berth near Aden. He took a donkey to the Pyramids. He was shocked by Palestine. "For three days I saw nothing but humbug and tinsel, lying and cheating, ugly women, sand-fleas and dogs." He was revolted by Bethlehem, "disgusted at being taken down two flights and shown an old wet cave as the place where the Saviour was said to have been born." He visited Balaklava in the Crimea and reported that the Charge of the Light Brigade had been "a terribly exaggerated affair, so far as massacre was concerned."

When he returned to New York in July 1856, the *Herald* greeted him with sixteen full columns of his letters from abroad and James Gordon Bennett met him with the request that he run for Congress. But the wanderlust was, for the moment, more important to him than politics.

In 1856 he returned to Europe with his wife and infant daughter, taking up residence in Paris at the Grand-Hôtel du Louvre, in the rue de Rivoli. He contracted to write a series of financial articles for *Merchants' Magazine* and determined to become a linguist like the German businessmen he had met in the East. He already knew German. Now he hired a Catholic priest to tutor him in French and Italian. When he wasn't studying he was trying to enter European society. He mingled with French counts, Spanish dukes, and tsarist princes, and felt what he learned from them "made up for the loss of a college career." He was childishly happy to be invited to a formal ball given by Napoleon III in the Tuileries. There were four thousand guests, many waltzing to an orchestra led personally by Johann Strauss. Train was pleased to meet the Emperor's current mistress and to speak to the Empress Eugénie in French.

He did not remain in Paris long. He went to Rome, where a fiery Italian delegation welcomed him as a liberator. He was certain they mistook him for Garibaldi, but it turned out that they knew who he was. Nevertheless, he wanted no part of their violence. "The curious thing about the affair," he reflected later, "was that here, as everywhere, these people regarded me as a leader of revolts—Carbonari, La Commune, Chartists, Fenians, Internationals—as if I were ready for every species of deviltry. For fifteen years, five or six governments kept their spies shadowing me in Europe and America."

In 1857 he went to Russia armed with a social message from a mutual friend to the Tsar's younger brother, the Grand Duke Constantine. Train tracked the Grand Duke to his country residence in Strelna, near St. Petersburg. After that he was royally treated. He found Moscow the most impressive city he had ever seen. "There is something primitive and prehistoric about it. . . . I was astonished to find in the Kremlin a portrait of Napoleon at the battle of Borodino."

But Train was more than a tourist. In every country he carefully made business contacts. It was after his return to Paris from Moscow that one of these contacts paid off handsomely. And soon Train was embroiled in the first of several financial jugglings that were to make him a millionaire.

He had met Queen María Cristina of Spain, one of the wealthiest women in the world. He had also met her financial adviser, Don José de Salamanca, the Spanish banking giant. Train swiftly made use of these acquaintances. He learned that when the United States had bought Florida from Spain, part of the purchase money had been deposited to the Queen's credit in the Bank of the United States. After the bank was liquidated, the Queen's cash assets were invested in forty thousand acres of Pennsylvania real estate, land rich in coal and iron ore.

It troubled Train that these forty thousand acres were lying unexploited. He had long had an idea that a rail link should be constructed between the Erie Railroad and the Ohio and Mississippi Railroad, thus uniting the East and the Midwest. Now he saw that this link could be built across the Queen's property in Pennsylvania, enriching her holdings a hundredfold. He approached her, and she was interested. It was all the encouragement Train required.

He darted in and out of Paris, London, New York, and Pennsylvania, trying to pull the deal together. He needed solid financing. He tried to see the Queen's banker, Don José de Salamanca. He had no luck until he offered to lend him a million dollars. Salamanca's interest was piqued. But, instead of lending the Spaniard a million, Train walked out with Salamanca's signature on notes for a million. With this money pledged, Train wangled $2,200,000 worth of credit from manufacturers of iron in Wales. With the financing completed, Train permitted the Queen's representative in London, James McHenry, who had made a fortune exporting dairy products from America, to take over and push the project to completion.

Train collected $100,000 in commissions. The four hundred miles of the Atlantic and Great Western Railroad were built across three states, including the Queen's acres. The railroad proved a terrible failure. It went into receivership three times in thirteen years—before it finally became a success as part of the Erie Railroad. In the end, the Queen saw no profits. And the invincible Don José de Salamanca had nothing to show for his gamble beyond a sea of red ink—and a town named Salamanca in New York.

Train, however, was heady with his coup and certain that he could make more money by concentrating on transportation. Impressed by horse-drawn streetcars in Philadelphia and

New York, he decided to promote them, with a few innovations of his own, in Europe. England, especially, seemed a likely place. Train had long been appalled by the snail's pace of its carriage traffic. Further, he felt that English labor sorely needed a cheap means of public transportation.

He took his radical ideas to Liverpool. They were promptly rejected by the authorities, who felt that his trams would clutter the thoroughfares and provide unfair competition for the omnibuses. He moved on to neighboring Birkenhead, and there found that an old shipbuilding friend was chairman of the city commissioners. By promising many concessions—among them that he would rip up his tracks and repair the streets at his own expense if the system proved a nuisance—Train was given permission to proceed with a "horse tramway." He laid four miles of tracks, provided spacious streetcars, each drawn by horses, and inaugurated the line on August 30, 1860. The tramway was an immediate sensation.

Certain that he had overcome all opposition, Train stormed into London. But there he ran into a stone wall. The omnibus people, fearing competition, and the gentry, objecting to overcrowded passages, vigorously opposed him. Train fought the harder, and finally by his eloquence gained permission for an experimental two-mile track from Hyde Park to Bayswater.

Though the omnibus drivers tried to sabotage him by wrecking his rails with their vehicles, and though the gentry had him jailed once for creating a nuisance, Train might have succeeded but for an unfortunate accident. One day a small boy was run down by a tram. The uproar was tremendous. Train was arrested for manslaughter. Though he was acquitted, the bill authorizing extension of his streetcar lines was voted down in Parliament.

Undeterred, Train continued to promote his street railways. Glasgow and Birmingham rejected them; Staffordshire allowed him to construct seven miles of track. Gradually, Train broke down resistance, and eventually he saw his streetcars spread throughout Great Britain and then to Copenhagen, Geneva, and Bombay.

Train's battle for cheap transportation in England was a minor skirmish compared with another battle he fought, against the British upper classes on behalf of the Union cause in the Civil War. It was the eve of Fort Sumter. English nobility, distrusting the North's radical democracy, feeling kinship for the South's culture, allied itself with English industrialists, who needed Southern cotton, in backing the Confederacy. Only the inarticulate British masses, who sensed that Lincoln's ideals were their own, sided with the Union.

If the British people were inarticulate, George Francis Train was not. He appointed himself their spokesman. He took to the public platform, wrote pamphlets, and published a newspaper in an effort to keep England from going into the Civil War on the side of the South.

His speechmaking was shrewd. He realized that many British laborers could not afford to hear him and that many white-collar workers would not want to hear him, so he offered to speak gratis on behalf of local charities. Into his appearances he injected the atmosphere of a revival meeting. Often he led off by singing "De Camptown Races," then invited the audience to join him in the chorus. It was fun. And what followed was often fun, too. After the bombardment of Fort Sumter, Train told listeners: "We invented railways and Mississippi steamboats. We have invented a new kind of war, fighting without killing anybody—forty hours of bombardment and no bloodshed."

Because the Union had no voice in the London press, Train financed his own propaganda sheet, the *London American*, published at 100 Fleet Street in a building decorated with the Stars and Stripes. The paper, which Train claimed had received a $100 contribution from Secretary of State Seward, frankly expounded the Northern cause and reprinted all of its publisher's speeches.

Two incidents early in the war transformed Train's campaign from one of wit to one of intemperate bombast, and dangerously imperiled his person. The first was the reporting of the first Battle of Bull Run by the austere London *Times*. The second was the outcry of the entire English press against the boarding of the British mail-steamer *Trent* by Union Navy men.

The Times had sent its renowned correspondent, William H. Russell, a veteran of the Crimean War and the Sepoy Mutiny, on a tour of the United States. Russell reported that most Americans, influenced by Irish immigrants, disliked England. He made sly innuendoes about certain American democratic institutions such as the "street-railway-car." He met Lincoln and found himself "agreeably impressed with his shrewdness, humor, and natural sagacity," but doubted that he was a gentleman. All of this alarmed Train, but did not ruffle his sense of humor. As he remarked from one rostrum: "I can tell you, gentlemen, it is a notorious fact when *The Times* takes snuff all England sneezes."

Then came Bull Run. The citizenry of the North was demanding action. Union troops, in great number, were prematurely sent marching on Richmond. Between Washington and Richmond were four rivers and many streams. One of these streams, thirty miles west of Washington, was called Bull Run. There the outnumbered Confederate soldiery engaged the advancing Army of the Potomac in the first major clash of the war.

From Washington spectators in wagons, ladies in carriages, and politicians on horseback hurried to a nearby hill to watch the progress of the battle. Among these spectators was Russell. As the day wore on, military wagons approached the spectators. Then came Union soldiers fleeing in great disorder and confusion, insisting that they were being pursued by Confederate cavalry. "I spoke to the men," Russell wrote, "and asked them over and over again not to be in such a hurry. 'There's no enemy to pursue you. All the cavalry in the world could not get at you.' But I might as well have talked to stones." Russell reported that when he challenged the cowardice of one Union soldier, the man tried to shoot him, but his pistol jammed. Two days later, in Washington, Russell continued to watch the retreat, "the jaded, dispirited, broken remnants of regiments passing onward, where and for what I knew not."

To Train, reading these accounts in London, Russell seemed to be viciously slanting his news—blaming the defeat at Bull Run on Northern inability and fear rather than on inexperience. At once Train struck out at *The Times* correspondent in print and on the lecture platform. He labeled the correspondent "Munchausen Russell" and "The English Libeler." He accused Russell of being a drunk and a liar. He attacked Russell for presenting "an eye-witness picture of a battle that he not only never saw, but was not within some miles of." He attacked him as a poor reporter who worked in a fog of intoxication. "Under the impulse of champagne and good brandy, he can paint a battle scene; but how shallow, aside from this, how feeble, his correspondence generally appears." Actually, Train was unfair. Russell, if perhaps prejudiced, was an honest reporter. He did see a portion of the Battle of Bull Run. And though he did drink, his consumption was considerably less than that of Grant. Nevertheless, Train's attack on Russell was effective in helping counteract British anti-Union propaganda.

The *Trent* affair was another matter. It created universal resentment in England and gave Train much difficulty in his defense of the Union position. In 1861 the Union screw-sloop *San Jacinto*, commanded by Captain Charles Wilkes, intercepted the British steamer *Trent* 240 miles off Havana. In a violation of international law, of the kind of which the English themselves had been guilty in 1812, American seamen boarded the *Trent*, searched it for Confederate messages and mail, then removed by force four Southern passengers. The passengers thus abducted were John Slidell and James Mason,

Confederate commissioners to France and Great Britain, and their secretaries.

The English press cried insult and shouted for war. Train made speech after speech defending the Union position, but was constantly heckled. Nevertheless, he continued with his argument: "Let us have the evidence that Wilkes has broken the law. England might have the right of asylum, but if they went to war it would be a lunatic asylum." As time progressed, Train softened his defense. At last he admitted that Slidell and Mason should be given up—and indeed, five days later, Seward did surrender them, without apology, but with congratulations to England for "at last adopting the principles of international law for which the United States had long contended."

Perhaps Train's most practical service to the Union cause was in what he termed "my exposure of blockade running from British ports." In a stream of letters to the *New York Herald* Train revealed "the names of the men interested, the marks of the cargoes, and the destination of the shipments." This created intense feeling against Train, who, while he would not carry a gun, admitted that he carried a cane for use as a weapon.

Before this feeling against him could lead to violence, Train suddenly decided to return home. He had conceived a plan whereby he would end the Civil War. At least a dozen other individuals, mostly Peace Democrats, had tried and failed. But Train, as a relative by marriage to Jefferson Davis, felt that his presence and eloquence in Richmond would be enough. The only obstacle was in reaching the Confederacy. This obstacle, he felt, he could overcome when he received information that a ship named the *Mavrockadatis*, scheduled to sail from England to Newfoundland, was actually a blockade-runner heading for a Southern port. Train secured passage under the pseudonym of Oliver—and was surprised when the ship actually went to Newfoundland.

In Boston once more, Train was greeted enthusiastically

by the press, by hostesses, by organizations wishing him to speak. He took it all quite seriously. "I found that I had returned to my country the most popular American in public life," he recorded. He made several hasty, ill-conceived speeches. In one, after being presented by the Mayor of Boston, he implored his fellow Americans to ignore English culture. "Let us think for ourselves—for we are a superior race." In another address, after branding the English cowards, he announced that Lord Palmerston had murdered Prince Albert by feeding him draughts of poison, to satisfy his own ambitions. Most persons enjoyed the sensation of his remarks, but a few were sharply critical. The *Cleveland Leader*, while crediting him for helping his nation in the *Trent* affair, admitted: "Since his return to this country he has given daily recurring proofs of his total absence of both decency and common sense. He is afflicted with diarrhea of words more than any person we have ever known."

President Lincoln, however, was still grateful for Train's unofficial efforts on behalf of the Union in England. He invited Train to Washington. Train never forgot that he was "warmly received by the President," as well as by members of the Cabinet and a small group of senators. "I had heard very much, of course, about the freedom of speech of Mr. Lincoln, and was not, therefore, astonished to hear him relate several characteristic anecdotes. In fact, three of the most prominent men in the United States at that time were striving to outdo one another in jests—the President, Senator Nesmyth of Oregon, and Senator Nye."

Train and his wife were among the five thousand persons invited to Lincoln's second inaugural ball. Mrs. Train, her hair powdered gold, wore a gown of blue silk and lace, and appeared, it may be presumed, with some reluctance. She was a Southerner, sympathetic to the Confederacy, and remained a source of much irritation to her husband throughout the conflict.

About this time Train, though only thirty-three, began to promote what was to be his last major venture. It was his greatest undertaking, and, most likely, his most profitable one. The project involved the financing and building of the Union Pacific Railroad.

Train admitted that his idea grew out of his anger with the British for blocking his street railways. He was determined to get even. He saw his chance when the British opened the Suez Canal as a short cut to the Orient. He would compete for Far Eastern trade by building a transcontinental railway across the Rocky Mountains, thus giving America a shorter route to the Orient. He approached Commodore Cornelius Vanderbilt with his visionary project. Vanderbilt told him: "If you attempt to build a railway across the desert and over the Rocky Mountains, the world will call you a lunatic." Despite this warning, Train went ahead on his own.

In 1862 he obtained a charter from Congress to construct a road running from the Missouri River to California. When it came to raising the cash necessary to start the road, he was turned down everywhere. Then he remembered something from his foreign experience. "In Paris, a few years before, I had been much interested in new methods of finance as devised by the brothers Emile and Isaac Perrere. These shrewd and ingenious men, finding that old methods could not be used to meet many demands of modern times, invented entirely new ones which they organized into two systems known as the Crédit Mobilier and the Crédit Foncier—or systems of credit based on personal property and land."

Through the Pennsylvania legislature Train established the Crédit Mobilier of America. While the United States government financed the Union Pacific, it was the Crédit Mobilier that served as a trust to finance the actual construction of the railroad. Immediately, Train raised $1,400,000 from sixteen friends in Boston, including Cyrus H. McCormick and William H. Macy. He himself invested $150,000.

On December 2, 1863, ground was broken near Omaha for the first mile of the Union Pacific. Train was the only one of the original founders present. He made a speech and a glowing promise. "Ten millions of immigrants will settle in this golden land in twenty years," he said. "If I had not lost all my energy, ambition, and enterprise, I would take hold of this immigration scheme, but the fact is I have gone too fast, and today I am the best played-out man in the country." This self-analysis was not inaccurate, yet Train was businessman enough to buy himself 5,000 lots in Omaha. He realized that the railroad would make Omaha. Before his death, these lots were worth $30,000,000.

Train predicted that the Union Pacific would be completed by 1870. For this prediction, he complained, he was "denounced as a madman and a visionary." The road snaked its way West, laid by twenty thousand tough Irish and Chinese laborers guarded by federal troops against Indian raids, all under the leadership of General Granville M. Dodge, who had been an engineer with Sherman on the march to the sea. It was finished, not in seven years, as Train had predicted, but in six, when the last, golden, spike was driven in at Ogden, Utah.

Shortly after, Train left the Crédit Mobilier or was dropped from it. He claimed: "Through my suggestion and through my plans and energy . . . this mighty highway across the continent . . . was created." He said he had built the Union Pacific. He had not, of course. He had helped finance it and publicize it. The men who really built the road were Congressman Oakes Ames of Massachusetts and Thomas Clark Durant, the road's first vice-president.

Train had long been out of the Crédit Mobilier when it blew sky high in one of the greatest scandals of the time. The *New York Sun* made known the story in 1872. The stockholders of the government-sponsored Union Pacific had contracted with the stockholders of the Crédit Mobilier to build the road. But it so happened that the stockholders of the Union Pacific were also the stockholders of the Crédit Mobilier.

For every dollar the Crédit Mobilier spent in construction it charged the Union Pacific and the government two dollars. To prevent investigation, Congressman Ames carefully distributed free stock in Crédit Mobilier to fellow representatives and senators. This stock paid 625 per cent dividends within a year. Before the thievery was fully exposed the financiers of the Union Pacific had made themselves almost $44,000,000 in profits. The subsequent scandal ruined the reputations of the Vice-President of the United States and a great number of congressmen, and publicly embarrassed the entire Republican Party.

By the time the scandal took place Train had drifted far from the world of finance. He had become interested in politics and obsessed with a desire for publicity. Most journalists who spoke with him, while admitting his brilliance, felt that he was misdirecting his abilities. Several thought that he was losing his grip. "The Train of ideas," a reporter on *The Nebraskan* remarked, "sometimes lacks the coupling-chains."

The reporter on *The Nebraskan* was unusually perceptive. As a boy-merchant and young promoter Train had displayed remarkable talent. He was intelligent, clever, audacious, energetic, and inventive. But he lacked a central drive, a realistic goal. He was scatterbrained. He did too much too easily and too quickly. With concentration and purpose he might have made a solid reputation in any one of several professions —as a financier, an author, or a politician.

Gradually, over a period of forty years, he descended into the most pitiful unreality and eccentricity because he wanted only attention. When he could no longer win attention through normal accomplishment, he employed every extreme stunt that came to mind. He cultivated the art of astonishment. Instead of honest dissent, born of careful thought and conviction, he became contrary for the mere sake of sensation.

He actively entered politics in 1869 because he had a Messiah complex. But he was a Messiah without a message, having merely the forensic equipment and evangelistic fervor to communicate nothing. As a politician, he was a half-baked thinker, part democrat and part fascist, part genius and part fool, never really insane, but surely psychopathic.

After his Crédit Mobilier period he was wealthy. On his two-and-a-half acres at Newport he had a villa and a special building for bowling and billiards that cost $100,000. He had a $50,000 guesthouse for his father-in-law. He had six carriages, and he claimed that it cost him $2,000 a week to live. But after he plunged into politics he neglected his business, his family, and his home, and lost all three in the continuing affair with his ego.

It was in a Dublin jail—one of fifteen he occupied in his lifetime, usually for siding with revolutionary causes or assuming the bad debts of others—that Train first conceived, as he put it, "a feeling of confidence that I might one day be President of the United States."

1872 was a confusing election year, and Train hoped that he might benefit by the confusion. Ulysses S. Grant, a shy, highly moral man who liked whiskey, horses, cigars (he once smoked twenty-four in a day), and low company, was presented for re-election by the Republican Party. Grant's well-meaning incompetence had permitted a shocking carnival of corruption during his first term. Many high-minded Republicans had had enough of him. They determined to break away from the regular party and nominate their own candidate.

These Liberal Republicans met in Cincinnati, wrote a platform that severely indicted Grant, and then cast about for a man who could defeat him. George Francis Train thought he was that man. On the second day of the convention he rose and shouted: "All aboard! Get aboard the express train of George Francis Train!" There was a brief snake-dance by his admirers, but when the actual balloting began, few delegates got aboard. On the sixth ballot, the pink-faced, angular, crusading editor of the *New York Tribune*, Horace Greeley, who looked like somebody's grandmother, and whose slogan was "Turn the rascals out," was nominated for the presidency. Train was astounded. He had hoped, even at the eleventh hour, that "the people would see the futility of supporting Greeley, and of placing me at the head of the ticket."

But Train was not through. If no one would place him on an existing ticket, he would create a ticket of his own. And so he became the sole candidate of the Citizens' Party. His entry into the campaign, however, did not clear the air for the voters. Everyone, it seemed, was running for the presidency that year. When the regular Democratic Party agreed to affiliate with the Liberal Republican in support of Greeley, a die-hard group of Independent Democrats refused to go along. These Democrats nominated Charles O'Conor, a prominent New York attorney, as the first Catholic ever to run for the presidency. Meanwhile, the Prohibition Party offered the electorate James Black, of Pennsylvania. And, perhaps most startling of all, the Equal Rights Party convened in New York City to nominate Victoria Claflin Woodhull for president.

Of all the candidates, George Francis Train was the most tireless. Resplendent in a blue swallow-tail coat with brass buttons, he stumped the nation from coast to coast, delivering 1,000 speeches that earned him $90,000 in admission fees. "I went into the campaign as into a battle," he wrote later. "I forced fighting at every point along the line, fiercely assailing Grant and his nepotism on the one hand, and Greeley, and the spirit of compromise and barter that I felt his nomination represented, on the other." Grant ignored Train's broadsides, but Greeley was once sufficiently provoked to call him "an ass, a lunatic, a charlatan and a mountebank."

In his campaign oratory Train promised to increase immigration from Europe, build trade with the Orient, and smash corruption. Once, when he denounced a ring of grafters in New York, he was asked to name names. He replied: "Hoffman, Tweed, Sweeney, Fisk, and Gould . . . Tweed and Sweeney are taxing you from head to foot, while their horses are living in palaces . . . To the lamp-post! All those in favor of hanging Tweed to a lamp-post, say aye!" As a matter of fact, Train exposed William Marcy "Boss" Tweed and his Tammany Hall gang, who would steal $200,000,000 from New York City in six years, long before *The New York Times* and Thomas Nast took credit for the same feat.

Train's interviews, speeches, and writings during the course of the campaign became more and more unrestrained. He told one interviewer: "Of course you know that you are talking to the next President. I am also the greatest man in the world. I can give Buddha, Confucius, Moses, Mohammed, and all the rest of them, fifty on the string, and then discount them." His election-year literature called him the "man of destiny," ready and willing to rule the country with one hundred of America's wealthiest men as his advisers, and added that he was "an instrument in the hands of some mysterious power, to emancipate the people from the slavery of Party and the Fanaticism of ages." An editor of the *Washington Capital*, attending one of his speeches, decided that he should have been an actor, reporting: "He double-shuffles and stamps on the floor 'till the dust obscures him; he beats his breast, clenches his fist, clutches his hair, plays ball with the furniture, outhowls the roaring elements. . . . And yet he is not happy; no, he wants to be President."

President he could not be. Millions heard and enjoyed him, but did not take him seriously. When the votes were counted, U. S. Grant had 3,597,132. Horace Greeley had 2,834,125, Charles O'Conor had 29,408, James Black had 5,608, Victoria Woodhull had not been permitted to vote even for herself, and Train—well, as far as the statistics could be trusted, Train had no votes at all.

He was bitter. He voiced his bitterness. "I thought I knew something of the people, and felt confident that they would prefer a man of independence, who had accomplished something for them, to a man who was a mere tool of his party, a distributor of patronage to his friends and relatives. . . . But I was mistaken. The people, as Barnum has said, love to be humbugged."

It is difficult to think that he expected to win, or that he even took his three-year campaign for the Republican nomination and then for the presidency seriously. For late in 1870, when he was contesting for the nomination, he suddenly interrupted his campaign to take a trip around the world. True, he may have wanted to dramatize his candidacy by a spectacular feat. Or, as he claimed, he may have wanted to show his fellow Americans the value of fast transportation. But most likely, he wanted publicity for its own sake.

And so, at the age of forty-one, almost the age that Verne made Phileas Fogg, Train started westward in his race around the world to prove that the journey could be done in eighty days. Actually, he was away more than eighty days. He started from San Francisco early in August and did not return until late in December. While his traveling probably took eighty days, there was a two-month diversionary detour in France.

Train crossed the United States on the new Union Pacific he had helped to build. He gave 28 speeches in California, netting himself $10,000 and a host of new enemies. A talk he gave in San Francisco to industrialists and politicians was typical. "If I had been the Federal general in command of California at the time [of the Civil War]," he said, "I should have hanged certain men, some of whom are present."

On August 1, 1870, he boarded the *Great Republic* for Yokohama. When he reached Singapore he learned that Napoleon had been crushed at Sedan and that France was in a state of chaos. Nevertheless, he decided to proceed directly to France as the quickest route to his transatlantic connections in Liverpool.

After more than two months of travel, he arrived in Marseilles. No sooner had he settled in his suite at the Hôtel du Louvre et de la Paix, than delegates of the revolutionary Commune called upon him. "We have heard of you and want you to join the revolution," they told him. "Six thousand people are waiting for you now in the Opera House."

Train had never, previously, shown interest in the International. But there were people waiting to see and hear him. There was the promise of excitement and publicity. It was inducement enough. He hurried to the jammed Alhambra Opera House, where the audience chanted his name and the glory of the uprising. "When the shouting ceased," he recalled in his autobiography, "I told the people that I was in Marseilles on a trip around the world, but as they had called upon me to take part in their movement, I should be glad to repay, in my own behalf, a small portion of the enormous debt of gratitude that my country owed to France for Lafayette. . ."

In the next weeks Train took over completely. He spoke against the Prussians. He spoke against Léon Gambetta's Third Republic. He spoke on the average of seven times daily for twenty-three consecutive days. He led a march on the Marseilles military fortifications and helped run up the flag of the Red Republic. And finally, to give the Commune an experienced military leader, he summoned General Gustave Paul Cluseret from his Swiss exile. Cluseret had experience enough. He had fought for the North in the American Civil War, under General McClellan, and taken an active part in the Fenian Insurrection in Ireland. Now, handsome in a gold-laced uniform that Train purchased for him, he rushed off to the barricades in Paris. There, it might be added, he was arrested by the Commune itself for treason, eventually saved by government troops, and returned to Switzerland.

Meanwhile, Train remained in Marseilles, where he almost lost his life. One morning, observing soldiers marching beneath his hotel balcony, he mistook them for comrades of the Commune and shouted: "*Vive la Commune!*" Too late, Train realized they were government troops. They halted. Five riflemen stepped forward, knelt, and took aim at Train. Quickly Train snatched the flags of France and the United States off the balcony, draped them about his body, and shouted: "Fire, fire, you miserable cowards! Fire upon the flags of France and America wrapped around the body of an American citizen—if you have the courage!" The firing squad was ordered back into line, and the troops moved on.

Shortly after, Train left Marseilles. He did not get far. In Lyons he was arrested for revolutionary activity and thrown into jail. He smuggled a note out to his frantic secretary, George P. Bemis, which read: "Am in St. Joseph Prison and secretly incarcerated." Bemis, through the intervention of Alexandre Dumas, visited Train, then cabled President Grant, the *New York Sun*, and the London *Times* for help. After thirteen days in prison, during which he lost thirty pounds, Train was released and taken to Tours.

In the palace of the prefecture at Tours, he was ushered into the presence of the government leader, Léon Gambetta, who was seated at his desk. Gambetta did not stir. Train stood, waiting. "He made not the slightest signs of being aware that I was present. He did not even turn his face toward me. I did not learn until afterward that the distinguished Italian-Frenchman had one glass eye, and could see me just as well at an angle as he could full-face."

Huffily Train asked to be seated. Gambetta motioned him to a seat. Train, as audacious as ever, immediately changed his political allegiance. "Monsieur Gambetta," he began, "you are the head of France, and I intend to be President of the

United States. You can assist me, and I can assist you. . . . Send me to America, and I can help you get munitions of war, and win over the sympathy and assistance of the Americans."

Gambetta ignored this. He had something else on his mind. "You sent Cluseret to Paris," he said, "and bought him a uniform for three hundred francs."

"You are only fairly well informed, Monsieur Gambetta. I paid three hundred and fifty francs for the uniform."

"Cluseret is a scoundrel."

"The Communards call you that."

The interview was over. Train was expelled from France. He resumed his journey around the world, chartering a special train to the Channel, and catching the ship *Abyssinia* in Liverpool for New York. Back home again, he crowed to the press that he had made the journey in eighty days. No one ever really counted the days. The record was accepted and publicized, and soon enough Phileas Fogg was born.

Train's record did not last two decades. In November 1889 the diminutive, intense sob-sister for the New York *World*, Nellie Bly, who had feigned insanity to expose conditions on Blackwell's Island and had gone down in a diving bell and up in a balloon to obtain feature material, left New York on a 24,899-mile trip around the globe. Exactly seventy-two days, six hours, and eleven minutes later she reached New York on a special train from San Francisco, while ten guns saluted her from the Battery and her paper's headline shrieked: "Father Time Outdone!" Race horses, babies, songs, and games were named after Nellie Bly, who remained a legendary figure until her death in 1922.

But all the vast publicity accorded her irked George Francis Train. An upstart of a girl in ghillie cap and plaid ulster had destroyed one of his few remaining claims to fame. He felt that he must preserve his reputation as a traveler. At once, he got in touch with the New York *World* and requested sponsorship of a new trip around the globe. The

World was not interested in breaking its own record. Train then wired a friend in Washington, the editor of the *Tacoma Evening Ledger*, asking him to arrange $1,000 worth of lecture engagements. The editor of the *Ledger*, remembering that Train had selected the site on which Tacoma was built ("There is your terminus," he had once told officers of the Northern Pacific), and realizing the trip might put the community into print, arranged $4,200 worth of lectures.

Train was sixty-one years old when he left Tacoma by steamer for Vancouver. Over five hundred persons saw him off for Japan. The sixteen-day passage was rocky. Train was unaffected, but reported that a fellow passenger, Lafcadio Hearn, was seasick all the way. The trip was filled with small adventures. He was detained in Japan for lack of a passport. "At Nagasaki, the Consul told me that no foreigner could get a passport in less than three days. I said I'd get one in less than three seconds or see the Mikado or burst the empire. I went to Tokyo and got my passport in 30 minutes." A cyclone cost him thirty hours en route to Singapore. At Calais he faced another obstacle. "I found that there was no boat I could catch. I telegraphed to Dover for a special boat and was told I could have one for forty pounds. All right. The boat came, but there were many people who desired to come, so they charged the others 17s. 6d. a head and charged me nothing; forty pounds saved." In New York he was stalled thirty-six hours trying to obtain space on a train. At last he chartered a special Pullman for $1,500 and sped west. When he was delayed in Portland another five hours through mismanagement, he refused to attend a banquet in his honor. He went directly to Tacoma, returning to his starting point after sixty-seven days, twelve hours, and two minutes of travel. He had settled his score with Nellie Bly.

But still he was not through. Two years later, when he was offered an opportunity to improve upon his own record, he could not resist. A new community in Washington, Whatcom, located on Puget Sound, wanted to advertise itself and offered to finance Train around the world. He made the journey, without mishap or delay, in sixty days flat. It was his last adventure as Phileas Fogg.

During both of these trips, Train was, in the eyes of the law, a lunatic. The chain of events that led to this absurd designation began one day in November 1872. Train had been addressing a group in Wall Street on his candidacy for president when a friend handed him a newspaper that announced the arrest of Victoria Woodhull. It appeared that Mrs. Woodhull, the very same woman who was his rival for the presidency, and her attractive sister, Tennessee Claflin, had been jailed for obscenity (for their exposure of Henry Ward Beecher's love life) at the instigation of the puritanical dry-goods salesman, Anthony Comstock. At once Train determined to play Don Quixote—"like a true errant knight, he flew to our side as a champion," Mrs. Woodhull said—and like Cervantes's errant knight, Train emerged from the joust with the label of lunacy.

Train brought out a new edition of a paper he had once published in Omaha, *The Train Ligue*, and presented, under sensational headlines, three columns of quotations from the Holy Bible relating to sexual intercourse. "Every verse I used was worse than anything published by these women," he stated. He was inviting arrest, and he did not have to wait long. New York detectives, spurred on by Comstock, found him in his apartment and hustled him off to the Tombs.

Train was deposited in a cubicle off the second tier, a section of the Tombs known as Murderers' Row. Among his fellow inmates, he recorded later, was "the famous Sharkey, who might have got into worse trouble than any of us, but who escaped through the pluck and ingenuity of Maggie Jordan." William J. Sharkey, who helped elect Train the president of Murderers' Row, was indeed in worse trouble than the others. He was under sentence of hanging for having killed a debtor named Dunn with a derringer. But fortunately for Sharkey, the Tombs was sloppily managed. Just as Train was permitted to wear a sealskin overcoat and receive reporters, so Sharkey was allowed to have daily visitors in his cell, which was furnished with walnut table, chaise longue, canary, and carpeting. His most regular visitor was his mistress, an accomplished pickpocket named Maggie Jordan. One day she brought Sharkey a green veil, woolen dress, black cloak, high-heeled shoes, and a pilfered visitor's pass. He walked out in this disguise and retired to Cuba for the rest of his days.

Train needed no Maggie Jordan to assist his escape. The government realized it had a tiger by the tail. The obscenity charge was weak and the government was eager to forget it. Police were instructed to leave Train's cell door open, lose him in the halls, make deals with him, anything to get rid of him. Train would not budge. He was in the Tombs, and there he would sit until he was properly tried.

After fourteen weeks, the government decided to try him on the grounds of insanity. Three doctors examined him. One declared him sane; the other two thought him obsessed on several subjects. All agreed that he was "of unsound mind, though harmless." A jury concluded that he was quite sane. Finally the government decided to try him on the charge of obscenity. But his lawyer, perhaps at the advice of Train's family, pleaded insanity. Hastily, the judge instructed the jury to bring in the verdict "Not guilty on the ground of insanity." Enraged, Train leaped to his feet and roared at the judge: "I protest against this whole proceeding. I have been four months in jail, and I have had no trial for the offense with which I am charged. Your Honor, I move your impeachment in the name of the people!" The judge threatened to pack him off to the State Lunatic Asylum in Utica, then thought better of it and released him as "a lunatic by judicial decree."

Thereafter, he began to call himself The Great American Crank and played the role to the hilt. Years before, in Omaha, suffering some fancied insult from the manager of the Herndon House, he had marched out of a banquet vowing to get even. Within a few hours, he had purchased an empty lot across the street for $5,000, sketched the crude plan of a new and better hotel on the back of an envelope, and offered a contractor $1,000 a day if he would deliver the completed building in sixty days. When Train returned from a vacation sixty days later, the three-story, 120-room Cozzen's Hotel, constructed at a cost of $60,000, was standing, ready for business.

Similar impulses had occurred to him from time to time in his early years. But in the last two decades of his life they took hold of him completely. When he heard that the mammoth Columbian Exposition of 1893 was doing poorly in Chicago, he rushed off to save it. The Midway, under Edison's new electric bulbs, had its share of oddities. Swami Vivekananda, from India; Ida Lewis, a lighthouse keeper who had rescued twenty-two persons; Comanche, a horse that had been the only survivor of Custer's Last Stand; Susan B. Anthony, Lillian Russell, and Snapper Garrison were all on display. But none created more of a stir than George Francis Train as he led a grand march up the Midway with a Dahomey belle from the African village on his arm.

Every unorthodoxy attracted Train. He became a vegetarian. After all, had not Plato, Shelley, Voltaire, Schopenhauer, and Thoreau been vegetarians? He dined on cereals, boiled rice, and fresh fruits, and believed that if he ate enough peanuts he would live to be 150. As he explained: "Having eaten no meat, eggs, fish, oysters, poultry, or animal food of any kind for many months, all the ancient argument, antagonism, ferocity of my nature has died out, and yet I am in savage health and terrible mental vigor."

In public he would not shake hands with friends. Instead, he shook hands with himself, as he had once seen the Chinese do. Nor would he communicate with acquaintances except by writing on a pad. These were means, he said, of storing up his psychic force. He invented a new calendar, based on the date of his birth and his age, and he announced he was running for Dictator of the United States.

Toward the end he was alone and he was poor. His wife, supported by a trust fund he had left her, died in 1879. His villa was long gone. And he had lost his Omaha properties through foreclosure, though he maintained that they had been taken from him illegally and that he would still be worth $10,000,000 when he chose to become sane.

He supported himself by writing and speaking. His old friend Darius Ogden Mills had built the first of a chain of low-cost hostelries, the Mills Hotel No. 1, in New York City. Train rented a tiny room in the hotel, furnished with bed, chair, dresser, and several crates crammed with his papers. His room cost him twenty cents a night, his dinners fifteen cents each, and he claimed that he needed no more than three dollars a week to live. In this room he did his writing. He sold political articles, written in blue and red pencil, to newspapers. He published *Train's Penny Magazine*, a weekly which sold for two cents, and in its pages inveighed against religion, mail-order houses, the Spanish-American War. And, at the request of D. Appleton and Company, he dictated, working an hour and a quarter a day for twenty-eight days, his autobiography, *My Life in Many States and in Foreign Lands*. In this volume he laid claim to a prodigious inventiveness. He insisted that he had suggested, or conceived, the perforation of postage stamps, erasers on lead pencils, steps on carriages, and the canning of salmon. He tried, also, to explain his role as the original Phileas Fogg. "I have lived fast," he wrote. "I have ever been an advocate of speed. I was born into a slow world, and I wished to oil the wheels and gear, so that the machine would spin faster and, withal, to better purposes."

But to the very end his real livelihood came from addressing audiences in person rather than writing for them. Though his fee was reduced to $100 a performance, he appeared regularly in Boston, Omaha, Chicago, and San Francisco. He still made an impressive figure on the platform, with his receding white hair grown long, his flowing mustache, his handsome, dark face. Often he affected a curious costume for his lectures, wearing a military coat, a communist red sash, a string of Chinese coins, and carrying a green umbrella. In his lectures he continued to provoke his listeners. At the Boston Music Hall he called Boston "a backwoods town" and Harvard a school for incompetent football players. But more often he expounded his creed. "My religion is my conscience, my belief is the brotherhood of man. Everything is worth having, nothing is worth worrying over; that philosophy is a sure cure for all diseases."

During his speaking tours Train met and conversed with all sorts of weird personalities, some of whose eccentricities made him seem staid by comparison. The most colorful of these cornered Train in his Occidental Hotel room, in San Francisco when he was lecturing on the *Alabama* controversy. England had built the cruiser *Alabama* for the Confederacy, and the *Alabama* had destroyed eighty Union merchantmen and one warship before it was finally sunk off Cherbourg. More than three years before, an international tribunal had met to find England guilty of a "breach of neutrality" in building, equipping, and permitting the escape of the *Alabama*. The tribunal had forced England to pay $15,-500,000 in gold in damages for depredations committed by this vessel and two others against Union shipping. Instead of the fine, Train was demanding the invasion of Canada and the seizure of British Columbia as more fitting reparations.

He had finished just such a lecture in San Francisco when he was visited by Joshua Norton, self-proclaimed Emperor of the United States and Protector of Mexico. Norton I, attired in his blue military coat topped with gold epaulets, demanded that Train keep hands off British Columbia. Train would not listen. Then Norton changed his tactics. He said that if Train persisted with the invasion, he would guarantee to deliver peaceably Vancouver Island for $1,200.

It was an interview that might have been invented by Lewis Carroll. In the end, Train threw Norton out, and His Highness published a notice in the *San Francisco Herald* forever banning Train from his Empire.

As the lecture tours became more infrequent, Train spent most of his days on a bench in Madison Square, sunning himself, feeding squirrels and pigeons, and playing with the youngsters who romped on the grass. He loved children, told them stories, bought them sweets, and took them to circuses. He told them, as he had told his own offspring: "Treat all with respect, especially the poor. Be careful to injure no one's feelings by unkind remarks. Never tell tales, make faces, call names, ridicule the lame, mimic the unfortunate, or be cruel to insects, birds, or animals." And when his book was done, the year before his death, he dedicated it to the little people who were his last friends and who believed in him—"To the children, and to the children's children, in this and in all lands, who love and believe in me, because they know I love and believe in them."

He was seventy-five years old when he died of Bright's disease on the night of January 19, 1904, in New York City. For two days hundreds of people crowded into the funeral parlor for a last glimpse of him. Most of them were little people carrying flowers.

Before his burial in Brooklyn, his physician, Dr. Carlton Simon, in collaboration with an alienist, Dr. Edward C. Spitzka, removed his brain for study. They found it was a remarkably heavy brain. It weighed 1,525 grains or 53.8 ounces. It was found to rank twenty-sixth among the brains of 107 famous persons. George Francis Train would have been pleased beyond measure to know that it was heavier, even, than the brain of Daniel Webster.

IV

The Free Lover Who Ran for President

> *"I advocate Free Love in its highest, purest sense, as the only cure for the immorality, the deep damnation by which men corrupt and disfigure God's most holy institution of sexual relations."*
>
> VICTORIA WOODHULL

When that greatest of Athenian orators, Demosthenes, after failing to lead his fellow Greeks in a successful revolt against the Macedonians, fled to a temple on the isle of Calauria and there took his life by biting off a portion of a poisoned pen, he could hardly have imagined how soon and for what purpose he would return to the earth he had so reluctantly left. Yet, a little more than two thousand years later, in the summer of 1868, in the unlikely city of Pittsburgh, Pennsylvania, Demosthenes returned to inspire another orator to undertake a revolt against puritanical convention which would rock America for a decade and more.

The hostess to Demosthenes' resurrection was an attractive, aggressive, outrageous young lady named Victoria Claflin Woodhull. For some years previous, Mrs. Woodhull, who had been raised on mesmerism and had been much addicted to trances, had consorted with an anonymous apparition clad in a Greek tunic. This friendly spirit-creature materialized frequently and made extravagant promises to Mrs. Woodhull of future wealth and power. He answered all her questions, except one. He would not reveal his identity.

But in Pittsburgh, where Mrs. Woodhull, her lively sister, and her zany family were earning a meager livelihood out of spiritualism, magnetic healing, cancer cures, and prostitution, the apparition in the Greek tunic appeared once more and at last revealed his identity. He traced his name, Mrs. Woodhull later related, on a marble parlor-table, and its eerie brightness illuminated the entire gloomy room. His name was Demosthenes. And, having overcome this final formality, the old Attic orator imparted to Mrs. Woodhull a crucial instruction that was to change her life. He ordered her to travel to a house at 17 Great Jones Street, New York City, and enter it, and occupy it, and know that thereafter only good and great events would befall her.

Apparently, and not unexpectedly, Demosthenes was sufficiently persuasive to send Mrs. Woodhull scurrying to the house on Great Jones Street near Broadway, in New York City. She entered it, found it furnished and to let, and explored it. In the library all was intact except one book lying loose on a table. Curiously she picked up the book, glanced at the title, and what she saw, she admitted, was "bloodchilling." The book was entitled *Orations of Demosthenes.* Mrs. Woodhull promptly rented the house, sent for her relatives, and prepared to make her mark.

Whether or not her next step was stimulated by one more visitation from the ether world is not known. More likely, Mrs. Woodhull took her immediate future into her own hands. Her Greek vision had promised her wealth and power. She was hardheaded enough to know that these she might obtain only through use of her natural advantages, which included sexual appeal, mystical experience, and unlimited audacity. At thirty Victoria Woodhull was a handsome, clever, brash woman, who looked chic and exciting in shirts and in shapely checkered dresses cut daringly short (to the calves). Samuel Gompers, first president of the American Federation of Labor, remembered her as "a slight, sparkling little creature, with expressive brown eyes and short brown hair." Her sister, Tennessee Celeste Claflin, a gay, somewhat coarse girl aged twenty-two, was even more beautiful, less intelligent, and certainly less inhibited.

In her own person, and in that of her younger sister, Victoria Woodhull saw sufficient assets for the founding of a fortune and a national reputation. The question was: where to begin? The answer came immediately: begin at the top. For in New York in 1868 the one person at the top was Commodore Cornelius Vanderbilt, the richest man in the United States, whose principal interests in his seventy-fourth year were females of sexual appeal who were not too swift of foot and anyone else of mystical experience who would give him assurance of health and longevity. To reach him required only unlimited audacity.

Undoubtedly, the idea of meeting the bluff, bewhiskered old Commodore originated in Mrs. Woodhull's fertile brain. She decided to effect the introduction through her male parent, Buckman Claflin, who, though a disreputable, one-eyed monster, was still her father and would lend the entire enterprise an air of respectability. Thus, Mrs. Woodhull and her hoydenish sister were chastely escorted to the mansion in Washington Place and announced as famous miracle-healers from the Midwest.

It is not surprising that they were promptly admitted. Commodore Vanderbilt was an ailing man who had become impatient with conventional medicine and was now employing the services of a Staten Island seer and an electrical wizard to give him hope and comfort. He was ready to listen to almost anyone. Mrs. Woodhull quickly explained that she was a successful medium, and that her sister Tennie was a magnetic healer who gave patients strength through physical contact. This last, as well as the provocative appearance of his fair guests, convinced the blasphemous old Commodore that he must put himself in their hands.

However, let it be remarked at once that Commodore Vanderbilt was neither an easy nor a pliable patient. He was tough, he was ruthless, and he was nobody's fool. He had pyramided possession of a single sailboat, purchased when he was sixteen, to the ownership of a hundred steamers servicing the East Coast and to the final control of the New York Central Railroad. Through instigating price wars, indulging in stock-market trickery, and bribing courts and legislatures he had accumulated $100,000,000 in his prime, and almost doubled the sum before his death. "Law?" he once bellowed. "What do I care about law? Hain't I got the power?"

Obviously such a man would not be easy to please. Yet, by some miracle of understanding, Victoria Woodhull reduced this blustering giant to the position of intimate friend and patron. When she realized his need for sex—indeed, few housemaids escaped his lust—she fed him the willing and vigorous Tennessee. The magnetic treatments, whereby Tennessee laid her hands on the Commodore's hands and passed electrical energy from her body into his, proceeded magnificently. Tennessee was soon in his bed, installed as his mistress. He called her his "little sparrow" and she called him "old boy."

A year and a half of Tennessee's special brand of magnetic healing softened the Commodore for Victoria Woodhull's special purposes. The idea of how she might best use the Commodore came to Mrs. Woodhull from her lover of four years, a bemused Civil War veteran and fellow spiritualist named Colonel James H. Blood. It was the astute Blood who realized at once that the Commodore might aid his protégées in that art at which he was past master—the art of making money by speculation. The Commodore possessed great stock holdings, manipulated shares by the thousands, dominated Wall Street as no other man did. Might he not be of greatest value in support of a brokerage firm?

On January 20, 1870, the *New York Herald* announced, incredulously, the opening of a new brokerage house—Woodhull, Claflin and Company—operated solely by two pretty and fashionable lady partners. Their headquarters, the newspaper continued, were in parlors 25 and 26 of the Hoffman House. Parlor 25 was furnished with reception chairs and piano, and decorated with oil paintings and a photograph of Commodore Cornelius Vanderbilt, beside which hung a framed inscription reading, significantly: "Simply to Thy cross I cling." To its description the *Herald* added a comment: "The notion prevails among the lame ducks and old foxes of Wall Street that Vanderbilt, the oldest fox of them all, is at the bottom of the experiment."

If this announcement created a furor, it was as nothing compared to the excitement generated among investors and members of the exchange when Victoria Woodhull and her sister invaded Wall Street itself. For soon enough Hoffman House was found too confining, and the ladies opened new business quarters at 44 Broad Street. Seven thousand visitors, fascinated by the oddity and by the silent partnership of Vanderbilt, flocked to their offices in the first week. When the traffic did not abate, the proprietors were obliged to post a notice in their vestibule reading: "All gentlemen will state their business and then retire at once." Gentlemen were admitted by a uniformed doorman to a front office furnished with leather sofas and walnut desks, which was separated by a glass-and-wood partition from a rear cubicle reserved for female customers. Mrs. Woodhull and her sister, fresh roses in their hair and gold pens cocked jauntily on their ears, were cordial to legitimate customers, but evasive with the press. They were in business for themselves, they said. They would not discuss their patron. "Commodore Vanderbilt is my friend," said Tennessee, "but I will not say anything more concerning that matter." The press was, for the most part, generous in its praise, and headlines referred to the sisters as the "Lady Brokers," the "Queens of Finance," the "Bewitching Brokers," the "Vanderbilt Protégées." Banks and financial firms respectfully came calling, and were impressed, and the new business boomed.

In three years, by Victoria Woodhull's public estimate, the

new brokerage house "made seven hundred thousand dollars." Where did these huge profits come from? One historian has been unkind enough to remark that "it is to be suspected they sold much more than railroad shares." But even the Everleigh sisters of Chicago, more expert at handling fleshly commodities, had never been able thus to make almost three quarters of a million dollars profit in three years. It may be said with some certainty that the great bulk of the profits earned by Woodhull, Claflin and Company came not from sex, but from brains. And the brains belonged to Commodore Vanderbilt. For during those exciting financial years he constantly provided the eager sisters with inside market information. In 1857 the Commodore, having disposed of his steamships, became a director, and later president, of the New York and Harlem Railroad. The stock in this line, which went from central Manhattan to Albany, the Commodore purchased at $9 a share. By bribing the City Council to extend the line, then by outwitting Daniel Drew, who was selling short, the Commodore sent the stock rocketing up to $179 a share. Mrs. Woodhull, lady broker, was his spiritual solace during this coup, and her own profits in the Harlem were almost half a million dollars.

When the Commodore determined to acquire control of the Erie Railroad, which ran from New York to Chicago and competed with his own New York Central, he took Mrs. Woodhull along for the ride. It was a rocky road. Gould and Fisk reached the directors of the Erie first, had them issue $10,000,000 worth of bonds, had these converted into 50,000 shares of stock, and dumped the lot on the market. The Commodore bought and bought, while Fisk joyfully chortled: "We'll give the old hog all he can hold if this printing press holds out." When the Commodore learned that he had been tricked, he forced Gould and Fisk to make the stocks good and to buy back $5,000,000 worth of them.

Finally, on that September day in 1869 known as Black Friday, Mrs. Woodhull was able to profit once more with the

Commodore's assistance. Gould, after encouraging President Grant to keep the nation's large gold-reserve locked up in Treasury vaults, bought $47,000,000 worth of free gold and drove its price up from the $132 required in greenbacks to purchase $100 in gold to $150 and to $162.50. The Exchange was in a panic. Angrily Grant released $4,000,000 in government gold, and Wall Street had its Black Friday as the price of gold plummeted down to $135. On that terrible day, the Commodore handed out loans of a million dollars to help settle the market. Through his advice, Mrs. Woodhull had sold at $160, and at enormous profit, before the final panic took place.

As time passed, the Commodore was being subtly, gently drawn away from the influence of Victoria Woodhull by his second wife, Frank C. Vanderbilt, a tall, dignified, religious Alabama girl. She barred entrance to all spiritualists, and surrounded her sickly husband with orthodox physicians and a Baptist pastor. Mrs. Woodhull did not mind. She already had what she wanted from the Commodore. She had wealth. Now she went after that which she desired even more—power.

On April 2, 1870, in the pages of the *New York Herald*, she made a proclamation that amazed the metropolis and would soon enough make her a national figure. "While others argued the equality of woman with man," she declared, "I proved it by successfully engaging in business. . . . I therefore claim the right to speak for the unenfranchised women of the country, and believing as I do that the prejudices which still exist in the popular mind against women in public life will soon disappear, I now announce myself as candidate for the Presidency."

It is unlikely that there ever existed, before the advent of Victoria Claflin Woodhull, a presidential candidate with a background so unstable, chaotic, and scandalous. She was born September 23, 1838, in the squalor of the frontier town of Homer, Ohio. She was the seventh of ten children, and she was named Victoria in honor of Great Britain's new queen. Her father, Reuben Buckman Claflin, was an uncouth conniver who earned a poor living as a surveyor and a postmaster. Her mother, Roxanna, was a strange, martial creature, probably of German-Jewish descent, probably conceived out of wedlock by a governor of Pennsylvania. Long years later, Victoria told the *Philadelphia Press* that she was raised "in a picturesque cottage, white painted and high peaked, with a porch running round it and a flower garden in front." She was raised in a broken-down shack on an unkempt hill, and every room of the shack from basement to parlor was filled with beds for the squalling children and relatives.

Victoria's mother, who believed in fortunetelling and the spirit world, conducted her unruly household after the precepts of that Austrian mystic, Friedrich Mesmer, who preached that human cures could be accomplished by occult force. Mrs. Claflin preferred Mesmer to the local physician, and three of her children died in their infancy. When Victoria was three years old, a housekeeper also died. Victoria saw her lofted on high by several muscular angels, and promptly swooned. Thereafter she was in constant touch with supernatural beings. Angels were her only friends, excepting the visions of two sisters who had died in childhood and with whom she continued to play. "She would talk to them," a friend reported, "as a girl tattles to her dolls." By her eleventh year she had had only three years of formal education. Her teachers found her uncommonly intelligent. Before she could continue her learning, a painful episode forced her abruptly to leave school and Homer, Ohio.

Buckman Claflin, a man who ordinarily had little interest in his possessions, suddenly had a change of heart one day in 1849. He took out insurance on his wooden grist-mill. As he had hardly funds to feed his family, and since the mill lay rotting of disuse, the precaution seemed oddly extravagant. One week later, when he was on a business trip ten miles away, the grist mill went up in flames. Claflin returned to collect his insurance. He was met not by an agent bearing the benefits of his premium, but by a vigilante committee of leading citizens. He found himself accused of arson and fraud. He was given the quick choice of the hemp or exile. Within the hour he departed for Pennsylvania. In the week following, the town raised money for the rest of the family and sent them packing.

Thus, necessity forced Roxanna Claflin, and Victoria and the rest of the hungry clan, to call upon their resources of invention. They formed a medicine show and sold a complexion oil made of vegetable juice. In the community of Mount Gilead, Ohio, where they were evicted from their first boardinghouse because Victoria evoked spirit music, they prospered briefly. And there, in 1853, when she was sixteen years of age, Victoria married Dr. Canning Woodhull.

She had met him two years earlier, at a Fourth of July picnic, and had seen him more or less steadily thereafter. He has been referred to as a "young dandy" and a "gay rake" and a "brilliant fop" who treated Victoria "abominably." Most latter-day judgments have been derived from a biased biography of Victoria written by Theodore Tilton after he had become her lover. Tilton declared that Victoria had been forced into the marriage by her parents. "Her captor, once possessed of his treasure, ceased to value it. On the third night after taking his child wife to his lodgings, he broke her heart by remaining away all night at a house of ill-repute. Then for the first time, she learned to her dismay that he was habitually unchaste, and given to long fits of intoxication."

As a matter of fact, Dr. Woodhull was anything but the cloven-footed devil depicted by the prejudiced Tilton. He came from a respectable Rochester, New York, family. He had been well educated in Boston. He had planned to acquire great riches during the gold rush to California, but had fallen ill in Ohio, and had remained there to resume his practice of medicine. When the Claflins rode into Mount Gilead he was a bachelor who dreamed of a peaceful home and a large family. He thought Victoria would help him fulfill that dream, but he miscalculated the character of his mate, and the mistake ruined his life. The problem in Dr. Woodhull's eleven years of discordant marriage was that he had bargained for a wife and had gotten a self-absorbed St. Joan who, like the Maid, heard voices and had a destiny (inspired by excessive devotion to the writings of George Sand) higher than that of the kitchen. Nevertheless, the restless and ambitious Victoria spent sufficient time with Dr. Woodhull to bear him two children—a boy, Byron, who lost his wits when he stumbled out of a second-story window, and a girl, Zulu Maud, who was to be the comfort of Victoria's later years.

Soon after her marriage Victoria decided that Ohio restricted her natural abilities. She induced her befuddled husband to abandon his practice and take her to California. There, through the recommendation of an actress named Anna Cogswell, she obtained a small role in a stage comedy entitled *New York by Gas Light.* This play led to others. But Victoria's progress was slow, and soon enough she realized that her future lay in a different form of entertainment. For in the East two other performers, Margaret and Katherine Fox, of Hydesville, New York, had attained a meteoric rise without ever once appearing in grease paint.

The Fox sisters had heard weird rappings at night "as though someone was knocking on the floor and moving chairs." Addressing overflow audiences that included such reputable personages as Horace Greeley, James Fenimore Cooper, and William Cullen Bryant, the sisters were interpreting the rappings as communications from the spirit world. Though a conclave of conservative medical men in Buffalo announced that the so-called rappings were created by the sisters themselves by cracking their knee and ankle joints, lay audiences refused to be so easily disillusioned. Seances became the rage, and accomplished mediums were much in demand. In California this need finally reached the ears of

Victoria Woodhull, who had long before communed with spirits for mere pleasure, but who now determined to forego her amateur status for an opportunity to share the large sums being offered to expert spiritualists.

Victoria, trailed by her sodden husband, caught up with her family in Cincinnati, where they were treating the gullible with a new cancer cure. When Victoria explained her plan the entire family was in agreement. A house was rented. A sign was posted, reading: "Tennessee Claflin, and Victoria Woodhull, Clairvoyants." The sisters gave noisy seances, at a dollar a head, and even attracted so famous a client as Jesse R. Grant, the father of Ulysses S. Grant. To the conjuring up of good spirits, the ladies added fortunetelling and magnetic healing. Their youth and attractiveness brought in a preponderance of male customers, who were prepared to pay far more for closer communion with their mediums. Apparently Victoria and Tennessee were not above practicing prostitution. The combination of soothsayer and whore might have enriched Victoria enormously had not Tennessee crudely spoiled the game. When Tennessee began to employ for the purposes of blackmail information gained as seer and strumpet, she was sued.

The Woodhulls and the Claflins left Cincinnati in great haste, and began a spiritualistic tour of Illinois, Kansas, and Missouri. In St. Louis, Victoria found true love. She had been invited to appear before the local Spiritualist Society to defend her doctrines against the attack of a clergyman. As spiritualism, which already had from three to four million followers in the United States, had somehow attracted persons interested in free love, feminine emancipation, and social reform, it was not surprising that Colonel James Harvey Blood was also in the audience. Though ostensibly Blood was covering the debate for the *St. Louis Times*, the real motive for his attendance was his interest in socialism and advanced social theory. Blood, a handsome veteran of the Civil War who had been wounded five times, was married and the father of two children. Disenchanted by his wife's materialism, by his job, and by the avaricious men it brought him in contact with, he sought comfort in a private vision of utopia. When Victoria Woodhull on the debate platform spoke of the same utopia, Blood was impressed. And when she spoke of the slavery of wifehood, when she announced that there was no such thing as sin, he knew he must meet her.

To meet her, Blood pretended to be a client needing advice. His delicacy was not necessary. According to Tilton, it was Victoria who at once saw a soulmate in Blood and seduced him forthwith. "Col. James H. Blood . . . called one day on Mrs. Woodhull to consult her as a Spiritualistic physician (having never met her before), and was startled to see her pass into a trance, during which she announced, unconsciously to herself, that his future destiny was to be linked with hers in marriage. Thus, to their mutual amazement, but to their subsequent happiness, they were betrothed on the spot by 'the powers of the air.'"

After that impromptu betrothal, Victoria and Blood lived as lovers. Blood abandoned St. Louis and his family to travel with Victoria to Chicago. Victoria also permitted the cuckolded, unprotesting Dr. Woodhull to accompany her, and assigned him to the task of looking after their children. In Chicago, after much legal difficulty, Victoria divorced Dr. Woodhull on the charge of adultery, and Blood divorced his wife after agreeing to a substantial settlement. Victoria and Tennessee rented a house on Harrison Street and performed as oracles. When neighbors suspected that they were also performing as women of easy virtue, the police were summoned. There being no proof of prostitution, the law accused them of "fraudulent fortune-telling." Once again the menage was on the road. In Pittsburgh, Victoria saw the light on the marble table which spelled the name Demosthenes —and the vision that was to lead her to Commodore Vanderbilt.

Having acquired, through Vanderbilt's friendship and advice, a profit of $700,000 by stock speculation (though she complained that her business and family expenses amounted to $300,000 a year) and assured of an income of $50,000 annually from her thriving brokerage firm, which recommended investments in subway projects and silver mines, Victoria turned her full attentions to promoting her candidacy for president of the United States. Probably no one, not even Victoria, could properly define her real purpose in competing for the nation's highest office. In an age when women in America had not even the vote (except in the Wyoming territory) her candidacy was regarded as pure eccentricity. Her real purpose undoubtedly was colored by a need for publicity and attention, and an honest desire to dramatize the rising clamor among women for equal rights and a single moral standard.

However, Victoria's candidacy would have died stillborn had it not been for the astute direction of two men who cleverly guided her every action. One was, of course, Colonel Blood, who saw in his mistress a mouthpiece for his own ideas on fiat money, female emancipation, and labor reform. The other, a newcomer to Victoria's growing circle, was the aged, bearded Stephen Pearl Andrews, a brilliant and renowned scholar, philosopher, and anarchist.

Andrews, the son of a Baptist minister, had college degrees in law and medicine. He had taught in a ladies' seminary in New Orleans, had narrowly escaped lynching in Houston for his abolitionist views, and had become an advocate of Isaac Pitman's system of shorthand, which he introduced into the United States. An extraordinary linguist, he knew thirty-two languages, including Chinese, on which he published a textbook in 1854. When he had enough of learning languages, he invented one of his own called Alwato, a forerunner of Esperanto based on his own interpretation of the different meanings of sounds. As he grew older, Andrews became more deeply interested in sociology. He conceived an anarchistic

VICTORIA WOODHULL
about 1872, when a candidate for president

EMPEROR NORTON I
about 1869,
from a photograph by "Helios" (Eadweard Muybridge?)

perfect state that he called Pantarchy. According to the dictates of Pantarchy the governing body took care of one's children and one's property, leaving the individual free to live as he wished. Quite naturally, as the government "had no more right to interfere with morals than with religion," Andrews's utopia advocated free and natural love.

As spiritualism was one more expression of revolt against convention, hundreds of spiritualists subscribed to Andrews's Pantarchy. But Andrews, a sweet, sincere radical, wanted not hundreds, but thousands to follow his new way. In Victoria Woodhull, with her daring and originality, he saw a useful ally. If she would be president, she must have a platform. Why should her platform not embody the tenets of Pantarchy? Andrews managed to meet her and to enchant her (she thought him the corporeal representation of her beloved Demosthenes). Soon Andrews joined Blood in laying out a campaign that would promote her name—and their own ideas.

After a series of articles in the *New York Herald*, signed by Victoria Woodhull, but written by Andrews and Blood, advocating a universal government and a universal language—published as a book in 1871 under the title *Origin, Tendencies, and Principles of Government*—it occurred to Victoria that she could not depend on the New York press to continue to publicize her radical views. If she was to gain speedy prominence, and successfully propagandize her theories, she must have her own newspaper. She had the necessary capital and she had the staff. Consequently, on May 14, 1870, appeared the first number of a sixteen-page, slick-papered journal called *Woodhull & Claflin's Weekly*. Beneath its name the five-cent newspaper bore the legend: "Progress! Free Thought! Untrammeled Lives!" And then, in smaller print, the promise: "Breaking The Way For Future Generations."

Among the financial advertisements that crowded the first issue was a statement of policy. The *Weekly* would refrain from "scurrility in journalism." Instead, it would be "devoted to the vital interests of the people." Above all, it would "support Victoria C. Woodhull for president with its whole strength" and would "advocate Suffrage without distinction of sex." The articles in the first issue, as well as in the issues that followed in the next four months, were tame, restrained, ladylike—this, curiously, because two male idealists with little sense of showmanship were writing the copy. There were stories praising Commodore Vanderbilt, deploring women's "voluptuous" fashions, and supporting business training for young ladies. There was a serialization of a novel by George Sand.

This editorial gentility did little to draw attention to Victoria, and it was costing a fortune. In September 1870 Victoria herself decided to take a more active part in publishing the newspaper—and, at once, the paper was front-page news. Immediately, and for two years after, the *Weekly* gave its faithful readers their five cents' worth and more. Article after article appeared supporting free love, abolition of the death penalty, short skirts, vegetarianism, excess-profit taxes, spiritualism, world government, better public housing, birth control, magnetic healing, and easier divorce laws. Fearlessly Victoria advocated legalized prostitution, exposure of Wall Street's financial swindlers, and compulsory classes in physiology for women. At her insistence the *Weekly* featured the first full version of the Communist Manifesto published in English, self-help articles on the subject of abortion, Thomas Carlyle's views on labor—and every letter that backed Victoria for president. Circulation became national, and reached a high of twenty thousand.

It was not enough for Victoria to plead her progressive ideas in print. She insisted upon practicing them, too. It was an era when women did not patronize public resturants unescorted after dark. Victoria, accompanied only by Tennessee, brazenly seated herself in Delmonico's one evening at seven o'clock and demanded service. Charles Delmonico refused to serve her. "I can't let you eat here without some man," he said. Whereupon Victoria sent Tennessee outdoors to locate a cab driver and bring him to the table. They were served.

It was an era when women did not participate in rude labor-movements. Victoria joined Section 12 of the International Workingmen's Association, which had been organized in 1864 by Karl Marx. The membership of Victoria and her followers was viewed with concern by Samuel Gompers. "Section 12 of the American group was dominated by a brilliant group of faddists, reformers, and sensation-loving spirits," observed Gompers. "They were not working people and treated their relationship to the labor movement as a means to a 'career.' They did not realize that labor issues were tied up with the lives of men, women, and children—issues not to be risked lightly."

Finally, it was an era when women talked and agitated about equal rights, but did nothing more about them. Victoria was the first to take direct action in Washington. Her motives in planning to storm the nation's capital may not have been entirely altruistic. She was beginning to realize that her newspaper was not influential enough properly to promote her person or her theories. To acquire a wider audience she knew that she must air her views in the capital. Diligently she studied the records and personalities of congressional leaders, seeking one man who stood above the rest. When this man visited New York, Victoria went to see him. He was General Benjamin Franklin Butler, the pudgy, cross-eyed representative from Massachusetts. As military governor of New Orleans after the Civil War, he had been commonly known as Beast Butler and the Bluebeard of New Orleans for his uncavalier attitude toward Southern womanhood. Though his management of the city had been above reproach, his brusque management of its female population left much to be desired. When the belles of New Orleans insulted Northern soldiers, Butler retaliated by declaring that each female offender "be treated as a woman of the town plying her avocation." While this put a prompt end to all obvious gestures of contempt, the Southern ladies still turned their backs to Butler when they saw him, which provoked his memorable remark: "These women know which end of them looks best." Yet, as a congressman the General proved more considerate than his colleagues toward American women in general. He believed not only in justice toward colored citizens and in the good sense of fiat or greenback money issued on faith in government, but also in equal rights for women. It was this last that gave Victoria Woodhull her hope.

Victoria apparently had no difficulty in convincing Butler to support her plan. She wished to present a memorial on behalf of woman suffrage to the Senate and the House of Representatives. Butler thought this a splendid idea. It is said that he wrote the memorial and then had the House Judiciary Committee invite Victoria to appear in person and read it to them.

Victoria, attired in an attractive Alpine hat, blue necktie, and dark dress, arrived in Washington prepared to address the august representatives on the morning of January 11, 1871. It was a decisive appearance for her, and the arrangement of the timing (surely at her own suggestion) had behind it a Machiavellian purpose. For, as Victoria well knew, on that very morning the influential National Woman's Suffrage Association, led by Susan B. Anthony, Isabella Beecher Hooker, Elizabeth Cady Stanton, and Paulina Wright Davis, was about to begin its third annual convention. Victoria sensed that, by her dramatic and highly publicized appearance, she was accomplishing what no member of the suffrage movement had yet accomplished. If her memorial impressed the committee of men, it might impress the association of women. And thus, with one stroke, Victoria might overcome female resistance to her radicalism and eccentricity and take over the suffragette following as her very own.

Certainly her instinct was correct. For when members of the committee assembled behind their long table in the crowded room, Susan B. Anthony, Isabella Beecher Hooker, and Paulina Wright Davis were on hand, anxiously watching.

At last Victoria was introduced. She rose gracefully, respectfully, and in a clear, musical voice began to read aloud her brief memorial. After stating that she had been born in Ohio, that she had been a resident of New York for three years, that she was a citizen of the United States, she went on:

"The right to vote is denied to women citizens of the United States, by the operation of Election Laws in the several States and Territories . . . the continuance of the enforcement of said local election laws, denying and abridging the right of citizens to vote on account of sex, is a grievance to your memorialist and to various other persons, citizens of the United States, being women . . .

"Therefore, your memorialist would most respectfully petition your Honorable Bodies to make such laws as in the wisdom of Congress shall be necessary and proper for carrying into execution the right vested by the Constitution in the Citizens of the United States to vote, without regard to sex."

It was an impressive reading. Victoria's simplicity, modesty, and feminity won the hearts of the members of the committee, but not their heads. Later, with two dissents, they voted against the memorial as being outside the province of Congressional action. The two dissents were made by Loughridge, of Iowa, and, of course, General Butler, of Massachusetts, whose minority report to the House vigorously backed Victoria's demand for equal rights. But if Victoria failed to win over the Judiciary Committee, she won a battle almost as important that morning. For the suffragette leaders, who had seen her and heard her at last, saw and heard not a strident Jezebel, but a restrained and refined lady who voiced more effectively than they their deepest yearnings. Immediately, without hesitation, they congratulated Victoria and invited her to attend the Suffrage Association convention that afternoon and address the delegates.

The association convened at Lincoln Hall in Washington. Victoria was seated on the platform with Susan B. Anthony and the other renowned feminists. When she was introduced by Isabella Beecher Hooker, who cautioned the audience that it was to be Mrs. Woodhull's first public address, Victoria appeared faint and needed assistance to come forward. She reread the content of her memorial and spoke briefly of the reaction it had made upon members of the Judiciary Committee. The suffragettes applauded her and welcomed her as their newest heroine.

When the convention broke up, the acceptance of Victoria Woodhull as a legitimate suffragette hung briefly in the balance. From all corners of the country, followers of the movement protested. But the new friends Victoria had made in Washington remained staunch. When several persons called Victoria an infamous woman, Susan B. Anthony snapped back that "she would welcome all the infamous women in New York if they would make speeches for freedom."

In New York, Victoria tried to consolidate her new power and respectability. She made a mild defense of woman suffrage at the Cooper Institute and followed this with several windy lectures on labor reform. But her main effort was directed toward gaining the support of many still reluctant suffrage leaders, among them Mrs. Lillie Devereux Blake, president of the New York State Association. Victoria asked Mrs. Blake to call. Mrs. Blake called, accompanied by her husband, Grinfill Blake, and was met by both Victoria and the ever uninhibited Tennessee. Mrs. Blake recorded the experience in her diary: "In the evening went to Woodhull and Claflin's, where we had a curious time." The curious time was elaborated upon, later, in a memoir, by Mrs. Blake's daughter, Katherine D. Blake:

"I remember vividly that the next morning she [Mrs.

Blake] said at the breakfast table, 'Grinfill! You know you behaved disgracefully last night!'

"His reply was, 'Well, Lillie, my dear, if you will take me to a house where there are not chairs enough to sit on, so that a pretty plump young lady [Tennessee] with nothing on but a Mother Hubbard comes and sits on the arm of my chair and leans over me, you must expect me to put my arm around her.'"

Thereafter, Mrs. Blake was an implacable enemy. She kept her distance, and her husband distant, from Victoria. She also withheld all suffragette support from Victoria. Presently she began to receive anonymous letters which, according to Katherine D. Blake, warned her "that unless she paid $500 her misdeeds would be 'shown up' in Woodhull and Claflin's scurrilous paper." Mrs. Blake put the blame for blackmail squarely on Victoria's shoulders, accusing her of having "had similar letters written to many other people." Others, too, accused Victoria of resorting to blackmail to bludgeon antagonistic suffragettes into compliance, though Victoria always vehemently denied the charges. At any rate, by this time she realized that she could not overcome all resistance to her candidacy. She had to be satisfied with the support of the liberal element of the feminist movement, and she moved quickly to exploit this support.

The anniversary of the launching of the suffrage movement was scheduled to be celebrated in Apollo Hall, New York City, on May 11, 1871. Victoria, who had found her stage presence at last, made a ringing, emotional bid for followers and front-page attention. "If the very next Congress refuses women all the legitimate results of citizenship," she cried, "we shall proceed to call another convention expressly to frame a new constitution and to erect a new government. . . . We mean treason; we mean secession, and on a thousand times grander scale than was that of the South. We are plotting revolution; we will overthrow this bogus Republic and plant a government of righteousness in its stead."

The good effects of this speech were nullified in five days by a public scandal instigated by Victoria's mother. Some months earlier, Dr. Canning Woodhull had appeared at the three-story house at 15 East Thirty-eighth Street which Victoria maintained for herself and her relatives. Since the divorce Dr. Woodhull had lost himself in alcoholism. He was impoverished and he was ill, and he begged Victoria for help. She took him in to care for their two children. She did not think it unusual that her lover, Colonel Blood, remained under the same roof. But Roxanna Claflin thought it unusual, and she saw her chance to get rid of Blood. She hated him. She thought that he had filled Victoria's head with high-flown ideas, that he had taken her from the happier life of the medicine show and spiritualism, and that he was using her only for her money, which might better be diverted to the Claflins. Moreover, Blood had little respect for Mrs. Claflin and had often threatened her.

In a fine frenzy Mrs. Claflin went to the police. At the Essex Street station she swore out a complaint against Colonel Blood for assault and battery. "My daughters were good daughters and affectionate children," she told the law, "till they got in with this man Blood. He has threatened my life several times. . . . I say here and I call Heaven to witness that there was the worst gang of free lovers in that house in Thirty-eighth Street that ever lived. Stephen Pearl Andrews and Dr. Woodhull and lots more of such trash."

The case went to court. Colonel Blood said that he had never laid a hand on Mrs. Claflin. Once he had threatened to "turn her over my knee and spank her." That was the extent of it. He insisted that he was Victoria's husband, though there was no proof of it. When asked if he and Dr. Woodhull occupied the same bedroom with Victoria, he would not reply. Victoria appeared in defense of her lover. "Colonel Blood never treated my mother otherwise than kind. . . . Sometimes she would come down to the table and sit on Mr. Blood's lap and say he was the best son-in-law she had. Then again she would abuse him like a thief." Tennessee testified that Colonel Blood rescued her from the evil influence of her mother and family. "Since I was fourteen years old, I have kept thirty or thirty-five deadheads. . . . I have humbugged people, I know. But if I did it, it was to make money to keep these deadheads." Dr. Woodhull wobbled up to the stand to state that, notwithstanding Mrs. Claflin's charges, it was she who was actually threatening poor Blood. In the end, the judge threw the case out of court —and into the lap of the press.

The press, less interested in mother love than in free love, was fascinated only by the fact that a presidential candidate, female, was keeping two lovers, male, in her bedroom at the same time. As far away as Cleveland, the *Leader* branded Victoria "a vain, immodest, unsexed woman" and a "brazen snaky adventuress." And in New York, for all who knew her to read, Horace Greeley wrote in the *Tribune:* "Let her be the one who has two husbands after a sort, and lives in the same house with them both, sharing the couch of one, but bearing the name of the other (to indicate her impartiality perhaps) and cause and candidate will be so fitly mated . . . that there will be no occasion even under the most liberal and progressive enlightened regime to sue for their divorce."

In her *Weekly*, Victoria lashed out, first at Greeley, then at all who mocked and criticized her. "Mr. Greeley's home has always been a sort of domestic hell . . . the fault and opprobrium of domestic discord has been heaped on Mrs. Greeley. . . . Whenever a scold, a nervous, an unreasonable, or even a devilish tendency is developed in a wife, it is well to scrutinize closely the qualities of the husband." As for the rest of them, let them cower in their glass houses. "At this very moment, awful and herculean efforts are being made to suppress the most terrific scandal in a neighboring city which has ever astounded and convulsed any community . . . We have the inventory of discarded husbands and wives and lovers, with dates, circumstances and establishments."

Still Victoria was not done. Her blood boiled at the injustice of being so severely and universally condemned and censured. She must let more persons than the readers of her *Weekly* know her true feelings. She must be vindicated in their eyes. Thus, on May 20, 1871, she addressed a letter, or "card" as such communications were then called, to the editor of the *New York World*, with a copy written out for *The New York Times*. Two days after its receipt it was published prominently in the *World*. It was not, as we shall see, just another angry protest. For in its content was an elaboration of that "most terrific scandal in a neighboring city," previously mentioned by Victoria in her *Weekly*, which would rock all of America and bring an idol crashing down from his high pedestal. Victoria's memorable revelation began:

"Sir: Because I am a woman, and because I conscientiously hold opinions somewhat different from the self-elected orthodoxy which men find their profit in supporting, and because I think it my bounden duty and my absolute right to put forward my opinions and to advocate them with my whole strength, self-orthodoxy assails me, vilifies me, and endeavors to cover my life with ridicule and dishonor.

"This has been particularly the case in reference to certain law proceedings into which I was recently drawn by the weakness of one very near relative and the profligate selfishness of other relatives."

Victoria went on to admit candidly that she did, indeed, dwell "in the same house with my former husband . . . and my present husband." She could not, she said, do otherwise, for Dr. Woodhull was ill and needed her support. Despite this charity, "various editors have stigmatized me as a living example of immorality and unchastity." Victoria said she was always prepared for criticism, but on this occasion her enemies had gone too far.

"I know that many of my self-appointed judges and critics are deeply tainted with the vices they condemn. . . . I advocate Free Love in its highest, purest sense, as the only cure for the immorality, the deep damnation by which men corrupt and disfigure God's most holy institution of sexual relation. My judges preach against free love openly, practice it secretly; their outward seeming is fair, inwardly they are full of 'dead men's bones and all manner of uncleanliness.' For example, I know of one man, a public teacher of eminence, who lives in concubinage with the wife of another public teacher, of almost equal eminence. All three concur in denouncing offenses against morality. 'Hypocrisy is the tribute paid by vice to virtue.' So be it. But I decline to stand up as the 'frightful example.'"

Several hours after the publication of this letter, Victoria sent a message to Theodore Tilton, a "public teacher" who was editor of the *Golden Age* magazine. She asked him to call upon her, at once, at her office. He appeared, at once, wary and puzzled. Victoria handed him the morning edition of the *World*, folded open to her letter.

Victoria indicated the letter. "I wish you would read it aloud."

He read it aloud. He read all of it, including the exposure of "a public teacher of eminence, who lives in concubinage with the wife of another public teacher, of almost equal eminence." He finished lamely, and looked up.

"Do you know, sir, to whom I refer in that card?" asked Victoria.

"How can I tell to whom you refer in a blind card like this?"

"I refer, sir, to the Reverend Henry Ward Beecher and your wife."

Tilton showed his surprise, not at the knowledge of his

wife's infidelity, about which he already knew, but at the realization that her infidelity was public property.

Victoria watched him. "I read by the expression on your face that my charge is true."

Tilton did not deny that it was true. When Victoria went on to review the affair in detail, he was forced to agree that her account, though "extravagant and violent," was substantially accurate. Tilton had to face an ugly fact: his pious wife's adultery, begun three years before and made known to him only eleven months before, could no longer be kept secret.

The scandal had had its beginnings on that day in 1855 when Reverend Henry Ward Beecher, pastor of the wealthy Plymouth Church in Brooklyn, officiated at the wedding of a worshipful member of his flock, the darkly attractive, charming Elizabeth Richards, to a handsome, twenty-year-old journalist named Theodore Tilton.

In the fifteen years following the wedding, the short, stocky, dynamic Beecher became the highest-paid preacher in America. He received $20,000 a year from the grateful Plymouth Church. He collected an additional $15,000 annually from writing and speaking tours. His colorful sermons made him not only a god to the three thousand Congregationalists who packed his church every week, but also a Republican of national prominence. Though he frowned upon the free-love theories held by Victoria Woodhull and her followers, he considered himself liberal and open-minded. He permitted the celebrated atheist Robert Ingersoll to address his congregation. He defended his Jewish brethren against the anti-Semitism of Judge Henry Hilton in the notorious Saratoga hotel boycott of Joseph Seligman. He tried to auction a slave woman from his pulpit to publicize his sister's book, *Uncle Tom's Cabin*. He was a man of magnetic personality, and his followers were fanatically devoted to him. Yet, for all of his success and acclaim, he was a lonely and restless person. An early marriage had bound him to a thin-lipped, disapproving, forever unamused New England wife named Eunice Bullard. She gave him nine children and little else. Her conversation, Beecher admitted, was "vapid" and "juiceless." Eventually, Beecher turned from his unhappy wife to the company of more admiring women. And finally, as an outlet for his needs and desires, he settled upon the wife of his protégé and closest friend.

Elizabeth Richards had, in a sense, been a product of Beecher's teaching and of his fervor. She had gone to school with one of his daughters and she had been a member of his church for fifteen years. When she met young Tilton she brought him into the church. Tilton was the eternal juvenile. Greeley dubbed him "Boy Theodore." The son of a carpenter, Tilton was educated at New York City College. Upon leaving school he became a reporter on the *New York Observer*. Though tall and strong, he possessed an air of feminine softness. He was brilliant, he was idealistic, and he was weak.

The year after his marriage Tilton fell under Beecher's influence and patronage. Through the pastor's intervention Tilton became editor, and then part owner, of the *Independent*, his salary climbing from $700 to $15,000 a year. Tilton and Beecher became close companions, and the lonely pastor was constantly in the Tilton home.

Beecher had always been aware of Elizabeth Tilton, first as an awed member of his congregation, then as the wife of his best friend. But soon enough he began to consider the warm, slight brunette as something more than a friend. And Elizabeth Tilton, now "Lib" to her pastor, found herself drawn closer to Beecher because of problems that had arisen with her husband. Tilton had become a fanatic abolitionist and had abandoned religion for free thought. Too, it was rumored that he was neglecting his wife for the company of other women. One of these women was a pretty, sixteen-year-old girl, Bessie Turner, who was employed to help care for his five children. Tilton had much affection for this girl, and on a night in 1867 he entered her bedroom lightly clad and slid into bed beside her. According to Miss Turner, Tilton whispered "that if I would allow him to caress me and to love me as he wanted to do that no harm should come to me, and that a physical expression of love was just the same as a kiss or a caress."

In August 1868 Elizabeth Tilton lost a son by cholera. If ever she needed consoling, this was the time. But her husband was off on a lecture tour. At last, she went to see Beecher at his home. She said that she needed him. As it turned out, he needed her as much. And that night, in her diary, Elizabeth wrote: "October 10, 1868. A Day Memorable." The most detailed account of the illicit affair was later made public by Tilton himself:

"She then said to me . . . that this sexual intimacy had begun shortly after the death of her son Paul . . . that she had received much consolation during that shadow on our house, from her pastor; that she had made a visit to his house while she was still suffering from that sorrow, and that there, on the 10th of October, 1868, she had surrendered her body to him in sexual embrace; that she had repeated such an act on the following Saturday evening at her own residence . . . that she had consequent upon those two occasions repeated such acts at various times, at his residence and at hers, and at other places—such acts of sexual intercourse continuing from the Fall of 1868 to the Spring of 1870 . . . that after her final surrender, in October, 1868, he had then many times solicited her when she had refused; that the occasions of her yielding her body to him had not been numerous, but that his solicitations had been frequent and urgent, and sometimes almost violent. . . ."

Tilton was able to reveal these details because he had heard them from his wife's lips on the evening of July 3, 1870. Conscience-stricken, she had at last broken away from Beecher and decided to confess all to her husband. She told him that her fall had been encouraged not by "vulgar thoughts," but by gratefulness to Beecher for his kind attentions in her bereavement and by his authoritative insistence that the act was not sinful. Through the year-and-a-half affair, she said, she had been in a "trance." She made him vow to keep his knowledge secret. And he agreed.

But *secret*, as we know, is probably the most elastic word in English usage. Tilton, his reaction varying between hurt and happy martyrdom, unburdened himself to a close friend, Martha Bradshaw, a deaconess of Beecher's church. He then repeated the same story to Henry Bowen, his publisher, whose own wife had once been seduced by Beecher. As for Elizabeth, she expiated her sin further by disclosing it to her hysterical and talkative mother, Mrs. Nathan B. Morse, who in turn gossiped about it to intimate friends.

When Victoria Woodhull revealed to Tilton her own full knowledge of the scandal, he thought at once that she had heard it from Mrs. Morse. He was wrong. Victoria had heard the scandal on May 3, 1871, from her fellow suffragette Elizabeth Cady Stanton during a private chat on marriage and free love. Not long before, Mrs. Stanton had been personal witness to the discord at the Tiltons, and she told Victoria about it.

It appeared that Tilton had dined with Mrs. Stanton and Mrs. Bullard at the latter's home. They planned to discuss the policy of *The Revolution*, a sufferage newspaper, which Tilton was helping them edit. But Tilton had no mind for journalism that evening. When the talk turned to marriage reform, Tilton exploded with a tirade against the influence of Beecher. He said that he despised "the damned lecherous scoundrel." And he told the startled ladies his reasons.

This was the morsel of gossip which Mrs. Stanton passed along to Victoria Woodhull. Had Mrs. Stanton held her tongue, it is possible that there would never have been a Beecher-Tilton case in American history.

When Theodore Tilton left Victoria Woodhull's presence that late morning of May 22, 1871, he realized that he was faced with a single difficult duty. He must preserve his wife's reputation and his own by convincing Victoria that the scandal must not be exposed to further publicity. To this end, employing the principals involved, the services of his pen, and even his own sexuality, Tilton for more than a year sought to divert Victoria from any indulgence in sensationalism.

Tilton, despite Elizabeth's protests, took Victoria to meet her, to prove to Victoria that his wife was really decent and deserved no injury. When he brought Victoria into the house, and introduced her, he said to his wife: "Elizabeth, Mrs. Woodhull knows all." Elizabeth was troubled. "Everything?" Tilton nodded. The rest of the meeting went smoothly. As Elizabeth sewed she discussed her opinions on many subjects, and later presented her guest with a volume of verse.

Next, Tilton went to Henry Ward Beecher and advised him to receive Victoria and "treat her with kindness." Apparently the pastor was agreeable, for Tilton was able to write Victoria: "My dear Victoria . . . you shall see Mr. Beecher at my house on Friday night. He will attend a meeting of the church at ten o'clock and will give you the rest of the evening as late as you desire."

Victoria was waiting in the Tilton parlor when Beecher arrived. She greeted him warmly, arms extended. They discussed the subject of marriage, and Beecher agreed that it was "the grave of love." Victoria chided him for not preaching what he believed, and he replied, uncomfortably: "If I were to do so, I should preach to empty seats and it would be the ruin of my church." Now she came to the topic uppermost in her mind. She wanted his public endorsement. She had written him, the day before, that she was scheduled to speak at Steinway Hall and "what I say or shall not say will depend largely upon the result of the interview." Bluntly she asked him to appear on the platform with her and introduce her. Beecher recoiled at the request. She was going to discuss free love, and he would have no part of it. Victoria called him "a moral coward." It is possible she threatened him. At any rate, as she recalled it, he immediately climbed "upon the sofa on his knees beside me, and taking my face between his hands, while the tears streamed down his cheeks, he begged me to let him off." When Victoria remained unmoved and repeated that she might yet expose his infamy, he exclaimed: "Oh! if it must come, let me know of it twenty-four hours in advance, that I may take my own life." Years after, Victoria confessed to one of her associates that "she herself had had sexual relations both with Tilton and with Beecher."

When Victoria finally appeared at Steinway Hall on the evening of November 20, 1871, it was not Beecher, but Tilton who introduced her. This pacified her sufficiently to make her omit, in her talk on social freedom, any mention of the scandal. As it turned out, her speech proved inflammatory enough. She called marriage laws "despotic, remnants of the barbaric age in which they were originated." She predicted that free love would be the religion of the next generation. There was considerable heckling from the vast, unruly audience, and during the speech some voice bellowed: "Are you a free lover?" Victoria left her text to shout back: "Yes! I am a free lover!" Half the audience cheered, the other half booed. Angrily, speaking extemporaneously, Victoria went on:

"I have an inalienable, constitutional, and natural right to love whom I may, to love as long or as short a period as I can, to change that love every day if I please! And with that right neither you nor any law you can frame have any right to interfere. . . ."

Tilton continued to conciliate Victoria in every way. He wrote lectures for her. He wrote, and rewrote, from notes supplied by Colonel Blood, a nauseatingly saccharine biography of her entitled "An Account of Mrs. Woodhull," which was printed as a special *Golden Age Tract*. Finally, after swimming with her at Coney Island and spending long evenings conversing with her, Tilton became Victoria's lover. Whether this consummation of their intimacy was a studied effort by Tilton to placate her, or the natural result of his proximity to her seductive person, we will never know. But the affair occurred, and Victoria acknowledged it publicly several years later, much to Tilton's embarrassment and his wife's distress. A reporter on the *Chicago Times* asked her for an opinion of Theodore Tilton.

"I ought to know Mr. Tilton," Victoria replied frankly. "He was my devoted lover for more than half a year, and I admit that during that time he was my accepted lover. A woman who could not love Theodore Tilton, especially in reciprocation of a generous, overwhelming affection such as he was capable of bestowing, must be indeed dead to all the sweeter impulses of our nature. I could not resist his inspiring fascinations."

"Do I understand, my dear Madame," asked the incredulous reporter, "that the fascination was mutual and irresistible?"

"You will think so," said Victoria, "when I tell you that so enamored and infatuated with each other were we that for three months we were hardly out of each other's sight day or night. He slept every night for three months, in my arms. Of course we were lovers—devoted, true and faithful lovers."

However, Victoria disengaged herself from Tilton's embraces long enough to set in motion a new scheme that might enhance her chances of becoming president of the United States. She mentioned to Mrs. Stanton, Mrs. Hooker, and other gullible feminists that the Suffrage Association would be wise to create its own political party and sponsor its own candidates for public office. The idea thrilled the suffragettes, and at once they printed announcements summoning delegates to a convention at Steinway Hall on May 9 and 10, 1872. "We believe that the time has come for the formation of a new political party whose principles shall meet the issues of the hour and represent equal rights for all." To these announcements, at Victoria's suggestion, Mrs. Stanton appended the all-powerful name of Susan B. Anthony.

Miss Anthony was lecturing in Illinois when she picked up the latest issue of the *Woodhull & Claflin's Weekly* and read that she was sponsoring a new political party. She perceived, at once, Victoria's ulterior purpose. Victoria was making a daring bid to reorganize the suffragette movement so that she might take it over. Miss Anthony acted with firmness and dispatch. She telegraphed the association to remove her name from the list of sponsors. She told them that she was coming to New York on the first train to protect their interests. She wrote them: "Mrs. Woodhull has the advantage of us because she has her paper, but she persistently means to run our craft into her port and none other."

Once in New York, Miss Anthony made it known that none of Victoria's vast and varied following, which has been organized as the Victoria League, would be eligible to attend the suffragette convention. Mrs. Stanton thought Miss Anthony unreasonable, but Miss Anthony would not budge. If there was to be a suffrage convention, it would be for legitimate suffragettes only.

The suffrage convention began on schedule in Steinway Hall, with Miss Anthony in the chair and Mrs. Stanton delivering the keynote address. Victoria was nowhere to be seen. As the business of the meeting continued into the night, and neared adjournment, there was a sudden commotion backstage. Dramatically Victoria Woodhull materialized, determined to be heard by the great assembly.

As Miss Anthony rushed to block her way, Victoria faced the audience and made a motion that the convention adjourn and reconvene the following day in Apollo Hall, which she had leased for her supporters. From the floor, someone seconded the motion. Hastily Victoria called for a vote, and was answered by a scattering of ayes. But Miss Anthony was equal to the crisis. She spoke rapidly and strongly. There could be no vote, for there had been no motion by a legitimate member of the Suffrage Association. "Nothing that this person has said will be recorded in the minutes," she cried. "The convention will now adjourn to meet tomorrow at eleven o'clock *in this hall.*" Victoria tried to be heard again, but Miss Anthony overrode her, shouting to the janitor to turn down the gas lights. In a matter of minutes the hall was darkened, emptied of delegates, and Victoria was alone. Defeated at her own game, she had lost the support of the suffrage movement forever.

The following morning, when the Suffrage Association, cleansed and chastened, met again, it unanimously elected Susan B. Anthony as its leader. Elsewhere, a determined Victoria Woodhull and her aides were busily herding 660 followers—defected suffragettes, spiritualists, socialists, members of Section 12 of the International, free lovers, and freelance cranks—into Apollo Hall for the purpose of creating a vigorously new political party.

Judge Reymart, of New York, presided. He introduced Stephen Pearl Andrews, who moved that the new convention call itself the Equal Rights Party. His motion was carried. Then other orators took over. There was a speech in favor of a minimum wage. There was a poem that deplored bribery and corruption. And, by evening, at last there was Victoria.

To thunderous applause she spoke against the corporations, against the Vanderbilts and Astors, against the two-party system, against the republic of men. With evangelical fervor she reached the climax of her address:

"From this convention will go forth a tide of revolution that shall sweep over the whole world. What does freedom mean? The inalienable right to life, liberty and the pursuit of happiness. What is equality? It is that every person shall have the same opportunities to exercise the inalienable rights belonging to the individual. And what justice? That the alienable rights belonging to individuals shall be jealously guarded against encroachment. Shall we be slaves to escape revolution? Away with such weak stupidity! A revolution shall sweep with resistless force, if not fury, over the whole country, to purge it of political trickery, despotic assumption, and all industrial injustice. Who will dare to attempt to unlock the luminous portals of the future with the rusty key of the past!"

The moment had come. Judge Carter, of Ohio, leaped to the edge of the platform. "I nominate Victoria C. Woodhull for president of the United States!" he shouted. "All in favor of the nomination say aye!" Apollo Hall trembled under the roar of ayes. Hundreds were on their feet, screaming, cheering, waving hats, handkerchiefs, as Tennessee Claflin, herself a candidate for Congress, led four hundred Negro soldiers and a band up the chaotic aisles.

When the tumult had been stilled, and order restored, Victoria made a short, modest speech of acceptance and thanks. The chair then opened nominations for vice-president. A man in the audience offered up the name of a prominent redskin, Chief Spotted Tail. An emancipated woman shouted that Colonel Blood belonged on the ticket with Victoria. Moses Hull, of Kentucky, nominated Frederick Douglass, a onetime fugitive slave who had acquired an international reputation as a reformer, author, and lecturer. "We have had the oppressed sex represented by Woodhull," stated Hull. "We must have the oppressed race represented by Douglass!" The candidates were put to a vote, and it was Douglass for vice-president by an overwhelming majority.

Later, when ratification of the ticket occurred, Tennessee's band played again. The music was "Comin' thro' the Rye." But the words, boomed forth by hundreds of hoarse voices, were new and exciting:

Yes! Victoria we've selected
For our chosen head:
With Fred Douglass on the ticket
We will raise the dead.
Then around them let us rally
Without fear or dread,
And next March, we'll put the Grundys
In their little bed.

But the flush of recognition was only briefly enjoyed by Victoria. Though a Kentucky congressman soberly announced that female agitation might give Mrs. Woodhull his state by twenty thousand votes, the Suffrage Association made it clear that their female members and their members' husbands were going to boycott the Equal Rights Party. Though Colonel Blood estimated that the shrewd nomination of Douglass might give Victoria the lion's share of the four million Negro votes, Douglass himself quickly shattered this dream. According to Mrs. Blake's diary, "Douglass knew nothing of the performance until, horrified, he read about it in the morning papers." At once he wrote an open letter to the press declining the nomination. The New York papers, as one, ridiculed Victoria in cartoon and print. Official sources were even less tolerant. The Governor of Massachusetts made it clear that he would not permit Mrs. Woodhull to campaign in Boston. "You might as well have the undressed women of North Street on the stage there."

Immediately it became apparent that by legitimizing her candidacy for president, Victoria had weakened her position. Before the nomination, she had been regarded as a progressive, if somewhat bold, eccentric. With the nomination, and a following that did not include the more stable suffragettes, she was regarded as a potentially dangerous radical. The rent on her brokerage house was raised $1,000 a year, and it had to be shut down. *Woodhull & Claflin's Weekly*, neglected and already in debt, lost the support of Commodore Vanderbilt. Financial advertising was withdrawn, and the periodical was temporarily suspended. The landlord of the house on Thirty-eighth Street, hinting outside pressure, asked Victoria and her family to leave the premises. Neighbors were muttering about prostitution, and certain people had objected to Victoria's muckracking against the "rottenness of the social condition." No hotel or boardinghouse would take her in, and one night she and her family were forced to camp in the street. At last, relatives located a residence, but Victoria's troubles continued to mount.

Theodore Tilton had had enough of pacifying and loving the presidential candidate, and he was through. He said that he broke with Victoria because he resented her public remarks against suffragettes who were his old friends. She said that she broke with Tilton because he preferred to support Horace Greeley, rather than herself, for the presidency. Meanwhile, two of Beecher's most respected sisters savagely fought Victoria in print. Earlier Catharine Beecher, resentful of Victoria's hints at scandal, had warned her: "Remember, Victoria Woodhull, that I shall strike you dead." She struck through her more famous sister, Harriet Beecher Stowe, who had become wealthy and world renowned twenty years before on the publication of *Uncle Tom's Cabin.* The puritanical Mrs. Stowe, who had only recently raised a storm of protest in England by charging Lord Byron with incest (in defense of Lady Byron, who was her friend), now set her sights on Victoria. She published a series of sharp articles against Victoria in *Christian Union,* and she published a novel in which a thinly disguised Victoria was portrayed in anything but a flattering light. Victoria was stung. Angered by defeat and persecution, she decided to retaliate in such a way as to wound her enemies and regain her position of national prominence on the eve of the elections.

It was September 11, 1872, and Victoria, despite the Governor's ban, was in Boston to address the American Association of Spiritualists. Though she was president of the organization, she wished to speak about something more earthly than spiritualism. For the first time naming names, she revealed the adulterous affair between Beecher and Elizabeth Tilton. "Henry Ward Beecher suffered severely," wrote the *Memphis Appeal.* "She said . . . he preached every Sunday to his mistresses, members of his church, sitting in their pews, robed in silks and satins and high respectability!" Though Boston and New York papers covered her speech, only one dared mention it in print. The *Boston Journal* reported that a "prominent New York clergyman was personally accused of the most hideous crimes."

Met by this conspiracy of silence, Victoria took matters into her own hands. If the popular press would not be honest, then she would "ventilate the scandal" in her own periodical. With the assistance of Blood and Tennessee she revived *Woodhull & Claflin's Weekly*, and on the morning of October 28, 1872, she had her sensation at last. She headlined the entire issue, dated five days later: "THE BEECHER-TILTON SCANDAL CASE. The Detailed Statement of the Whole Matter by Mrs. Woodhull."

She wrote: "I intend that this article shall burst like a bomb-shell into the ranks of the moralistic social camp." She pretended that her story had been originally given to a Boston paper, which had suppressed it. She repeated everything that she had heard from Mrs. Stanton and from Tilton. She made it plain that she did not disapprove of Beecher's affair with Elizabeth—after all, she was an advocate of free love. What she objected to was his sanctimoniousness. But she tried to be understanding of Beecher's passion. "With his demanding physical nature, and with the terrible restrictions upon a clergyman's life," she could not see fit to condemn him entirely. She even went so far as to praise "the immense physical potency of Mr. Beecher . . . Passional starvation, enforced on such a nature, so richly endowed . . . is a horrid cruelty. . . . Every great man of Mr. Beecher's type, has had in the past, and will ever have, the need for and the right to, the loving manifestations of many women."

But, continued Victoria, Beecher had given grave offense to Tilton. When Tilton learned of his wife's unfaithfulness, he tore the wedding ring off her finger and smashed Beecher's framed picture. Beecher, Victoria concluded eleven columns later, was "a poltroon, a coward and a sneak" for not owning up to his clandestine affair.

The uproar that followed was tremendous. Newsboys hawked the weekly through the city, and over one hundred thousand copies were sold. As copies became scarce, single issues began to sell for ten dollars each, and finally for forty. Beecher was confronted with the scandal. A friend wanted reassurance that the whole thing was a fraud. "Entirely!" said Beecher. His attitude made it clear that he was above the battle. "In passing along the way, anyone is liable to have a bucket of slops thrown upon him," he remarked. But if he pretended to ignore the exposé, Anthony Comstock did not. This part-time guardian of the nation's morals read the story after midnight and felt it to be a "most abominable and unjust charge against one of the purest and best citizens of the United States." When Beecher refused to sue for libel, or for anything else, Comstock himself instigated criminal action. The morning after publication, he sought out the United States District Attorney, who was a member of Beecher's congregation, and demanded that Victoria and her sister be arrested for sending obscene printed matter through the mails.

The deputy marshals found Victoria and Tennessee in a carriage on Broad Street with five hundred new copies of their weekly beside them, waiting to be arrested. A prohibitive bail of $8,000 was placed on each, and they were hustled into a cramped cell of the Ludlow Street Jail. After a month without trial, they were released on bail, then rearrested on another charge and again released on bail, and finally arrested a third time when Comstock discovered that they were sending reprints of their scandal edition through the mails. After six months of confinement, Victoria and Tennessee were granted a jury trial. Their savior proved to be none other than Congressman Butler, who had first brought Victoria to public prominence in Washington. He had helped write the law against sending obscene material through the mails and now explained that it was meant to cover only "lithographs, prints, engravings, licentious books." In court Victoria's attorney pointed out that the offending weekly was none of these. The jury agreed and found the sisters "Not guilty."

But to the editorial writers of *The New York Times*, Victoria was still guilty. In attacking Beecher so unfairly she had "disgraced and degraded . . . the female name." It was not until three years later that Victoria saw herself partially vindicated. After Beecher's backers, accusing Tilton of slander, had drummed him out of the Plymouth Church by a vote of 210 to 13, and after an examining committee of the church had completely exonerated their beloved pastor, Tilton was moved to act. He instigated suit against Beecher for $100,000 for alienation of his wife's affections, and on January 11, 1875, in Brooklyn, the great scandal at last came to trial. Tilton testified that Beecher had seduced his wife, and for a year and a half "maintained criminal intercourse" with her. He presented letters to prove that the good pastor had told his wife that she was not properly appreciated by her husband and had suggested that they find other ways to express their love beyond "the shake of the hand or the kiss of the lips." Beecher, for his part, admitted affection, denied adultery, and, after 112 days of wrangling and 3,000 pages of testimony, got a hung jury (with a vote of 9 to 3 against Tilton after 52 ballots). Beecher's followers gave him a hero's welcome. The *Louisville Courier-Journal*, like most of the press in sentiment, branded Beecher "a dunghill covered with flowers."

Though Beecher had hoped to become president, his ambitions for public office were destroyed by the scandal. Yet, he held his following, and his lecture audiences even increased, enabling him to count on as much as $1,000 a speech. As the accused, he had survived nicely. Victoria Woodhull as his accuser fared not half so well. The scandal she had brought to light had done little to aid her in her bid for the presidency. She was behind bars, in the Ludlow Street Jail, on November 5, 1872, when Grant was easily re-elected president. Victoria received no electoral votes and but "few scattered popular ones." At first she blamed her crushing rejection on the corruption of the Grant machine. "If Jesus Christ had been running against this man," she told a San Francisco audience, "he'd have been defeated." Later she sensed that her theories and reforms were too advanced for the general public.

For a while, wracked by illness and exhaustion, she persisted with her lectures on free love. Though well attended, they no longer generated the old excitement. As always, Victoria continued to live her personal life without regard for public opinion. She had several affairs. One was with a nineteen-year-old college boy whom she had hired to help manage her lectures. His name was Benjamin R. Tucker, and in 1926 he revealed the extent of his involvement to Emanie Sachs, who published it in *The Terrible Siren.* Though he was shy, he professed to believe in Victoria's doctrines, and tried not to appear surprised when she kissed him or sat on his lap. One Sunday morning he entered her parlor to find her stretched on a lounge. "After some conversation," wrote Tucker, "she said: 'Do you know, I should dearly love to sleep with you?' Thereupon any man a thousandth part less stupid than myself would have thrown his arms around her neck and smothered her with kisses. But I simply remarked that were her desire to be gratified, it would be my first experience in that line. She looked at me with amazement. 'How can that be?' she asked." The arrival of Colonel Blood interrupted any further discussion. But when Tucker returned that afternoon, Victoria was still waiting to seduce him. "Mrs. Woodhull was still obliged to make all the advances; I, as before, was slow and hesitating. . . . But, despite all obstacles, within an hour my 'ruin' was complete, and I, nevertheless, a proud and happy youth."

Victoria, apparently, was insatiable, for young Tucker was obliged to return for the same purpose that night and frequently in the days that followed. But when Victoria insisted upon making this promiscuity a family affair, Tucker revolted. "One afternoon, when I was walking up town with Victoria from the office, she said to me suddenly, 'Tennie is going to love you this afternoon.' I looked at her wonderingly. 'But,' I said, 'I don't care to have her.' 'Oh, don't say that,' she answered; 'nobody can love me who doesn't love Tennie.' " With that, Tucker fled.

Though Victoria expected tolerance toward her own affairs, she demanded faithfulness on the part of her lovers. When in 1876 she learned that Colonel Blood had been attentive to several young females, she was outraged. She told him that she was tired of supporting him and asked him to leave. Though they had not been married, Victoria formally divorced Blood on the complaint that he had consorted with a prostitute. Except for one occasion, years later, when she silently passed him on the street, she never saw him again—and long after, she learned that he had died on a gold-hunting expedition to Africa, far from the utopian world of free love and fiat money he had so long adored.

At about the time of Blood's departure from her home, Victoria began to lose interest in radicalism and reform. Her ideals seemed as tired and passé as her person. Her existence seemed to have lost all point and purpose. Once the noble Demosthenes had guided her toward the path to wealth and power. She had tasted both and found them bitter. Now her deepest yearning was to find peace, normality, and refuge in some placid orthodoxy. And so, in her thirty-eighth year, she abandoned Demosthenes for Jesus Christ.

The startling conversion first became apparent on the editorial page of the *Weekly*, which was appearing erratically again. A standard quotation from John Stuart Mill on "the diseases of society" was abruptly replaced by more soothing words from St. Paul. Also, a series of interpretative articles on the "Book of Revelations" crowded out shrill arguments on equal rights. Finally Victoria canceled her popular lectures on the prostitution of marriage for lectures, well punctuated with Biblical references, on her discovery that the Garden of Eden was in the body of every married woman.

Before this vague and confused exploration into religion could go any further, an event occurred that completely changed Victoria's life. On the morning of January 4, 1877, after shouting for his wife to sing him some hymns, the mighty Commodore Vanderbilt expired. In death, as he had in life, he rescued Victoria from need and oblivion. The Commodore's will left over $100,000,000 to his heirs. Of this total, $95,000,000 went to his eldest son, William, and the remaining paltry $5,000,000 to his other son, Cornelius, and his eight daughters. The indignant minority sued on the grounds that the deceased had been mentally incompetent at the time the will was written. Though Cornelius settled for $1,000,000 out of court, the eight Vanderbilt daughters fought on. To prove their father's incompetence, they consulted, among many others, Victoria Woodhull, who had once been his medium.

In the clash over the Commodore's will, Victoria saw a golden opportunity to recoup her fortune. The Commodore had left her nothing, though he had left Tennessee an oil painting and had entrusted to both sisters "certain large sums" to be used in advancing the cause of spiritualism. Victoria made it known that the Commodore owed her more than $100,000, the residue of an old, unfulfilled business deal.

While there exists no documentation on what happened next, it seems obvious that William Vanderbilt, as main heir and defendant, took the hint. Rather than have Victoria testify against his interests by recollecting the Commodore's mental lapses, William paid off.

In 1876 Victoria had turned to Christ for salvation, but in 1877 it was the Commodore who saved her. We do not know the precise sum she extracted. Figures ranging between $50,000 and $500,000 have been mentioned. But a condition of William's deal apparently was that Victoria and Tennessee remove their persons from American soil at once and for the duration of the contest over the will. And so, late in 1877, with new wardrobe, new servants, and six first-class staterooms, Victoria and Tennessee sailed for England.

Arriving in London, Victoria leased a fashionable suburban home and decided to make herself known by resuming her platform appearances. She had posters printed which announced the forthcoming personal appearance of "the great American orator." On an evening in December 1877 she addressed a large audience at St. James's Hall. Her subject was "The Human Body, the Temple of God," and though it concerned varied problems of motherhood and heredity, there was at least one male member of the assemblage who listened with rapt attention. His name was John Biddulph Martin, the rich and aristocratic son of a rich and aristocratic father. Victoria's appearance and her personality moved him deeply. "I was charmed with her high intellect and fascinated by her manner," Martin recalled later, "and I left the lecture hall that night with the determination that, if Mrs. Woodhull would marry me, I would certainly make her my wife."

Soon enough, Martin succeeded in meeting the astonishing American "orator." It was not surprising that Victoria found him agreeable, and that she could reciprocate his affection. She wanted security, acceptance, love, and all of these John Biddulph Martin could promise in abundance. At thirty-six—Victoria was then thirty-nine—Martin was a full partner of the prosperous Martin's Bank, at 68 Lombard Street, London, a firm that traced its origin back to 1579. Beyond this major inducement, Martin possessed several others. He had been an athlete at Oxford, and despite his age and beard, he still had the trim appearance of an athlete. He was a quiet man, devoted to culture and scholarship, and Victoria was his first real love.

If Victoria hoped for a quick, happy ending to a tumultuous career, it was not to be so simple. Martin's parents, at Overbury Court, were appalled by his choice for wife. Had they thought to investigate Victoria, they would not have had to go beyond their daily newspapers. The press, if restrained, made it plain that Mrs. Woodhull's past had been checkered. She had been twice married and twice divorced, the elder Martins incorrectly learned. She had crusaded—horror of horrors—for free love. She had been the inmate of an American jail. And her name had been linked with such public scandals as the Beecher trial and the Vanderbilt-will case. Were these the qualifications for an English banker's wife? Evidently not. The elder Martins made their disapproval clear. Their son was desolate; their future daughter-in-law was indignant.

Like the ancient Chinese emperor who burned all history books and records so that history might begin with him, Victoria Woodhull now desperately and grimly set out to obliterate her past. She had been, she insisted, the editor of *Woodhull & Claflin's Weekly* in name only. Colonel Blood had written those reprehensible articles on free love, and Stephen Pearl Andrews had exposed the Beecher-Tilton scandal, all without her knowledge. While she did, indeed, believe in the emancipation of women, all else credited to her pen and tongue were the grossest falsehoods. Her own life, from birth, had been one of chastity and conformity.

It took six years to convince the elder Martins. At last, probably worn down by Victoria's persistent chatter about purity and by their son's endless romantic pleadings, they withdrew threats of disinheritance and gave their consent. On October 31, 1883, at the age of forty-five, Victoria Claflin Woodhull became Mrs. John Biddulph Martin, London lady and legal mistress of a gray, stately residence at 17 Hyde Park Gate.

But for Victoria, in all her eighteen years of contented marriage, the fight to suppress or revise her shocking and eccentric past was never done. When some of the wives of Martin's friends cut her dead, Victoria offered 1,000 pounds reward for a list of those in "conspiracy to defame" her. Just as book publishers print excerpts of good reviews of their best authors, Victoria printed and circulated broadsides containing good character references taken from carefully screened American sources.

When a friend found two pamphlets on the Beecher-Tilton scandal, with ample references to the part played in it by Victoria Woodhull, on the shelves of the British Museum, and reported it to Victoria, she begged her husband to act. On February 24, 1894, Martin brought suit against the trustees of the British Museum for libel. The trial, such as it was, lasted five days. Defended by a peer of the realm, Victoria was described as a victim of constant persecution—married by force to "an inebriate" at an early age, unjustly incarcerated merely because she had taken "a strong view" of Reverend Beecher's adultery, maligned because she had bravely sought to elevate the status of her sex. The British Museum, which had never before been brought to court for libel, was represented by a renowned attorney who was also one of its trustees. Though his cross-examination of Victoria was relentless and detailed, her answers were so discursive and vague as to make the usually attentive London *Times* confess to its readers that it could not grasp her testimony. In the end the jury agreed that libel had been committed, but with no intent at injury, and awarded Victoria twenty shillings in damages.

Ever vigilant, Victoria continued to incite her husband to

defend her good name even when foul aspersions were cast from great distances. Time and again, Victoria took Martin from his coin collection and from the history of his family's bank that he was preparing, and induced him to accompany her to America to have justice done. When the *Brooklyn Eagle* featured a series of popular articles by the stern and exacting Thomas Byrnes, celebrated police inspector, on infamous female intriguers, and when one of these intriguers turned out to be Victoria Woodhull, she hastened to New York with Martin for a showdown with Byrnes. Despite her protests of "a great injustice," despite Martin's demands for retraction, Byrnes would not budge. Facts were facts, and he had published facts. Martin was dismayed. "I'm very sorry you will do nothing." Byrnes was stone. "I am sorry, too, but I am a public official and any statement I make I may be held responsible for. And you have the courts to which you can have recourse at once." Whereupon Victoria and Martin retreated to finish their battle in the press. They told reporters that Byrnes had been cordial and apologetic. Byrnes heard this with "no little surprise" and announced that he had been neither cordial nor apologetic.

But not all of the Martins' married life was spent commuting to America in Victoria's defense. There were happier days in the English years when Victoria sponsored brilliant dinners and evenings at Hyde Park Gate for her growing number of London friends and followers. And, while she occupied herself by again running for president of the United States in 1892 (mostly by correspondence), by planning an autobiography she never wrote, and by publishing a proper monthly called *The Humanitarian*, John Martin basked in the reflected pleasure of her activity, stirring himself only to fulfill his obligations as head of the Royal Statistical Society.

In his fifty-sixth year Martin fell ill. After a slow recovery he was advised to vacation at Las Palmas, in the Canary Islands, off Africa. There, in a weakened condition, he contracted pneumonia, and on March 20, 1897, died. Victoria's daughter, Zulu Maud, wrote his obituary for *The Humanitarian.* "Theirs was a perfect union," she concluded, "marred only by persecution."

Four years later, Victoria, possessed now of an inheritance valued at over $800,000, sold her home at Hyde Park Gate and moved to her late husband's country manor at Bredon's Norton, Worcestershire. Her ancient valley-residence, thickly populated with servants, looked out upon a vast estate and the river Avon. Without her husband's restraining influence, she quickly reverted to form. While he was still alive she had in her monthly denounced socialism and all advanced ideas. Now, at sixty-three, insisting that a "charming woman has no age," she plunged into a whirl of reform.

Victoria gave over a portion of her estate to an amazon project called Bredon's Norton College, in which young ladies were invited to study agriculture. She flayed the English school system as outmoded and opened her own progressive kindergartens for village youngsters in the vicinity. She again patronized spiritualism and presided at a salon for those who believed as she believed. In 1912 she offered an antique silver trophy and $5,000 to the first person who would successfully fly the Atlantic Ocean. In 1914 she contributed $5,000 toward the purchase of Sulgrave Manor, the home of George Washington's English ancestors, built in 1531, which was presented to the Anglo-American Association. In 1915, with World War I under way, she worked for the Red Cross and at fund-raising campaigns for Belgians and Armenians, and sent Woodrow Wilson a stiff cable reading: "Why is Old Glory absent from shop windows in England today when other flags are flying?"

At war's end she was very old and very alone. Her daughter was ever beside her, but Tennessee remained her closest friend. Tennessee, brash and amoral as ever, had fared well in the English climate. In 1885, during a seance with a wealthy, elderly English widower named Francis Cook, she disclosed that the late Mrs. Cook was urging her husband to marry his medium. The wedding took place at once. Cook, who amassed his money importing shawls from India after Queen Victoria made them fashionable, possessed an expensive house near the Thames and another in Portugal. When he was knighted, Tennessee became Lady Cook. The title did not inhibit her. Upon her husband's death in 1901 she was left a fortune of $2,000,000, and she disposed of it with reckless philanthropy. She traveled regularly to the United States, scolding Theodore Roosevelt in person for not doing something about woman suffrage, attempting to establish a chain of homes for reformed prostitutes in the South, trying to build a "school for fathers" on Long Island, and endeavoring to raise a female army of 150,000 in 1915. She died in January 1923, and though she left a tearful Victoria $500,000 richer, she deprived her of the last link to the past.

Victoria knew that her time was near. But she would not accept the fact. She felt most alive during afternoons when in her white sports-car she urged her nervous chauffeur to drive at recklessly high speeds. In her manor house she tried to ward off death with innumerable eccentricities. Like Train, she refused to shake hands with visitors for fear that they might contaminate her. At nights she avoided her bed as she would a coffin, preferring to sleep in a rocking chair.

But on the morning of June 20, 1927, while English women were awakening and American women were going to sleep, all fully possessed of the equal rights for which she had so long fought, death came to Victoria Claflin Woodhull Martin. In three months she would have been ninety years old. Her epitaph had been prepared long years before, by an admiring editor in Troy, New York. He had written history's verdict in a sentence:

"She ought to be hanged, and then have a monument erected to her memory at the foot of the gallows."

V

The Forty-Niner Who Abolished Congress

"We do hereby Order and Direct Major General Scott, the Commander-in-Chief of our Armies, immediately on receipt of this our Decree, to proceed with a suitable force and clear the Halls of Congress."

JOSHUA NORTON

On April 15, 1876, Dom Pedro II, who had the appearance of an Old Testament patriarch and was to be the last emperor of Brazil, disembarked in New York for a three-month visit to the United States. Though Secretary of State Hamilton Fish was on hand to meet him, the studious South American sovereign insisted that he wished no official receptions, but preferred to do his sight-seeing as a private citizen.

Within two days, at his own request, Dom Pedro was on a train to the Far West, eagerly peering through his window for glimpses of redskins or Mormon harems. In San Francisco he attended a performance of *King Lear*, visited Chinatown, translated several Hebrew scrolls in a synagogue on Sutter Street, and generally did as he pleased. But when the University of California, across the bay, solicited his attendance at an official reception in his honor, he who had once remarked: "If I were not an emperor, I should like to be a schoolteacher," found that he could not refuse. As it turned out, it was fortunate that he accepted the invitation. For it was on the California campus that Dom Pedro was welcomed, for the first time since his arrival in the United States, by one of his own rank and station who would give him his best understanding of democracy.

The ceremonies in the University of California assembly hall were about to begin when Dom Pedro, seated beside the institution's president and most learned professors, was suddenly surprised by the approach of another guest, more royal, more regal, than himself. The visitor, a bearded, stocky, serious, middle-aged man, was attired in a black, high hat surmounted by a green ostrich-plume, a frayed, blue long-tailed coat replete with gold epaulets and brass buttons, a pair of outsized shoes slit at the sides, and a heavy saber dangling from his waist. Soberly he ascended the platform, and, though uninvited, took an empty seat near the dignitaries. The audience of students buzzed and giggled. Dom Pedro was seen to blink at the newcomer. Hastily an introduction was effected—and thus Dom Pedro, to his utter amazement, found himself exchanging formal courtesies with one who was described as "His Imperial Highness, Norton I, Emperor of the United States and Protector of Mexico."

Though Norton's true identity was soon revealed to the Emperor, he was no less astonished. For of all the sights he would see and the men he would meet during his 9,000-mile journey through the United States—the admirable water-supply system in Chicago, the appalling insane-asylum in St. Louis, the delightful dinner with Longfellow in Cambridge, the gracious interviews with President Grant, the visits to Mammoth Cave and Sing Sing Prison and the Centennial Exhibition in Philadelphia—no one and nothing would prove more memorable than this chance acquaintance with North America's self-appointed Emperor. Norton I, as Dom Pedro would learn, had publicly abolished both houses of Congress and both major political parties, had printed his own bonds and levied his own taxes, and yet not only had been tolerated by his more democratic Americans, but also had often been sheltered, fed, and clothed at their expense. In the person of this improbable being, Dom Pedro saw perhaps the truest representation of American democracy at work which he was to see in his entire three-month visit.

Emperor Norton had lived fifty-seven years and reigned benevolently seventeen of them before he met, in the Brazilian ruler, the first and last royal personage he was to know in his lifetime. But unlike Dom Pedro, Emperor Norton was of plebeian stock. His father, John Norton, an English Jew, was a farmer. His mother, Sarah, was of humble parentage. Joshua Abraham Norton, the second of two sons, was born in London on February 4, 1819. His only relationship to royalty was that, at birth, he became a subject of George III.

In 1820, when Joshua Norton was two, his family joined four thousand other English colonists in a pioneering migration to Grahamstown, South Africa. There his father bought and tilled a farm, and eventually helped found Algoa Bay, now known as Port Elizabeth. By the time Joshua Norton was twenty, his father had expanded his interests to part ownership of a general store in Cape Town which specialized in ships' supplies. Of young Norton's African years we know little. He enlisted for a short term as a colonial soldier. He worked as a clerk in his father's store. When his father began to outfit vessels of his own, he took charge of a two-masted brigantine and in 1844 sailed it to Peru and Chile, where he lost money on the venture.

When Joshua Norton was thirty his father followed his mother to an early grave. The business that Norton inherited proved of little value, and he soon liquidated it and sailed for Brazil, where he is thought to have made quick profits on several merchandising investments. Meanwhile, near the city of Sacramento in far-off California, a workman had discovered gold on Captain John Sutter's properties. Immediately the great gold-rush was on, and almost a quarter of a million persons were on the way to California. Norton heard the sensational news in Brazil. Without roots, with a normal hunger for sudden wealth, he decided to participate in the gamble.

With $40,000 in savings and inheritance in his trunk, Norton boarded the small German schooner *Franziska* at Rio de Janeiro. He and six other passengers endured 101 monotonous, impatient days at sea. But on the bleak, cold Friday morning of November 23, 1849, their little vessel plodded past the Golden Gate and lay at anchor amid the numerous abandoned and neglected ships dotting San Francisco Bay.

Norton, tall and imposing in his purple cape, joined his fellow passengers in a longboat and was rowed ashore at Montgomery Street, the very center of the business district. The sight that met his eyes as he proceeded into the boom town was unforgettable. Only a year before, San Francisco had been a sleepy village of several hundred inhabitants and fifty adobe huts. Overnight it had been transformed into a bustling, unruly, filthy Mecca for gold diggers. Canvas tents, rude lean-tos, wooden shanties, and brick hotels housed twenty thousand visitors. The muddy, winding streets, filled with rubbish, cluttered with unpacked merchandise, crowded with wagons pushing to the mines, were flanked by an incredible variety of stores, brothels, warehouses, and saloons. In the jammed streets, raucously shoving and pushing, were not only native Americans, white, black, brown, and red, but also pigtailed Chinese, turbaned Hindus, serape-covered Spaniards, Australians, Malayans, Italians, Russians, and Scandinavians. Amid the influx of foreigners the fastidious and very English Joshua Norton was hardly noticed at all. He located a hotel and signed the register, giving his occupation as "traveling merchant."

If Norton intended to become a forty-niner, he soon enough sensed that El Dorado was more readily accessible in the business life of San Francisco than in the backbreaking and precarious gold-fields of Upper California. As the population increased from 20,000 to 90,000, as the demands for food, clothing, construction material, and mining supplies grew louder, Norton realized that a fortune might be made by shrewd trading. But this was a risk even for an experienced businessman like himself. The commodity market was utterly unpredictable. Importing was a costly business. One's judgment had to be sound, for lack of storage space required immediate auctioning of goods. If a scarcity existed at the moment, tremendous profits were possible. If the market happened to be glutted, great losses were inevitable. Still, the population was growing, the need was insistent, and Joshua Norton decided to chance it.

In less than two months Norton opened an office at 242 Montgomery Street, overlooking the city's main thoroughfare, and hazarded his $40,000 in speculation. As a commission agent he bought and sold, for himself and for others, mines, buildings, and extensive lots of real estate. Eventually he and a partner named Robertson built a huge store-and-warehouse on which was painted "Joshua Norton & Company." They imported coal, bricks, and beef, held their goods until they were in demand, and then unloaded at great gain. In May 1851 a ten-hour fire wiped out eighteen city blocks, the entire business district, and, of course, the wooden structure of Joshua Norton & Company. Shortly after, having dismissed his partner, Norton erected a building of his own just one block from his old location. He dealt successfully in coal, tea, flour, coffee, and rice. In the end, his enthusiasm for rice was to lead to his financial downfall and his elevation to royalty.

By early 1853 he had amassed a fortune of $250,000. Now he evolved a scheme that would make him even wealthier. As the owner of California's first rice mill he had been keenly aware of periods when the community suffered gaping shortages of flour. He had seen the price of unhusked rice jump from 4 cents a pound to 32. A shortage loomed again. China had banned exportation of rice to California, and San Francisco's meager supply was rapidly dwindling. Norton determined to corner the rice market. Aware that complete control would enable him to set his own price on this staple commodity, he began to buy every kernel of rice in the vicinity. Then, to protect his immense holdings, he began to buy every shipment of rice that came to port. When a South American vessel, owned by three Peruvians named Ruiz, arrived with 200,000 pounds of rice, Norton absorbed the entire cargo for $25,000, of which sum he paid down $2,000 in cash. When other shipments followed, Norton absorbed these, too.

Then, suddenly, it seemed that every nation was pouring rice into San Francisco. In less than a month, three more vessels arrived, all laden with barrels of rice, one of them carrying 250,000 pounds of it. Norton no longer possessed sufficient funds to absorb the flood and contain the price. He was obliged to allow these and other shipments to be auctioned on the open market. He had purchased his rice at 13 cents a pound, and now he saw the commodity dip to 8. It fell as low as 3 cents before he was able to dispose of his holdings.

He was almost bankrupt. Swiftly his difficulties compounded. Late in 1853 another fire razed five hundred buildings, among them Norton's new store-and-warehouse. He viewed the disaster, remarked one observer, "as a man dazed by a tremendous grief." Meanwhile, he still owed a balance of $23,000 to the three Peruvians. Arguing that the rice had been inferior in quality, he refused to pay. He was promptly sued, and after almost three years of nerve-racking legal disagreement a jury awarded the Peruvians $20,000 in damages. During those painful years, Norton halfheartedly tried to re-establish himself as a broker in gold dust, but the effort failed miserably. When he lost his lawsuit there was nothing to do but to declare bankruptcy. In November 1856 his assets, worth $15,000, were disposed of by the sheriff, and his debts were listed in the district court as amounting to $55,811.

He was only thirty-eight, but his mammoth failure seemed to deprive him of all energy and ambition. He wanted no more of commerce and competition. Injured in pride and pocket, his head filled with fancied persecutions, he withdrew to the privacy of his expensive room in the Tehama House to brood on the world's wrongs. When he could no longer afford the room he moved to a cheap boardinghouse and supported himself by working as a clerk for a Chinese rice company and by receiving some aid from the British consulate.

Eventually he quit his job and retreated to his room to meditate. Loyal business acquaintances and fellow members of the Pacific Club visited him regularly. Though deeply depressed, Norton remained quite sane. In his hermitage he read considerably and conversed with his visitors, and with the passage of time his personal losses receded. His new worry, and obsession, was the troubled state of the Union. The Dred Scott case was in the news. The Lincoln-Douglas debates were being publicized. Tension between North and South was building up. Norton felt that war was inevitable unless stern measures were taken. A democracy, loose and inefficient, could not cope with internal strife, he contended. Only the firm hand of monarchy, a monarchy such as England possessed, could guarantee peace. What America needed, Norton concluded, was an autocratic ruler. So often did he expound on this archaic argument, that eventually his callers began to refer to him, and address him, jestingly, as "His Gracious Highness" and "Emperor." And soon enough, he asked himself: why not?

On the evening of September 17, 1859, the editors of the *San Francisco Bulletin* informed their readers that "a well-dressed and serious-looking man" had visited them and "quietly left the following document, which he respectfully requested we would examine and insert." The document followed:

At the peremptory request and desire of a large majority of the citizens of these United States, I, Joshua Norton, formerly of Algoa Bay, Cape of Good Hope, and now for the last 9 years and 10 months past of San Francisco, California, declare and proclaim myself Emperor of these United States; and in virtue of the authority thereby in me vested, do hereby order and direct the representatives of the different States of the Union to assemble in Musical Hall, of this city, on the 1st day of February next, then and there to make such alterations in the existing laws of the Union as may ameliorate the evils under which the country is laboring, and thereby cause confidence to exist, both at home and abroad, in our stability and integrity.

NORTON I,

EMPEROR OF THE UNITED STATES.

Most historians who were to record the years of Norton's reign found it easiest to explain his ascension from businessman to monarch by stating that he had become "demented," a "mental derelict" because of his bankruptcy. There is no evidence that he was actually insane. While his distaste for business and his desire for attention led him to side-step reality, he was never completely out of touch with it. If many of his notions were fanciful, others were shrewd and sensible. Because his prosperity and happiness depended upon being noticed, he made himself noticed. And in his make-believe role he contrived to survive more comfortably than many who jeered him. Unable to contend with the pitfalls and pressures of the commercial world, he found a new profession and created half a world of his own. Like Napoleon Bonaparte (whom he detested), he crowned himself and established himself in a highly uncompetitive field. Thus, in 1859, encouraged by friends who could not believe he was serious, Joshua Abraham Norton, deposed businessman, emerged from seclusion as Emperor of the United States by popular demand.

Shortly after his astounding proclamation in the *Bulletin*, he appeared in public for the first time as Emperor. Gone were the somber, conventional trappings of the man of commerce. In their place was an outfit distinctly military. From the local Presidio, Norton had salvaged an officer's second-hand uniform. It was light blue, and trimmed with gold epaulets and brass buttons. On his head he wore a general's cap decorated in red, which he later discarded for the tall beaver-hat with the feather. In his buttonhole he wore a rose, and at his side a heavy saber acquired from a blacksmith. His feet were shod in navy boots cut open at the sides to give his corns more freedom. In fair weather he sported a walking stick, in rainy weather a colorful Chinese umbrella.

His first appearance in the streets of San Francisco created a gratifying sensation. He moved swiftly to consolidate this good will. Less than a month after his initial proclamation, another appeared in the *Bulletin*. The Emperor decreed that since "fraud and corruption prevent a fair and proper expression of the public voice," the moment had come for drastic action. Therefore, "We do hereby abolish Congress, and it is hereby abolished." When Washington took no notice Norton was incensed. A supplementary proclamation was made public. "We do hereby Order and Direct Major General Scott, the Commander-in-Chief of our Armies, immediately on receipt of this our Decree, to proceed with a suitable force and clear the Halls of Congress." Lest this was not clear, there was one more document to astound the citizenry. "We, Norton I, by the grace of God and the National Will, Emperor of the Thirty-three States and the multitude of Territories of the United States, do hereby *dissolve* the Republic of the United States of North America." With the suggestion that the governors of the states maintain order until he had taken over full control, Norton abolished "the Democratic and Republican parties" and prepared to stage his long-announced convention.

The convention was scheduled for February 1, 1860, in San Francisco's Musical Hall. A week before the meeting the hall burned to the ground. Undismayed, Norton announced that the convention would proceed four days later at the Assembly Hall. The *Bulletin* predicted a full house, and thought the meeting would "be a great day for California." At the last moment, either because he lacked money to pay for the hall or had forgotten to notify delegates, the convention was canceled. Nevertheless, Norton permitted his long-prepared opening address of welcome to be made public:

"At the request of a large majority of the citizens of the Republic, you have been directed to assemble here, this day, to ratify, alter, or reject, a proposed alteration of the form of your government. An alteration is demanded and insisted upon, or We should not have been entrusted with the authority to have called a Convention of the Nation for that object. . . ."

With the convention out of the way and his authority still unopposed, the Emperor turned to the very real and immediate problem of the privy purse. To rule a great nation—or, at least, to survive personally—required a considerable sum of money. Norton set his mind to this grim task at once. At first he wrote checks on banks in which he had no accounts. This indiscretion might have shortened his reign had not the sums been extremely modest and the bankers his old friends. Soon enough he hit upon a happier expedient. He conceived the idea of issuing "Bonds of the Empire." These came off the presses of Charles A. Murdock without charge, the printer having been promised the post of Chancellor of the Exchequer in return for the favor. Each bond, illustrated with a portrait of the Emperor as well as with reproductions of the Stars and Stripes and the California State Seal, was worth fifty cents. In twenty years the buyer was promised the repayment of his fifty cents with 5 per cent interest.

When the bonds did not suffice to meet his vast royal expenditures Norton was forced to resort to a system of taxation. Disdaining the bureaucracy of a revenue department, he both levied and collected the taxes himself. In an account book he noted the names of all prominent business houses and the amounts they were to be assessed monthly for the advantages of his rule. Regularly, in full court attire and with account book in hand, he called upon his subjects. Struggling shopkeepers got off with twenty-five cents; wealthy bankers were commanded to pay as much as three dollars. Resistance was rare, and on a profitable day the monarch would collect as much as twenty-five dollars. Sometimes, when he had a great project in mind, a project to promote national harmony or world peace, he would discuss a loan, at 4 per cent, for millions of dollars. On these occasions, according to the *Alta*, he would confront a friend and "attempt to negotiate a loan of several hundred million dollars, and depart perfectly contented with a two- or four-bit piece."

Yet, for all of his taxation and promissory notes, he could not have maintained his high position without insisting upon his royal prerogative of free rent, food, clothing, and transportation. During the greater part of his twenty-one-year reign, he lived in a single, musty room at the rear of the Eureka Lodging House. The rent was fifty cents a day, and it was paid by the Occidental Lodge F. & A. M., which the Emperor had helped found in more prosperous times. The interior of this, his court, he had furnished himself. It consisted of a chair and table set on a faded rug, an outdoor camping-cot, a pitcher and basin resting on a broken stand. On one wall was a portrait of the Empress Eugénie. On another wall, hanging from common nails, was his wardrobe. "There were many hats," reported a newspaperman who visited the room. "There was first an old stove-pipe hat resting side by side with a little plaster cast of himself on the table. Directly above, hanging in a row on the wall, were three more—the first a derby hat. Next to this hung an old army cap bound with red lace, and next in line a regulation army hat, also trimmed with red, and which had apparently once adorned the cranium of a martial bandmaster, as was attested by the lyre which graced its front. On the wall opposite, over the bed, hung the well-known sword of the Emperor, and in the corner, against the bed, stood four canes, the gift of devoted 'subjects.' "

His clothes were cared for by a Chinese laundryman, and when the Chinese refused to accept imperial bonds as payment, Norton's landlord assumed the expense. When his uniforms wore thin Norton approached San Francisco's leading men's shops for replacements. They were usually supplied. Once, when his attire was again threadbare, he went directly to his followers. "Know ye whom it may concern that I, Norton I . . . have heard serious complaints from our adherents and all that our imperial wardrobe is a national disgrace. . . . We warn those whose duty it is to attend to these affairs that their scalps are in danger if our said need is unheeded." The said need did not go unheeded long. Rather than have their beloved monarch's appearance bring disgrace upon his capital city, the San Francisco Board of Supervisors unanimously voted to outfit him at public expense.

The Emperor always ate out. Though his midday meals—usually taken at the free-lunch corner of a neighborhood bar—were light, he ate his dinners in the most fashionable restaurants. Though he always announced his rank upon being seated, he was known everywhere and never charged. He partook of full-course meals, was not shy about returning an entree improperly prepared, and frequently chastised waiters for inadequate service.

While he never traveled to the far-flung corners of his Empire, he was much in evidence about his capital city. He rode the municipal streetcars without cost. He was grateful for this free passage, but not beholden. He felt it his due. Once when a fellow passenger, an elderly lady, could not find her five-cent fare, Norton advised the conductor to move on. "Let her," he said, "be a guest of the Empire." On his occasional trips to Sacramento and other northern cities, his railroad or steamboat berths were occupied with the compliments of their owners.

Thus, unencumbered by the normal struggle for existence, Emperor Norton was able fully to enjoy the advantages of his lofty post. Day followed day through the years in placid parade. By force of habit he rose late, permitted a worshipful fellow boarder to help dress him, and then sauntered to the nearest bar for a light repast. In early afternoon he set out on foot to survey his happy dominion, often accompanied by wide-eyed children and almost always by two faithful dogs. These aged canines, city characters, were not of aristocratic pedigree. One, a black mongrel, was known as Bummer for his habit of cadging meals at taverns. The other, a dark-yellow collie, was known as Lazarus because he had risen to life after a near fatal fight. When Bummer was kicked to death by a drunk and Lazarus was poisoned, the San Francisco press published obituaries and the Virginia City newspaper carried a touching farewell by Mark Twain. Though reams of sentimental copy were to be produced about the Emperor's attachment to the dogs, these accounts were, for the most part, unauthorized and inaccurate. Norton had little affection for Bummer and Lazarus, but graciously allowed them to become part of his daily retinue.

On his strolls, accepting the bows and curtsies of his subjects, the Emperor inspected civic improvements, chatted with pretty girls (he had an eye for a well-turned ankle, but remained a bachelor without heir), discussed law enforcement with police, looked in on delinquent merchants, paused to relax at chess in the Mechanic's Library, attended a different church every week (so that there would be no wrangling for his favor among varied denominations), and constantly made his presence felt at all forums and political meetings.

During one election campaign, when a candidate for the Senate rose to appeal for votes, Norton commanded him to desist and be seated. "You don't have to speak further," Norton advised him, "because I hereby appoint you United States senator."

On another occasion, as Allen Stanley Lane has related in his biography, *Emperor Norton*, he participated in a discussion of free love sponsored by the Lyceum of Self Culture. Upon being introduced, he remarked somewhat enigmatically that 82 per cent of all infants born in America were destroyed. "Take twenty-five square miles of land," he continued. "Let it rain on that land twenty-four hours. Then turn every one of those drops of water into a baby. How many babies would there be?" It was not a rhetorical question. He demanded an answer. The dazed audience had none to give. Offended by this dim-witted reaction, Norton descended from the platform and marched out of the meeting.

During evenings, Norton was sometimes in evidence at the city's playhouses. When he made his grand entrance minutes before curtain time and strode majestically to the orchestra seat reserved for him by the management, the audience came to its feet en masse in silent tribute. But more often his evenings were spent contemplating the problems of Empire. In his quiet room, far from the temptations of frivolity, he would sit down to his wooden table, take up his pen, and scratch out his historic proclamations.

At an early date in his reign he decided that "Mexico is entirely unfit to manage her own affairs, the country being in a constant state of internal distraction, anarchy and civil war." To defend the peons from the avaricious Napoleon III, Norton appointed himself official "Protector of Mexico." But after the brutal execution of Maximilian, Norton withdrew his championship of the proletariat. A people who could murder an Emperor—dangerous precedent—was too "unsettled" to deserve his protection.

He tempered justice with mercy. When John Brown was tried, Norton decided that "Brown was insane" and should not be harshly judged. Learning that, despite his opinion, Brown had been hanged, Norton summarily discharged the Governor of Virginia from his office. During the Civil War he ordered Lincoln and Jefferson Davis to come to him in California so that he might mediate the dispute. When they ignored his imperial command he went over their heads to Grant and Lee. During the Franco-Prussian War he sided with the Prussians and gave Bismarck constant advice. When the war ended he took credit for the peace. Some of his decrees were translated into German and appeared in the Austrian press. One ill-informed Vienna railroad employee actually wrote Norton in 1871, requesting the post of American ambassador to Austria.

Of all of the Emperor's decrees, only one was to reflect his remarkable vision. For it was Norton who first suggested, in print, the San Francisco Bay bridge. Two problems, one personal and one municipal, motivated his inspiration. He enjoyed visiting Oakland, across the bay, but found the journey by ferry tedious and time consuming. Only a bridge could speed his commuting. Too, he was troubled by the rivalry between San Francisco and Oakland, each community wishing to become the terminus of the new Central Pacific Railroad. It was felt that the city failing to win the railroad terminal would be seriously deprived of commerce and population. Norton realized that a bridge might solve the problem. On August 18, 1869, he offered the *Oakland Daily News* the following proclamation:

"We, Norton I, *Dei Gratia*, Emperor of the United States and protector of Mexico, do order and direct, first, that Oakland shall be the coast termination of the Central Pacific Railroad; secondly, that a suspension bridge be constructed from the improvements lately ordered by our royal decree at Oakland Point to Yerba Buena. . . ."

Norton's venture into the technical field of engineering was met with cries of "crazy," but little more than a half century later, the bridge was constructed, and it spanned the bay just as Norton had suggested.

The great majority of his subjects appreciated his selfless interest in their welfare. Even the celebrated showed him marked respect. When Mark Twain returned in 1869 from the trip to the Mediterranean which was to produce *Innocents Abroad*, he announced that were he to make another such "pleasure excursion around the world and to the Holy Land" and had he "the privilege of making out her passenger list," he would include among his favorite companions Bret Harte, the elder James Coffroth—and Norton I of San Francisco.

In 1892, when Robert Louis Stevenson and his stepson, Lloyd Osbourne, published their novel *The Wrecker*, much of which was laid in San Francisco, they paid tribute to the city by recounting its treatment of a favorite son:

"Of all our visitors, I believe I preferred Emperor Norton; the very mention of whose name reminds me I am doing scanty justice to the folks of San Francisco. In what other city would a harmless madman who supposed himself emperor of the two Americas have been so fostered and encouraged? Where else would even the people of the streets have respected the poor soul's illusion? Where else would bankers and merchants have received his visits, cashed his cheques, and submitted to his small assessments? Where else would he have been suffered to attend and address the exhibition days of schools and colleges? where else, in God's green earth, have taken his pick of restaurants, ransacked the bill of fare, and departed scathless? They tell me he was even an exacting patron, threatening to withdraw his custom when dissatisfied; and I can believe it, for his face wore an expression distinctly gastronomical."

Though "the imperial government" of Norton I was more

indulgent than most autocracies, there were infrequent evidences of *lèse majesté* and rebellion through the years. Once, at Petaluma, California, the Emperor received telegrams of an inciting nature from Abraham Lincoln and Jefferson Davis. Again, there were several cables signed Victoria Regina, inquiring after his health and hinting at marriage. These and similar communications perpetrated by practical jokers plagued the Emperor throughout his reign. This type of irreverence toward royalty even infected the State Assembly at Sacramento. In January 1872 a pension bill in favor of General John A. Sutter was passed over vigorous opposition. In an effort to ridicule its passage, the enemies of the Sutter bill proposed one of their own: "The sum of two hundred and fifty dollars per month is hereby appropriated out of any funds in the State Treasury not otherwise appropriated for the relief of Emperor Norton the First. . . ." During the heated debate that followed, one Sutter supporter dared inquire: "Who is Emperor Norton the First, I would like to know?" Norton determined to answer the unbelievable question by making a personal appearance. Within a few days he charged into Sacramento, and began buttonholing legislators, explaining why they must support his monthly pension. But he was too late. His bill was already lost in the files of the Committee on Claims.

Most resistance to Norton came in the form of obstruction, and these rare flare-ups were most always the results of ignorance. On one train journey to Sacramento the Emperor made his way to the dining car for his evening meal. A new waiter thought his appearance suspect and refused to fill his order. The Emperor contained his temper and repeated his choice of menu. The waiter doubted that he had the money to pay for it. Money? The Emperor was apoplectic. He pounded the table with his cane, commanding the waiter to serve him before he disenfranchised the entire railroad. Fortunately a party of San Franciscans at a nearby table witnessed the scene and agreed that their ruler must be obliged at their expense. When news of this terrible incident reached the main offices of the Central Pacific the next day, the directors were hasty to make amends. They mailed Norton a lifetime free pass for use on Pullman or diner on any of their California trains.

Even more barbaric was the effort, on the night of January 21, 1867, to unseat him from his throne. A newly appointed and overzealous young policeman named Barbier arrested the Emperor on a charge of vagrancy. When the sputtering Norton revealed that he possessed almost five dollars, the officer revised his charge to insanity. Norton was dragged to the nearest station house and forced into a cell to await tests by the city alienist. The moment the Chief of Police heard of the mistaken arrest he personally released his monarch with profuse apology. The newspapers and periodicals of the West, in a single voice, denounced the outrage and extolled his reign. "Since he has worn the Imperial purple," said the *Alta*, "he has shed no blood, robbed nobody, and despoiled the country of no one, which is more than can be said of any of his fellows in that line."

As a new generation of loyal subjects grew to maturity they came to regard Emperor Norton as a romantic fixture. Their fathers had known his antecedents, but they themselves had not. And so they wondered, and conjectured fanciful beginnings, and embellished them in their gossip. To some he was a bastard son of Napoleon III or William IV of England. To others he was an heir discarded by George III. Norton heard these whisperings, and, in his dotage, did not deny them. An old friend who had known him in South Africa came visiting and asked him "to tell . . . how it was that he came by the title of Emperor, and why he wore the uniform he then had on." Norton, after extracting a promise of secrecy, confided that he had been born of French royalty, and sent to South Africa as a measure of safety, with one John Norton as his guardian.

On December 31, 1879, he published a proclamation heralding the New Year and offering up "prayers of thanksgiving to Almighty God." It was his last proclamation. On the early evening of January 8, 1880, he went out in a drizzle to attend a debate at the Academy of Sciences. He was in full uniform and in fine mood. At the age of sixty-two he walked still with vigorous stride. Those who saw him saw what Stevenson and Osbourne had seen—"a portly, rather flabby man, with the face of a gentleman, rendered unspeakably pathetic and absurd by the great sabre at his side and the peacock's feather in his hat." As he approached the building where the debate was to be held, he suddenly stumbled and collapsed to the sidewalk. A passer-by ran to his aid and propped him up while shouting to others for a carriage. Norton was unconscious when he was taken into the receiving hospital, and minutes later he was dead.

In the morgue they emptied his pockets, and the contents were more eloquent than any biography: three dollars in silver coins, a two-dollar-and-fifty-cent gold piece, a five-franc note dated 1828, a sheaf of cables signed by Disraeli, Parnell, Díaz, and the Tsar of Russia, a certificate giving him ownership of 98,200 shares of stock in a mine, and several copies of his own imperial script. "Le Roi Est Mort" was the headline in the *San Francisco Chronicle*.

His funeral was the funeral of an Emperor. His old friends and most loyal subjects, the members of the Pacific Club, defrayed the $10,000 expenses involved in what became a day of municipal mourning. Eight thousand men and two thousand women and children followed his rosewood casket to the Masonic Cemetery, beneath Lone Mountain, where he was affectionately put to rest.

Fifty-four years later, the Masonic Cemetery was one of several burial grounds abolished by law. The grandsons of those who had first buried their Emperor—now members of the Pacific Union Club—undertook the final task of reburial. The Emperor's remains were transferred to the Woodlawn Cemetery, just across the county line, and a marble tombstone was placed on the grave. On June 30, 1934, after the San Francisco Band had played, after infantrymen had exploded three volleys into the sky, after an American Legion bugler had finished taps, the inscription on the gravestone was unveiled: "Norton I . . . Emperor of the United States and Protector of Mexico . . . Joshua A. Norton 1819–1880."

His Majesty would have been mightily pleased, for history had remembered him, and his adopted homeland had recognized him at last.

VI

The Lady Who Moved Shakespeare's Bones

"Condemned to refer the origin of these works to the vulgar, illiterate man who kept the theatre where they were first exhibited . . . how could any one dare to see what is really in them?"

DELIA BACON

On April 25, 1616, an entry was made in the Stratford on Avon parish register of the burial of "will Shakspere gent." Across the flagstone placed over his wooden coffin, within the chancel of the church, was engraved a verse which, according to local tradition, had come from the pen of the deceased:

Good frend for Jesus' sake forbeare
To digg the dust encloased heare:
Bleste be the man that spares these stones
And curst be he that moves my bones.

Seven years after the actor-playwright had been laid to rest, there appeared in London a volume entitled *Mr. William Shakespeares Comedies, Histories, & Tragedies. Published according to the True Originall Copies.* This folio, edited and sponsored by Edward Blount, John Smithweeke, and William Aspley, and printed by William and Isaac Jaggard, was dedicated to the Earl of Pembroke and his brother the Earl of

Montgomery and "To the great Variety of Readers." The dedication, composed by two actors who had known Shakespeare well, explained that the book had been published "onely to keepe the memory of so worthy a Friend, & Fellow aliue, as was our SHAKESPEARE. . . ."

This was the first collected publication of all but one of Shakespeare's thirty-seven plays. Eighteen had never been printed before. The other eighteen had appeared individually in earlier authorized or pirated quarto editions, seventeen of them having been published during Shakespeare's lifetime.

With the distribution of the First Folio, the playwright's genius was at last on full display for his time and all posterity. For more than a century after Shakespeare's burial and his resurrection in the Jaggard volume, his authorship of the immortal works was accepted without question or doubt. No one disturbed Shakespeare's bones, literally or literarily, and no one directly disputed his authorship of the plays attributed to him in the First Folio. Then, gradually, the rumblings of surmise and suspicion began, instigated by scholars, critics, ordinary readers, and eccentrics who could not relate the brilliance and variety of Shakespeare's output to the few prosaic facts known of his middle-class life.

The first dissent was heard in 1771, when Herbert Lawrence, a surgeon and friend of David Garrick, issued a book entitled *The Life and Adventures of Common Sense: an Historical Allegory*. Lawrence contended that Shakespeare had plagiarized much of his best writing from a certain *Commonplace Book*. The extremely "pleasant and entertaining" composition in the *Commonplace Book* had been audaciously appropriated by "a Person belonging to the Playhouse; this Man was a profligate in his Youth, and, as some say, had been a deer-stealer. . . . With these Materials, and with good Parts of his own, he commenced Play-Writing, how he succeeded is needless to say, when I tell the Reader that his name was Shakespear." Though Lawrence's effort went into two English editions, and was translated and published in France and

Switzerland, his caustic remarks on the Bard caused little sensation.

The first half of the nineteenth century provided two mild doubters and one vigorous dissenter. In 1811 Samuel Taylor Coleridge delivered a series of lectures on Milton and Shakespeare (with an admitted preference for Milton) at the Philosophical Society in London. Discussing the plays of Shakespeare, he was incredulous that "works of such character should have proceeded from a man whose life was like that attributed to Shakespeare. . . . Are we to have miracles in sport? Does God choose idiots by whom to convey divine truths to men?" Coleridge was more willing to accept Shakespeare as thespian than as creator. "It is worth having died two hundred years ago to have heard Shakespeare deliver a single line. He must have been a great actor."

Twenty-six years later, a future prime minister of England, Benjamin Disraeli, announced his misgivings more indirectly. In his eighth novel, *Venetia*, brought out the year he finally won a Parliamentary seat, he had a fictional character remark: "And who is Shakespeare? We know as much of him as Homer. Did he write half the plays attributed to him? Did he ever write a single whole play? I doubt it."

However, the liveliest assault on Shakespeare's authorship occurred in New York during 1848. A book bearing the unlikely title of *The Romance of Yachting*, by Joseph C. Hart, belabored the Bard mercilessly. Hart's narrative cheerfully recounted his own adventures while on a sailing voyage to Spain. The sea change apparently worked wonders on his contemplative processes. En route he thought deeply, and when he came to record the physical highlights of his journey, he recorded also his varied meditations on the wrongs of civilization. One of his meditations, to which he devoted thirty-five pages, reflected his suspicions that Shakespeare as author was an impostor. "He was not the mate of the literary characters of the day," Hart wrote, "and none knew it better than himself. It is a fraud upon the world to thrust his surreptitious fame upon us. He had none that was worthy of being transmitted. The inquiry will be, *who were the able literary men who wrote the dramas imputed to him?*"

These isolated voices were heard by very few. But the few who heard them had a question of their own: if William Shakespeare had not written the thirty-six plays in the First Folio, who had written them? Lawrence had named a little-known book as their source. Coleridge and Disraeli had credited no one. Hart had, in passing, suggested Sir Francis Bacon. No real case had been made for any claimant to Shakespeare's place. From 1771 to 1852 the doubters had their nagging doubts and little else. But in 1852, with the emergence of a neurotic New England spinster named Delia Salter Bacon, the doubters suddenly had not one claimant, but several to Shakespeare's place.

Miss Bacon's livelihood came from teaching and lecturing to women on history and literature. For years she had been deeply immersed in the writings of the Elizabethan period, and her specialty was Shakespeare. The more she read of Shakespeare, the more she was troubled. "There was no man, dead or alive, that really on the whole gave me so much cause of offense with his contradictions," she once confessed in a letter to Nathaniel Hawthorne. "He appeared to be such a standing disgrace to genius and learning, that I had not the heart to ask anybody to study anything."

She came to think of Shakespeare, and eventually speak of him and write of him, as "Will the Jester" and "that Player" and "that booby" and "Lord Leicester's groom." She could not reconcile the deep philosophy and daring statesmanship she found in his plays with the "vulgar, illiterate . . . deer-poacher" who had been advertised as their author. With growing certainty she began to feel that Shakespeare had not written the plays credited to him, that his name had been borrowed to mask the identity of another. But what other? And why the elaborate masquerade?

She scanned the giants of the era, their activities, their writings, and suddenly, blindingly, the truth stood revealed. The plays that bore Shakespeare's name had been written in secret by a syndicate of creative men with a common purpose. The syndicate, she decided, consisted of Sir Francis Bacon (no ancestor of hers), Sir Walter Raleigh, Edmund Spenser, and several other "high-born wits and poets." These men were idealists and revolutionists. They possessed dangerous democratic ideas in a day when the divine right of kings and queens went unchallenged. Eager to promote liberty, equality, and justice, these men sought to propagandize their progressive views through popular plays performed for the masses.

This was Miss Bacon's startling, highly imaginative proposition. She did not announce it to the world at once. The news would be delayed four years while she reinforced her argument. But by 1852 it had become definite in her mind, and she could not resist circulating it among her students, her friends, and private audiences.

In that crucial year she was on the genteel lecture-circuit, addressing groups of ladies and their daughters in the better homes of New Haven, Boston, and Cambridge. The first recorded instance of her obsession with her new non-Shakespearean authorship theory dates from her Cambridge talks. A group of fine ladies had purchased tickets to attend Miss Bacon's lectures, first in the Brattle house and then in the parlor of the Farrar residence. Mrs. Eliza Farrar, married to a professor of mathematics at Harvard, and author of juvenile books, was responsible for Miss Bacon's appearance, and would later recall the impression it made.

Speaking without notes, Miss Bacon dwelt on ancient history and dramatized her account by means of pictures and maps. "In these she brought down her history to the time of the birth of Christ," wrote Mrs. Farrar in *Recollections of Seventy Years*, "and I can never forget how clear she made it to us that the world was only then made fit for the advent of Jesus. She ended with a fine climax that was quite thrilling."

At the conclusion of one such lecture, Mrs. Farrar remembered, several ladies lingered behind to have tea with Miss Bacon and to chat informally. During the conversation Miss Bacon mentioned a desire to visit England to search for proofs of her theory. Someone asked, with innocent curiosity, what theory Miss Bacon wished to substantiate. And immediately Miss Bacon was off in a bitter harangue against the "vulgar, illiterate" Shakespeare. Her listeners recoiled at the blasphemy, and Mrs. Farrar refused to encourage her protégée to discuss the subject further. Nevertheless, at every opportunity Miss Bacon continued to discuss it, until mention of Shakespeare became taboo among her friends. According to Mrs. Farrar, even Miss Bacon's hostess was forced to "put her copy of his works out of sight, and never allowed her to converse with her on this, her favorite subject."

One person, however, who met her in Cambridge and heard her discuss Shakespeare did not change the subject, but rather encouraged her and drew her out. Ralph Waldo Emerson in his forty-ninth year was much absorbed by the antislavery movement and occupied with speaking against the Fugitive Slave Law. But only four years before, in England, he had given some lectures entitled "Shakespeare," and he could still be interested by any academic debate on the Bard. In his journal for Wednesday, May 19, 1852, he wrote:

"I saw Miss Delia Bacon, at Cambridge, at the house of Mrs. Becker, and conversed with her on the subject of Shakspeare. Miss Bacon thinks that a key will yet be found to Shakspeare's interior sense; that some key to his secret may yet be discovered at Stratford, and I fancy, thinks the famous epitaph, 'Good friend, for Jesus' sake forbear,' protects some explanation of it. Her skepticism in regard to the authorship goes beyond the skepticism of Wolf in regard to Homer, or Niebuhr to Latin history."

Apparently Emerson had shown sufficient sympathy for Miss Bacon's ideas to invite her to expound them further. Three weeks after their meeting, when Emerson had returned to Concord and while Miss Bacon remained in Cambridge, she sent him what she called a "voluminous note . . . on this subject." Her outline stressed Sir Francis Bacon rather than a syndicate of writers as really Shakespeare, and she suggested publicizing her theory in print. Emerson was impressed. On June 12, 1852, he replied at some length: "I am deeply gratified to observe the power of statement and the adequateness to the problem, which this sketch of your argument evinces. Indeed, I value these fine weapons far above any special use they may be put to. And you will have need of enchanted instruments, nay, alchemy itself, to melt into one identity these two *reputations* (shall I call them?) the poet and the statesman, both hitherto solid historical figures."

Emerson thought that a magazine article, followed by a book, would best bring Miss Bacon's ideas before the public. He offered to assist her in securing publication. Miss Bacon was delighted and grateful, and she told Emerson: "Confirmations of my theory, which I did not expect to find on this side of the water, have turned up since my last communication to you. . . . Be assured, dear sir, there is no possibility of a doubt as to the main points of my theory. . . ."

Yet there must have been some tiny doubt. For the English trip had crystallized in Miss Bacon's mind as the necessary climax to her researches. She did not wish to set her ideas down on paper or publish them until she had visited St. Alban's, where Sir Francis Bacon had once lived, or until she had examined the Shakespeare collections in the British Museum, or until she had personally lifted the flagstone off Shakespeare's grave in the Stratford on Avon church and searched about his coffin for documents that might fully substantiate her case. She told Emerson that she must go to England for a year, no more, and at once he rallied to her cause.

She required contacts and money. Emerson was instrumental in helping her to obtain both. He supplied her with letters of introduction, notably one to his old friend Thomas

Carlyle. As to the financing of the English expedition, Emerson wrote to Hawthorne's sister-in-law, Elizabeth Peabody, and asked that prominent educator if she could assist in obtaining magazine serialization of Miss Bacon's projected book. "I can really think of nothing that could give such *éclat* to a magazine as this brilliant paradox." In short order the pages of *Putnam's Magazine* were opened to Miss Bacon for a series of articles to be drawn from her book. This gave promise of considerable income, but still it was not enough.

Emerson had one more idea. Miss Bacon would soon be in New York for a series of lectures. He suggested that she call upon an old friend of his, Charles Butler, who was wealthy, well-read, and fascinated by anything bizarre. Emerson arranged the meeting, and Miss Bacon called upon Butler. Like Emerson, Butler was won over. He would be her patron. If she must go to England, he would gladly finance the passage and support her for half a year.

On May 14, 1853, Delia Bacon boarded the steamer *Pacific* in New York harbor, and ten days later she docked in Liverpool, ready for the showdown with "that Player" who had, so long ago, warned such as she that they would be "curst" if they moved his bones.

How well she would move those bones, even she could not know. For by the time she was forced to leave England four years later, she had initiated a heresy in literature, a controversy in academic circles that would persist generation after generation, that persists even today after more than a century.

When she disembarked from her steamer at Liverpool on May 24, 1853, she had little realization of the din her visit would create in future years. She knew only the gnawing immediacy of her mission: to regain for honorable and brilliant men—Bacon, Raleigh, Spenser, and their associates—the acclaim that was rightfully theirs, but had been usurped, albeit unwittingly, by an unlettered actor who lay at rest beneath the floor of a village church, but who soon enough would rest no more.

Delia Salter Bacon's monomania was cast in the first fifteen years of her life. Her father, the Reverend David Bacon, was a descendant of an early Puritan who had once held military rank in England. He himself was made of the same sturdy stuff. Raised on a Connecticut farm, he became a fanatical Congregationalist clergyman. Turning his eyes westward, he saw his life's work. Accompanied by his adoring, delicate eighteen-year-old bride, Alice Parks Bacon, he headed into the wilderness and for five years preached to uninterested redskins in Detroit, Mackinac, and settlements in the back country.

His lack of success in converting savages to Christ brought on a crisis. Church funds were withheld, and he was left stranded. He found himself in the area of Ohio's Western Reserve, and there, faced with need to make a decision, he was divinely inspired. He realized his real mission: to establish a holy community where Eastern immigrants might support themselves in an atmosphere both devout and pure.

The word from on high was enough. He promptly purchased 12,000 acres of the richest forest land in the vicinity. Having no cash, he bought on credit. As he busied himself in constructing his own log cabin and subdividing his acres into smaller farm tracts, he corresponded with Congregationalist families in the East who wanted to move to Ohio and dwell in piety with their Reverend.

He called his religious utopia Tallmadge, and in this holy town, in the confines of the log cabin he had built, a girl whom he christened Delia Salter Bacon was born on February 2, 1811. There had been four children before her, and there would be one after her, but Delia alone would be infected by her father's fanaticism.

The burden of his growing family weighed heavily on David Bacon as he awaited the settlers who would relieve him of his indebtedness and fulfill his dream of a heaven on earth. But in short months his dream was shattered by a Congressional embargo on foreign goods which finally culminated in the War of 1812. The Connecticut parishioners who had planned to leave for Ohio changed their minds. And in the Western Reserve David Bacon had his promised land to himself.

When he could not meet his obligations, his creditors quickly foreclosed and repossessed his 12,000 acres, his skeleton town of Tallmadge, and his very residence. Crushed in spirit and deprived of livelihood, David Bacon led his large family on the weary 600-mile trek back to New England. There he dragged out six more years of defeat selling Bibles, occasionally teaching, sometimes delivering sermons. He was forty-six when he died in August 1817, when the girl child upon whom he had left the deepest impression was only six.

Without inheritance, and with a half-dozen mouths to feed, the widow Bacon distributed as many of her brood as she could among relatives and friends and moved to New York City to work as a milliner. Of the entire family it was thought that six-year-old Delia fared the best. She was accepted in a Hartford home that offered her, at least materially, such comforts as she had never known before. Her guardian, Mrs. Delia Williams, was the wife of a prominent attorney.

Delia Bacon lived with the Williamses for nine years. In many respects she found them generous. For one thing, they provided her with the best education then available for an unemancipated American young lady. In 1824 the clever Catharine Beecher, seeking occupation after the death of her fiancé, Professor Alexander M. Fisher, established a small school for women in Hartford. Though it never attained an enrollment of more than 150 students, it was to become nationally respected. One of its first pupils was the founder's younger sister, Harriet, who would become world famous as Harriet Beecher Stowe. Another was Delia Bacon. Many years later, Catharine Beecher would remember that Delia possessed one "of the most gifted minds" she had ever encountered in male or female society, and that "she was preeminently one who would be pointed out as a genius. . . ."

Her three years under Catharine Beecher and dutiful support until she reached maturity were the best Delia could hope for as a ward of the Williamses. She was lonely for love and companionship. These her guardians could not supply. They were well intentioned, but they were childless, and their regime was austere. "There can be no doubt of the calm and constant kindness of patronage which the fatherless child received here," Delia's nephew, Theodore Bacon, wrote later. "But its calmness may have been somewhat stern and grim."

In 1826 Delia Bacon left the Williamses to make her own way. She was fifteen years old, without capital and without connections, and possessed only of the learning imparted by Catharine Beecher. She had no choice but to exploit her single asset. She would emulate Miss Beecher. She would found her own academy for women and teach others.

It took Delia four heartbreaking years to learn that she was no Catharine Beecher. Aided by an older sister, she opened girls' schools in Connecticut, New Jersey, and New York, and everywhere she failed. In the end her eldest brother, Leonard Bacon, the successful pastor of New Haven's First Congregationalist Church, rescued her from debt and urged her to concentrate on instruction to the exclusion of business.

For the next decade and more Delia Bacon devoted herself to teaching. She returned to Hartford to accept employment as a pedagogue, then restlessly moved on to two other similar positions in New York State. She taught with only half a mind for her work. Its better half was given over to authorship. "From her childhood," noted brother Leonard, "she has had a passion for literature, and perhaps I should say a longing, more or less distinct, for literary celebrity."

When she was twenty years old, Delia began her struggle for "literary celebrity," responding to what Catharine Beecher had characterized in her as "the desire of human estimation, especially in the form of literary ambition." Early in 1831 the firm of A. H. Maltby in New Haven published a collection of three melodramatic, historical novelettes entitled *Tales of the Puritans.* The title page credited no writer, as the author had insisted upon anonymity. But when the imaginative if incongruous stories met with no adverse criticism, Delia stepped forward to acknowledge authorship. Under her pen the Puritans unbent, and were made to indulge in protracted love scenes and dashing swordplay. The book had a brief vogue among lady readers, and Delia was more than satisfied, admitting that it had been "written without experience, without knowledge of the subjects of which it treated, with scarcely a book to refer to beyond the works made use of in school."

Later the same year, with less trepidation and no anonymity, Delia submitted a short story, "Love's Martyr," in competition for a first prize of $100 being offered by the *Philadelphia Saturday Courier*. Perhaps it surprised her not at all that she was soon announced as the winner. But it may surprise many, reading of her victory more than a century later, to know the caliber of opposition she overcame. For among those Delia had defeated in the contest was an impoverished former West Point cadet, two years her senior, named Edgar Allan Poe. Though Delia's fiction was awarded the $100, one of Poe's several submissions, "Metzengerstein," was given the secondary honor of publication during January 1832 at space rates. With this appearance in print, Poe, who had already brought out three volumes of verse, made his debut as a writer of short stories.

Next, Delia decided to become a playwright. Her first offering, long planned, would be based on a dramatic episode that had occurred during the Revolutionary War. Delia had once read of an American girl, Jane McCrea, who had fallen in love with a British officer under General Burgoyne's command. Taken captive by a party of Indians, Jane McCrea offered them a sizable reward if they would release her to the British. The proffered reward provoked a violent disagreement among the redskins. Each Indian claimed to deserve the full ransom. In the heat of the argument one savage turned upon the source of the trouble, the captive girl, killed her, scalped her, and made off. When the murder became public it did much to arouse and inflame patriotic opinion against the British and their Indian allies.

Out of these tragic materials, Delia spun her romantic play. It was rejected everywhere for its verbosity, improbability, and amateurish pretentions. Undeterred, yet with some misgivings (for she warned in her foreword that her work was "*not a Play* . . . not *intended* for the stage" but was merely a "DIALOGUE"), she submitted the theatrical effort for publication.

The so-called dialogue, two hundred pages of wordy prose in blank verse, was served up to America's readers in 1839 as *The Bride of Fort Edward: A Dramatic Story*, by Delia Bacon. "It was a failure, every way," Delia's nephew recorded. "It brought debt instead of money, and no renown; but it did the great service of ending, for a time, her attempts at literary work, and turning her back to study and instruction."

After this debacle Delia embarked upon the most successful undertaking of her brief career—that of lady lecturer. It is more than likely she got the idea from observing the success of Margaret Fuller, feminist, critic, and gadfly. In this new endeavor Delia seemed to find herself at last. Her knowledge of literature and history, her eloquence and wit, supplemented by a small reputation gained with her first book and by contacts acquired through years of teaching and through her clergyman brother's high station, helped to increase the attendance at her lectures. She might have had a long and prosperous career—and "will Shakspere gent" might have rested undisturbed through all eternity—had not scandal and shame entered her life in the malevolent shape of Reverend Alexander McWhorter, student of divinity and cad.

It is difficult, at best, to reconcile the stiff image left us by her subsequent literary reputation, of a studious, single-minded Delia Bacon, with the softer, shimmering vision, which existed before her retreat into monomania, of a warm, womanly Delia Bacon enraptured by love, sacred and profane. But as all existing evidence confirms, Delia was a woman. Beneath the prim aspect of teacher and speaker, behind the sterility of her scholarship, lay hidden the normal passions, the hungers, the longings for a man's love.

She was not, by any means, unattractive. During her lecturing phase, as Mrs. Eliza Farrar recalled, she "was tall and commanding, her finely shaped head was well set on her shoulders, her face was handsome and full of expression, and she moved with grace and dignity." A friend of Delia's, Mrs. Sarah Henshaw, remembered her as "graceful, fair, and slight. Her habitual black dress set off to advantage the radiant face, whose fair complexion was that uncommon one which can only be described as pale yet brilliant." A daguerreotype of Delia taken in May 1853, when she was forty-two years of age, still exists. She sits reposefully, staring into the camera. She wears a bonnet, and a shawl is thrown over her black-satin dress. Her hair is black and flattened by a severe part in the middle. Her brow is high, her deep-set eyes seem darker than the blue-gray described by her friends, her nose is long and classically Grecian, and her generous mouth is drawn in a tight, amused smile. If the face seems more forbidding, more worn, than the description of it left by her friends, it must be remembered that the portrait was taken six years after the sitter had suffered deeply at the hands of McWhorter.

With a nice sense of respect and a poor sense of history, Theodore Bacon does not mention McWhorter by name in his biography of his aunt. His only comment is provocatively enigmatic. "When she was mature in age, she underwent a most cruel ordeal, and suffered a grievous and humiliating disappointment."

The ordeal began in 1846 when Delia was lecturing in New Haven, where her brother Leonard had replaced his friend and mentor, Dr. Nathaniel W. Taylor, as pastor of the First Church. At the hotel where Delia took her room and board she found herself often dining at the same table with another occupant of the hotel, a young man named Alexander McWhorter. She learned that McWhorter came from a wealthy New Jersey family and was a resident licentiate of Yale, studying under Dr. Nathaniel Taylor. Though there was a mutual attraction between Delia and McWhorter, she remained briefly aloof. Perhaps it was because they had not been formally introduced. More likely, it was because Delia was then thirty-five years old, and McWhorter twenty-three.

After a short time, Delia could no longer ignore McWhorter's formal attentions. Nor, as it turned out, did she any longer wish to. Learning that her fellow boarder was a student under her brother's respected friend Dr. Taylor, she felt free to respond to McWhorter's overtures. It was her custom to give nightly receptions in her parlor. To these she invited friends and acquaintances, and to one such affair she invited McWhorter. He attended and made it clear that his interest in his hostess was romantic rather than intellectual.

"His first visit was not his last," the *Philadelphia Times* reported rather sternly in 1886. "He was more than pleased with Delia Bacon's intellectual attainments—he was interested in her personal attractions. He called upon her frequently. He showed her marked attention. He acted as her escort in public. He professed for her a profound and lasting affection, and would not take 'no' for an answer. He even followed her to a watering-place, with no other excuse than to be near her. These two . . . were lovers. . . . Then, when he tired of the flirtation, as all men do who fall in love with women older than themselves, he turned viciously upon his uncomplaining victim and contemptuously characterized an affair, that had begun with baseness on his part, a literary intimacy."

Delia's flight to the hydropathic establishment—the "watering-place"—in Northampton, Massachusetts, had been made necessary by a bad case of nerves brought on by her family's cynicism toward young McWhorter's motives. At first troubled by the disparity in their ages, she had removed herself from the hotel and McWhorter's gaze by taking residence at her brother's house. McWhorter insisted upon visiting her. It was then, upset beyond endurance, that she escaped to Northampton. Again the gallant McWhorter followed. At last, assured of his devotion, Delia gave herself to the divinity student.

Their romance became the talk of New Haven. Relatives and friends alike were fearful lest their beloved Delia become a fallen woman. To rescue her reputation they let the word be spread about that Delia was engaged to marry McWhorter. When the news of his betrothal reached the philandering young licentiate, he was amazed. At once his heart, so recently warm, began to chill. In a panic, he publicly denied the engagement. To make sure he was understood, he ridiculed Delia, exhibited her passionate letters of love, and insisted that though she had proposed marriage to him no less than five times, he had never agreed to anything beyond friendship. Delia, immersed in a bad attack of vapors, could not believe that her beloved was acting so badly. But when her most private letters were quoted back to her, the scales fell from her eyes.

Delia's camp, led by brother Leonard, called McWhorter a practiced seducer, a brazen liar, and a disgrace to the cloth. McWhorter's camp, led by Dr. Taylor, called Delia the seducer, called her Phryne, Theodora, Messalina, or at the very least a sex-starved spinster who had attempted to entrap an artless and defenseless young Yale student. With the pastor of the First Church and its ex-pastor engaged in battle, all of New England's clergy felt called to arms. Men of God took opposite sides and gossip ran wild.

In defense of virtue, Leonard Bacon determined to have justice done. Young McWhorter had obtained a license to preach in the vicinity. Leonard Bacon demanded that the Congregational Ministerial Association revoke that license. His sister's seducer, he implied, was Satan incarnate. He would prove that McWhorter was guilty of "slander, falsehood, and conduct dishonorable to the Christian ministry."

The charges came to trial before a jury of twenty-three ministers. McWhorter put up a stout defense. His view, as Miss Beecher reported it, was that an older woman had ensnared "his unsophisticated affections." He swore that he "had never made a declaration of affection." In refutation Leonard Bacon revealed that he had seen "a real love letter" from McWhorter to Delia in which the divinity student had declared: "I have loved you purely, fervently." As his sister's keeper, Leonard Bacon regarded her suitor as anything but unsophisticated (rather, as a "clerical Lothario," the press reported in clarification). McWhorter had misled Delia and tampered with her affections, all with dishonorable intent. When he had attained his objective he had retreated, and then had attempted to protect his reputation by maligning a good and decent lady. By the time Delia took the stand there was little left to say. Usually eloquent, she was tongue-tied and soon in tears.

The twenty-three jurors consulted and voted their verdict. Twelve ministers found McWhorter not guilty. Eleven found him guilty as charged. By a narrow margin McWhorter had been vindicated, but he was admonished to practice what he preached. Delia's admirers, and there were many, never vindicated him or forgave him. Catharine Beecher published a book on the scandal sympathetic to Delia. And as recently as 1888, a disciple of Delia's, the Minnesota congressman and reformer Ignatius Donnelly had only contempt for "the base wretch who could thus, for the amusement of his friends, trifle with the affections of a great and noble-hearted woman."

After the trial Delia went to Ohio to recover and to bury herself in the books of another, and happier, age. When she returned to New England and her lectures, she was a new woman and she had a mission. For she had found in history a man she disliked even more than the faithless McWhorter. This man, she would soon announce, was William Shakespeare, pretender and mountebank.

An omnivorous reader, she knew the plays credited to Shakespeare almost as well as any Elizabethan scholar. Curious about the genius who had created these magnificent and varied works, she began to study Shakespeare's life. At once she was dismayed at how little was known of a writer so prolific and so great.

Delia learned that there was no contemporary record of Shakespeare's birth, schooling, or social life. There was evidence that his father had been a butcher, farmer, wooldealer, and glover. A bond dated November 28, 1582, gave proof of Shakespeare's marriage to Anne Hathaway. An assortment of documents indicated that he had performed as an actor at Court, had purchased a fine house in Stratford, and had been involved in many land investments. A hasty will, filled with erasures and interlineations, and made out three months before his death, bequeathed his biographers information on his family, friends, real estate, and "second-best bed," which last he left to his wife. This there was, and little more.

Delia found that most other information on Shakespeare came later and was secondhand. John Aubrey had mentioned some early education, but he mentioned it sixty-five years after Shakespeare's death. That Shakespeare had held the horses for the actors in the Earl of Leicester's company, and had later become one of the company, was not a fact, but a tradition. So was the story that he had been forced to depart Stratford after being caught deer-poaching on the estate of Sir Thomas Lucy. The deer-poaching episode was not published until ninety-two years after Shakespeare had died.

Delia was anything but satisfied. Question after question came to her mind about Shakespeare as human being and artist. The works were there for all to see, and they were the product of genius. But could this man have been that genius? If so, where was a record that he had ever attended school? Or owned a book? Or traveled abroad? How could he, whose parents were ignorant and whose station was low, have had so much knowledge of ancient history and of untranslated Greek and Latin classics? Where could he have learned of court manners and chivalric sports? How could he have acquired so technical a background in law, medicine, and military affairs? An actor and property holder, when did he find the time to pen two plays a year? And if he found the time, why did neither he nor his contemporaries ever mention or discuss his writing in personal letters? Where was one single bit of correspondence from Shakespeare to a publisher, fellow writer, critic, patron, or actor? Above all, why did no manuscript from his pen, no scrap of manuscript even, survive his time?

As Delia questioned and questioned, and probed and researched into the Elizabethan and Jacobean past, the certainty took hold of her that Shakespeare had not written the plays attributed to him. He had been used by someone more cultured, more talented, perhaps by several people, which would logically account for the incredible variety of plays. But who were the real authors and why had they used "that Player"?

Delia searched the writings of Shakespeare's contemporaries for clues. Then she returned to the plays. At once it all came clear. She found "underlying the superficial and ostensible text" of the plays a daring and liberal "system of philosophy." Later she would explain her next step to Hawthorne, and he would tell the world that "as she penetrated more and more deeply into the plays, and became aware of those inner readings, she found herself compelled to turn back to the 'Advancement of Learning' for information as to their plan and purport; and Lord Bacon's Treatise failed not to give her what she sought. . . ."

In short, Sir Francis Bacon had written the plays. To his name she quickly added names of collaborators—Sir Walter Raleigh and Edmund Spenser. And, as minor fellow conspirators in this playwriting syndicate, she included the "courtly company" of Sir Philip Sidney, Lord Buckhurst, Lord Paget, and the Earl of Oxford.

To Delia it seemed that Sir Francis Bacon was everything that the great plays suggested Shakespeare should have been. The plays required in one man the knowledge of aristocracy, politics, poetry, law, diplomacy, sport, travel, and philosophy. Bacon alone had such knowledge. His birth had preceded Shakespeare's by three years, and he had lived ten years after Shakespeare was dead. His father had been Queen Elizabeth's Lord Keeper of the Great Seal. He had studied at Cambridge before he was thirteen, and had prepared for the bar at Gray's Inn. He had visited France, had served as a member of Parliament, and had been appointed James I's Lord Chancellor in 1619. He had lived extravagantly, and this, perhaps, more than anything else had forced him to accept bribes from litigants. Once exposed, he confessed to twenty-three acts of corruption, for which he was banished from the court, fined, and sentenced to the Tower of London for two days. He was probably, as Pope remarked, "the wisest, brightest, meanest of mankind." His philosophical ideas were far in advance of his time. And his reputation as a writer was secure with the publication of *The Advancement of Learning* and fifty-eight brilliant essays.

But for all of Bacon's erudition and energy, Delia would not credit him with the entire output enclosed in the First Folio. Part of the authorship belonged, she was certain, to Sir Walter Raleigh and Edmund Spenser. Raleigh had antedated Shakespeare by a dozen years and survived him by two. The son of a gentleman, Raleigh had been to Oxford, to war, and to far-off Virginia. From his prolific pen flowed books of travel, history, and verse, and Jonson regarded him as the father of English literature. One of Raleigh's closest friends was Edmund Spenser, who also preceded Shakespeare by twelve years, and who died a full seventeen years before "that Player." Spenser, a Cambridge graduate, was widely read, scholarly, and religious. He had been a member of the Earl of Leicester's circle and a frequent visitor to Elizabeth's court. His poetry showed familiarity with Greek, Latin, and English argot. And, of course, he had written *The Faerie Queene*.

These three, then, and their friends, had promoted a mediocre actor named Shakespeare to immortality for their own ends. In an era when royalty was throttling free speech, these men had decided that the play was the thing, the only means by which they might safely disguise their ideas and incite the masses. "It was a vehicle of expression," said Delia, "which offered incalculable facilities for evading these restrictions." For example, why not a modern tirade against tyranny cloaked in the toga of *Julius Cæsar?* "If a Roman Play were to be brought out at all . . . how could one object to that which, by the supposition, was involved in it?"

By 1852 Delia had interested Emerson in her radical theory, and a year later, with the financial backing of his New York friend, she had gone to England to complete her researches firsthand and to announce her shocking find to the literary world.

Within four weeks of her arrival in London she had reached Thomas Carlyle by means of Emerson's letter of introduction. Carlyle, at fifty-eight, was at the height of his fame as a historian. His *French Revolution*, published sixteen years before, was already a classic, and he had just returned from Germany, where he had done research on a projected biography of Frederick the Great. Though dyspeptic, and often crabbed and uncivil, this crusty idealist was astonishingly kind to Delia and her obsessive theory. Perhaps his affection for Emerson, whom he had met twenty years before and whose friendship he cherished—or perhaps his curiosity over the fact that, as he would write, "there is an understanding manifested in the construction of Shakspere's Plays equal to that in Bacon's Novum Organum"—inspired his kindness. At any rate, he informed Delia: "Will you kindly dispense with the ceremony of being called on (by sickly people, in this hot weather), and come to us on Friday evening to tea at 7 . . . and we will deliberate what is to be done in your Shakspere affair."

Carlyle, his wife Jane, and a learned family-friend were on hand in the Chelsea house to greet their strange American visitor. Carlyle liked Delia at once for her "modest shy dignity" and her "solid character." Delia was delighted with the historian, though startled by his booming laughter. "Once or twice I thought he would have taken the roof of the house off." The tea proceeded nicely until, at last, Carlyle asked his guest to explain her Shakespeare theory. Delia explained. At once there was a tempest amid the teacups. Carlyle may have had reservations about Shakespeare and respect for Sir Francis Bacon, but nothing so heretical as this had he expected or, indeed, ever heard before.

"They were perfectly stunned," Delia wrote her sister. "They turned black in the face at my presumption. 'Do you mean to say,' so and so, said Mr. Carlyle, with his strong emphasis; and I said that I did; and they both looked at me with staring eyes, speechless for want of words in which to convey their sense of my audacity. At length Mr. Carlyle came down on me with such a volley . . . I told him he did not know what was in the Plays if he said that, and no one *could* know who believed that that booby wrote them. It was then that he began to shriek. You could have heard him a mile."

The argument continued into the evening. As discussion became more heated, Delia became cooler toward Carlyle. At last he, perceiving her hurt, retreated into gruff tolerance.

He promised to keep an open mind and assist her in every way. He would submit to *Fraser's Magazine* an article she had written on the theory if she, in turn, would consent to study original source material in the British Museum. "If you can find in that mass of English records," he told her, "*any* document tending to confirm your Shakspere theory, it will be worth all the reasoning in the world, and will certainly surprise all men."

As the months passed, Delia utterly ignored Carlyle's advice that she test her theory against seventeenth-century papers in the British Museum. She needed no proofs beyond those she already possessed through the method of inductive reasoning so beloved by her idol, Sir Francis Bacon. Her funds, supplied by Butler, were swiftly dwindling, and she knew that she must give her great theory to the world before they were gone. She worked day and night on a detailed, book-length exposition of her hypothesis. The early chapters she expected to serialize in *Putnam's Magazine* to fulfill her commitment, and with the money received from the magazine she expected to finance her work to its completion.

During the latter days of November 1853 Delia suddenly removed herself from London to lodgings at the nearby village of St. Albans. There, a short walk from Sir Francis Bacon's old estate and his tomb, she continued to write. Her only effort at further substantiation of her theory occurred when, through the help of Sir Edward Bulwer-Lytton, she attempted to have Bacon's coffin opened. Her request was refused. Feverishly—she was now suffering severe headaches and occasional hunger pangs—she returned to her book. Carlyle was all disapproval. "Miss Bacon has fled away to *St. Albans* (the *Great* Bacon's place)," he reported to Emerson, "and is there working out her Shakspere Problem, from the depths of her own mind, disdainful apparently, or desperate and careless, of all *evidence* from Museums or Archives . . . Poor Lady! I sometimes silently wish she were safe at home again; for truly there can be no madder enterprise. . . ."

By remaining in St. Albans, Delia had, in effect, burned her bridges behind her. It was a dangerous decision, but there seemed to be no choice. She had spent the money given her for survival. All that was left was the money set aside for her passage back to America. And now she began to spend that, too. As she explained defensively to Emerson: "I am living here as economically as I could in America; and as I think only of finishing my work, and have no other future . . . I do not see why I should spend so large a sum merely for the sake of being in America."

She lived meanly, dedicated and driven by her holy mission. She rarely went walking, never met a native of the community except by accident, subsisted on the cheapest of fare, and scratched out her pages of manuscript while huddled in bed for warmth. Finally, after eleven months of privation and solitude in St. Albans, and after a month in Hatfield, she packed her precious manuscript and fled the severe winter of the countryside to seek more habitable lodgings in London.

Armed with a list of advertisements from *The Times*, Delia hired a cab. The driver, quickly aware of her limited means, said that he knew of reasonable lodgings in Sussex Gardens. Delia was agreeable to anything. Thus, by good fortune, she met momentary salvation in the form of a kindly, overweight greengrocer named Walker, and his wife. Walker had an unheated flat to let over his shop. Grateful for a haven, Delia moved in, paid her fourteen shillings promptly each week, and worked steadily toward completion of her book. Soon her funds were gone. Walker, a gentleman of delicacy and a patron of the arts, did not evict her. Instead, he permitted her to stay on without payment for six months. When Delia borrowed ten pounds and sent it to Walker, he returned it.

Despite a letter from Carlyle recommending her "clear,

elegant, ingenious and highly readable manner," portions of Delia's book were being firmly rejected by the leading British publishers. Delia was filled with despair. But her black mood was of short duration. For suddenly from New York came the first ray of hope. *Putnam's Monthly* had received a chapter of Delia's book from Emerson. The editors liked it. They were featuring the chapter in their January issue, just six weeks off, and were prepared to pay her five dollars for every page of print. Moreover, they wished another chapter for their February issue, and as many more chapters as Delia desired to have serialized.

Deliriously happy, secure in the knowledge that this arrangement could support her comfortably in London until her masterwork was done, she prepared four more chapters amounting to eighty pages of manuscript, and posted them. But even before her editors had received the new material, Delia's first article was in print.

The opening feature in the January 1856 number of *Putnam's Monthly*, was entitled "William Shakespeare and His Plays: An Inquiry concerning Them." Delia devoted her entire first article to the task of maiming William Shakespeare. She referred to his authorship of the plays as the "great myth of the modern age." She felt "that deer-stealing and link-holding, and the name of an obscure family in Stratford" were not exactly the requisites for scholarship. She berated him as "the Stratford poacher" and she ridiculed him as "this Mr. Shakespeare, actor and manager, of whom no one knows anything else." For the defenders of the Bard, who resented the deer-poaching tradition, she had only the harshest words. "If he did not steal the deer, will you tell us what one mortal thing he did do? He wrote the plays. But, did the man who wrote the plays do nothing else? Are there not some foregone conclusions in them?—some intimations, and round ones, too, that he who wrote them, be he who he may, has had experiences of some sort? Do such things as these, that the plays are full of, begin in the fingers' ends? Can you find them in an ink-horn? Can you sharpen them out of a goose-quill? Has your Shakespeare wit and invention enough for that? . . . Had *he* no part of his own in time, then? Has he dealt evermore with second-hand reports, unreal shadows, and mockeries of things? Has there been no personal grapple with realities, here?" No, the "vulgar, illiterate man who kept the theatre where they were first exhibited" had not created the great plays. The very idea "has become too gross to be endured any further."

Delia went no further in this initial blast. She withheld the names of those whom she had discovered to be the real authors. She hinted only of "some friend, or friends, who could . . . explain his miracle to us."

The article was a success, and created sufficient agitation and controversy to warrant more of the same. Or so, at least, Delia was led to believe. But then, like a thunderclap, came the incredible news from New York that *Putnam's Monthly* had decided to cancel the rest of the series.

What had happened? The editors gave, as their official reason, the explanation that the four latest articles were too general and "make so little progress in the demonstration of the main proposition, that if given separately they would weaken rather than increase the interest in the subject."

Emerson agreed with the editors. Though he had regarded Delia as a "genius, but mad" and ranked her with Walt Whitman as "the sole producers that America has yielded in ten years," he had now become impatient with her repetition, verbosity, and lack of solid, factual refutation. "The moment your proposition is stated that Shakespeare was only a player, whom certain superior person or persons could use, and did use, as a mouthpiece for their poetry it is perfectly understood. It does not need to be stated twice. The proposition is immensely improbable, and against the single testimony of Ben Jonson, 'For I loved the man, and do honor his memory on this side idolatry as much as any,' cannot stand. Ben Jonson must be answered, first. Of course we instantly require your proofs. . . . I am sure you cannot be aware how voluminously you have cuffed and pounded the poor pretender, and then again, and still again, and no end."

If Delia found the cancellation of *Putnam's Monthly* difficult to bear, she found Emerson's sudden loss of faith in her even more crushing. Suddenly, in her eyes, Emerson was an unreasonable intellectual snob. He had never been interested in her, after all. He had sponsored her simply to share credit for her brilliant theory. As to his challenge that she answer Jonson's assertion that he honored Shakespeare's memory, that was typical Emersonian nonsense. Of course she could answer that challenge, if she wished. "I know all about Ben Jonson," she wrote. "He has two patrons besides 'Shakspeare.' *One* was Raleigh, *the other* was Bacon. The author of these Plays and Poems was his Patron." In short, Jonson knew that Raleigh and Bacon were really Shakespeare, so quite naturally he praised his patrons by praising Shakespeare.

Emerson's role in the disappearance of her precious chapters added fuel to her frenzy. He had asked his brother William, in New York, to pick up the rejected chapters and return them to Concord, whence Emerson expected to forward them to Delia. William dutifully picked up the chapters and gave them to a house guest named Sophy Ripley, who was returning to Concord. "She took the sealed parcel in her hands," explained Emerson, "and came down to the Staten Island ferry with my brother in his carriage, one and a half miles, and just before reaching the boat perceived that she had not the parcel." Miss Ripley could not find the chapters in the straw-covered bottom of the carriage, or on the road, or in the ferry. She advertised for the lost parcel, and offered a reward, but it was never found. Delia blamed the magazine editors. She even blamed Emerson a little. But she did not blame herself for having failed to make copies of her work. As her paranoia took stronger hold on her, she hinted darkly of a plot fostered by Shakespeare-lovers. "These are not the first of my papers that have been destroyed."

As a matter of fact, there were others to support Delia in her view. Her friends, and later her followers, believed that reasons other than mere repetition had made the editors of *Putnam's Monthly* cancel her series. Elizabeth Peabody thought that Shakespeare-scholars, led by Richard Grant White, had been so horrified by the heresy of the first article that they had descended upon Putnam's and talked them out of the rest of the series. Ignatius Donnelly, on the other hand, thought that the fault was to be found among Delia's own friends, who begged Putnam's to stop encouraging her eccentricity.

At any rate, Putnam's could no longer be depended upon, nor could Ralph Waldo Emerson. When the eighteen pounds Delia had received for her first article were spent, she was impoverished and at wit's end. She had been unable to pay her rent for a year. She was determined not to trouble Carlyle further. She had a letter of introduction to the wealthy, elderly bachelor, James Buchanan, who was American minister to Great Britain and who would in short months be elected president of the United States. Delia wrote Buchanan, asking to see him. He replied that he would call upon her. When he came, at last, she found him formal and remote and somewhat stuffy. She could not bring herself to ask his aid.

With Buchanan's departure all hope seemed to fade. Delia searched her mind for someone in all Britain who might come to the rescue of her person and her completed book. Then she remembered Nathaniel Hawthorne, the brother-in-law of her friend Elizabeth Peabody. She had never met him, but she knew that his old college-friend, President Franklin Pierce, had awarded him the well-paying consulship at Liverpool. Hawthorne, if anyone, would understand the plight of a fellow author. He had struggled, too. Of course, he was known to have an antipathy toward women who were aggressive, erudite, talkative. He had disliked Margaret Fuller intensely. "She had not the charm of womanhood," he had thought, and found her too excessively pushy for femininity, too clever, and too frank on the subject of sex. Would he, then, couple Delia's name with Miss Fuller's? Would he remember her writings, and the lectures, and the New England scandal, and draw away from her? Delia hesitated. But only briefly. Hunger and pain and defeat gave her courage.

On May 8, 1856, she sat down and wrote:

"Dear Mr. Hawthorne,—I take the liberty of addressing myself to you without an introduction, because you are the only one I know of in this hemisphere able to appreciate the position in which I find myself at this moment. . . .

"Of course it is not pleasant to me to bring this subject to the attention of strangers, as I have been and still am compelled to, for it seems like a personal intrusion, and like asking a personal favor. . . .

"For I want some literary counsel, and such as no Englishman of letters is able to give me. Mr. Carlyle has been a most cordial personal friend to me, but there are reasons why I could not ask this help from him, which would become apparent to you if you should look at the work at all. . . .

"The work admits of publication in separate portions. What I want is to begin to publish immediately a part of it, enough to secure the discovery. . . . I would not be willing to print any part of it till some friendly eye had overlooked it, if there were no other reason for delay. It is not hard reading. Would you be willing to take a part of it, a part which you could read in an evening or so . . . ?"

In Liverpool the fifty-two-year-old Hawthorne, sick of his consular job, "bothered and bored, and harassed and torn in pieces, by a thousand items of daily business," as he would write Delia, irritated by the beer-sodden British, might have been expected to possess little patience for another American in trouble. Yet, so sensitive was he to human loneliness and insecurity, and so decent and good were his instincts, that he was moved to reply to Delia at once. Within four days of writing him, she had her answer. He had heard of her several years before from Miss Peabody. And he had heard of her theory. He thought that he was too busy and preoccupied to be very helpful as critic or judge, but if she needed his reaction, or his assistance in securing a publisher, he was ready to serve her. There was only one condition, and in this Hawthorne was firm:

"I would not be understood, my dear Miss Bacon, as professing to have faith in the correctness of your views. In fact, I know far too little of them to have any right to form an opinion: and as to the case of the 'old Player' (whom you grieve my heart by speaking of so contemptuously) you will have to rend him out of me by the roots, and by main force, if at all. But I feel that you have done a thing that ought to be reverenced, in devoting yourself so entirely to this object, whatever it be, and whether right or wrong; and that, by so doing, you have acquired some of the privileges of an inspired person and a prophetess—and that the world is bound to hear you, if for nothing else, yet because you are so sure of your own mission."

Grateful, excited, and alive again, Delia sent portions of her book to Hawthorne. And with them an apology:

"I am sorry to have hurt your feelings with my profane allusions to the Earl of Leicester's groom, a witty fellow enough in his way. But long familiarity with the facts has produced a hopeless obduracy in my mind on that point. . . . I do not, of course, expect you to adopt my views until you find yourself compelled to do so, neither do I wish you to give the faintest countenance to them till you know fully what they are and their grounds."

Soon enough, Hawthorne had opportunity to become more fully acquainted with Delia's views. After reading portions of her manuscript he wrote her that he still was not a convert to her theory and that she made too much of the parallels she had found in Bacon and Shakespeare, writers' thoughts often being similar though they "had no conscious society with one another." However, he complimented her on her knowledge of Bacon and on "the depth and excellence" of her work.

Generously he offered her financial assistance, and when her pride restrained her from accepting, he sent the money anyway. Desperately as she needed his money, his literary help was what she sought most. And she told him so directly. "The way in which you can help me," she said, "will be to certify that you have read my book and that it is entitled to a publication."

Again Hawthorne understood her real need, and promised to do what he could. His own publisher in England was Routledge. This firm had sold "a hundred thousand volumes" of his books to their profit and his own, and he was certain that they would do anything he asked. But first he must meet Delia and discuss the matter with her. When could he call upon her? Delia was frightened. "I am unfit to see anyone. I have given up this world entirely. . . . Still, if you are kind enough to look after me when you come . . . I will put on one of the dresses I used to wear. . . ."

On July 26, 1856, Hawthorne went down from Liverpool to London, made his way to the grocery store in Sussex Gardens, met the fat, friendly Walker and his wife, and was escorted up three flights of stairs to Delia's flat. She was still asleep, though the hour was not early. Hawthorne guessed that her hermitlike existence had made her hours erratic. While Delia was being awakened, and nervously began to dress, her benefactor had time to study her parlor. Naturally he was drawn to her books first. They were piled high on a table, and each had some relation to her Shakespeare theory. There was Raleigh's *The History of the World*, Montaigne's *Essays*, Shakespeare's *Plays*, a volume of Bacon's letters, a pocket edition of the Bible, and several other works. Hawthorne settled down with Hazlitt's translation of Montaigne, and had been reading "a good while" when suddenly Delia appeared in the doorway.

Before her entrance Hawthorne had reflected on what her physical appearance might be. From her correspondence, from the fact that "she was a literary woman," he had conjured up an unattractive image: "I had expected . . . to see a very homely, uncouth, elderly personage." When Delia stood before him at last in person, he was agreeably surprised. He saw a woman "rather uncommonly tall," with "a striking and expressive face, dark hair, dark eyes, which shone with an inward light as soon as she began to speak." Though she was forty-five years of age, Hawthorne thought her aspect almost youthful and was sure that she had "been handsome and exceedingly attractive once."

There was no restraint. Their correspondence had made them friends, and they conversed quickly and easily. The talk soon turned to her theory and the publication of her book. Delia admitted that she was a recluse because she had no patience for meeting people not interested in her theory. She told Hawthorne that he was the fourth person to visit her apartment in all those months, and that except for a few evenings with Carlyle, and with Mrs. Farrar, who was visiting London, and business calls on the American Consul, she went out to see no one. She had even become estranged from her family in New England. They disapproved of her mission, and in an effort to bring her to her senses and force her to come home, they had ceased contributing to her support. Remembering this later, Hawthorne decided: "If taken from England now, she would go home as a raving maniac." He would write her family and tell them so—and do the best in his power "to supply her with some small means."

She was a brilliant talker. Speaking "in a low, quiet tone," she discussed "the authorship of Shakspeare's plays, and the deep political philosophy concealed beneath the surface of them." As he listened, Hawthorne thought that the plays were so varied and so deep that a hundred philosophies and truths could be discovered in them by anyone wishing to prove anything, but he refrained from speaking his mind for fear of provoking his hostess. As she went on and on, he was entranced by her presentation, but cynical about her argument. He contained his disagreement because he did not wish to debate the subject.

Next her conversation took a new turn that gave Hawthorne cause for dismay. The moment her book was accepted for publication, she said, she was going to open Shakespeare's grave in Stratford. "In Lord Bacon's letters, on which she laid her finger as she spoke, she had discovered the key and clew to the whole mystery," Hawthorne recalled. "There were definite and minute instructions how to find a will and other documents relating to the conclave of Elizabethan philosophers, which were concealed (when and by whom she did not inform me) in a hollow space in the under surface of Shakspeare's gravestone. Thus the terrible prohibition to remove the stone was accounted for. . . . All that Miss Bacon now remained in England for—indeed, the object for which she had come hither, and which had kept her here for three years past—was to obtain possession of these material and unquestionable proofs of the authenticity of her theory."

Hawthorne did not attempt to dissuade her from this macabre research. He felt sure that her "sturdy common-sense" would eventually keep her from attempting the sacrilege. The conversation finally turned to more practical matters. Hawthorne repeated his offer to submit her book to his own publisher. She bubbled with happiness. She would deliver the full manuscript in a week. She knew that Providence had brought Mr. Hawthorne into her life in this crisis.

More than an hour had passed. Hawthorne took his leave. As he left the grocery shop he was still under the spell of Delia's eloquence and fanaticism. But after a few blocks the sanity and bustle of English life about him knocked his "temporary faith" from his head and heart. By the time he reached Paternoster Row his meeting seemed an improbable dream. For a while he had been transported back into the Elizabethan era by sheer witchery, and had half believed what she had been saying, but now he was awake. Suddenly his promise to have her book published seemed extravagant and impossible. (Had not Elizabeth Barrett Browning, at a recent breakfast-party given in his honor, been "horrified" by Miss Bacon's theory?) Nevertheless, he had given his word. He would do what he could and hope for the best.

In less than a week Hawthorne had the thick manuscript. He had no time to read it, but turned it over to his wife. Sophia Hawthorne was impressed by its erudition. A few days later, Hawthorne took the book to London and laid it on Routledge's desk.

Hawthorne did not feel his labors on Delia's behalf were yet done. He was disturbed still by something that she had said about her family. He took it upon himself to address a lengthy letter to the Reverend Leonard Bacon in New Haven. He begged the clergyman not to think him impertinent for meddling in a family affair. But, he indicated, he felt it his duty to report on his relationship with Delia:

"I understand from her (and can readily suppose it to be the case) that you are very urgent that she should return to America; nor can I deny that I should give her similar advice, if her mind were differently circumstanced from what I find it. But Miss Bacon has become possessed by an idea, that there are discoveries within her reach, in reference to the authorship of Shakspeare, and that, by quitting England, she should forfeit all chance of following up these discoveries, and making them manifest to the public. . . . I will say to you in confidence, my dear Sir, that I should dread the effect, on her mind, of any compulsory measures on the part of her friends, towards a removal. If I may presume to advise, my counsel would be that you should acquiesce, for the present, in her remaining here, and do what may be in your power towards making her comfortable."

Leonard Bacon was deeply disturbed by Hawthorne's letter. He wrote his sister immediately. He tried to show restraint and good sense, but a more insensitive and intemperate communication cannot be imagined. His experience having been confined to giving advice on matters spiritual, he was ill equipped to hold forth on matters literary. He told Delia to concentrate on magazine articles and forget her book. He told her to limit her writings to Shakespeare's plays and forget the authorship theory. "You know perfectly well that the great world does not care a sixpence who wrote Hamlet." He warned her that she had yielded "to a delusion which, if you do not resist it and escape from it as for your life, will be fatal to you." He thought her theory a mere "trick of the imagination." But if she must persist with her book, he had one good, sound Yankee suggestion that might save all. "Your theory about the authorship of Shakspeare's plays may after all be worth something if published *as* a fiction."

Though infuriated by her relative's advice, Delia did not bother to fight back. For by the time she heard from Leonard she was already in Stratford on Avon, gathering all that remained of her wits to do battle with the real enemy. She had left London suddenly in late August with farewells to no one except Mrs. Eliza Farrar, and this of necessity.

Mrs. Farrar was entertaining guests one afternoon when a servant whispered to her that there was a strange lady at the door who would not leave her name. "On hearing this I went to the door," said Mrs. Farrar, "and there stood Delia Bacon, pale and sad. I took her in my arms and pressed her to my bosom; she gasped for breath and could not speak. We went into a vacant room and sat down together. She was faint, but recovered on drinking a glass of port wine, and then she told me that her book was finished and in the hands of Mr. Hawthorne, and now she was ready to go to

Stratford-upon-Avon." She revealed that the purpose of her mission was to open Shakespeare's grave. Mrs. Farrar pleaded with her to abandon the mad scheme. Delia would not listen. She wanted only Mrs. Farrar's help, and she would go. Mrs. Farrar gave her a sum of money and saw her off at the railroad station with heavy heart and a sense of impending tragedy.

In 1856 the market village of Stratford, in Warwickshire, was surrounded still by the "shadowy forests" and "plenteous rivers" and "wide-skirted meads" that the Bard himself had known and written about. Well-traveled country lanes led into the worn cobbled streets of the quiet, lovely old town. It was into this idyllic village that Delia Bacon dragged her sick and exhausted person on her last English journey. She was, she felt, more dead than alive, and her mind clung to reality by tenuous threads. Even her method of finding a lodging was somewhat fantastic, if fortunate. She saw an attractive cottage on High Street, near Shakespeare's last residence and the church that held his grave. She rapped on the door. The housekeeper told her that the lady of the house, Mrs. Terrett, was out. Delia said that she would wait. She forced herself inside and sat down, wracked with illness. Presently the owner of the cottage, Mrs. Terrett, a respectable old widow who lived on her income, returned. She was only mildly surprised. Though she had never had a boarder, or intended to have one, "she remembered, she said, that Abraham had entertained angels unawares." The kindly woman realized at once that her visitor was an American, and very ill, and she knew what she must do. She made Delia lie on the sofa, covered her, and went to make dinner. Later she agreed that Delia should have two front-rooms and all service for seven shillings a week.

It was more than four weeks before Delia had recovered sufficiently to leave her cottage and explore Stratford. She was attracted to the town at once. "I like Stratford," she wrote Hawthorne. "Shakespeare was right. It is a very nice comfortable place to stop in, much better than London for a person of a genial but retiring turn of mind." Hawthorne thought this was the only occasion on which he had ever known Delia to speak a word of praise for Shakespeare.

Though lulled by the old place, she was not unmindful of her true mission. But she had not yet the strength to move Shakespeare's bones. And then, suddenly, in her sixth week in Stratford she received the thrilling news that gave her all strength. Her book had been accepted for publication at last.

In an ecstasy of fulfillment, she wrote everyone. "Patience has had its perfect work," she wrote to Mrs. Farrar. "For the sake of those who have loved and trusted me, for the sake of those who have borne my burdens with me, how I rejoice!" Congratulations came back from friends and relatives and all were sincere. "Well done!" replied Carlyle. "This must be a greater joy to you than health itself, or any other blessing; and I must say that by your steadfastness you have deserved it! . . . My incredulity of your Thesis I have never hidden from you: but I willingly vote, and have voted, you should be heard on it to full length. . . ."

The printer and publisher, who had connection with *Fraser's Magazine*, was to be Parker—"you could not have a better Publisher," Carlyle assured her—and the editor of the manuscript was to be a most exacting gentleman named Bennoch. In her brief delirium of happiness Delia did not know, nor would she ever know, the actual circumstances behind her book's acceptance. Hawthorne had met with resistance to Delia's masterwork everywhere. Yet, out of his deep concern for Delia, he had persisted in this Herculean labor. At last the respectable Parker had agreed to publish under the conditions that Hawthorne lend his name to an introduction and that he bear the burden of $1,000 in printing costs. Hawthorne was amenable to both conditions, and preparations for publication went ahead.

In the six months that followed, Delia proved the most difficult of authors. She blocked Bennoch and Parker at every turn. They wished to call the volume *The Shakespeare Problem Solved*. Delia objected and supplied new titles with each new month. Until the eleventh hour there was no agreement. To the despair of all, she would not delete or rewrite a sentence, let alone a chapter. "Every leaf and line was sacred," sighed Hawthorne, "for all had been written under so deep a conviction of truth as to assume, in her eyes, the aspect of inspiration. A practiced book-maker, with entire control of her materials, would have shaped out a duodecimo volume full of eloquence and ingenious dissertation. . . . There was a great amount of rubbish, which any competent editor would have shoveled out of the way. But Miss Bacon thrust the whole bulk of inspiration and nonsense into the press in a lump. . . ."

As to an introduction by Hawthorne, Delia had hoped for one in the beginning and Parker had insisted upon it, but now suddenly she determined to stand alone. She had read Hawthorne's generous foreword, and she disapproved. She would gladly dedicate the book to him, but she would not accept his patronage in print. Bennoch and Parker pleaded with her. Hawthorne, exasperated, wrote: "I utterly despair of being able to satisfy you with a preface." He wanted no dedication. The foreword was a condition of publication. The foreword was favorable in every way. He told her that he had "merely refrained from expressing a full conviction of the truth of your theory. But the book will be in the hands of the public. Let the public judge; as it must. Nothing that I could say, beforehand, could influence its judgment; and I do not agree with your opinion that I have said anything likely to prevent your cause being heard." He suggested arbitration by Carlyle. Delia turned a deaf ear to his entreaties. Though the book was already set in type, Parker would not proceed unless Delia approved of the introduction. She refused and Parker, enraged, withdrew from the project entirely.

Suddenly her book was adrift again, and Delia was brought sharply to her senses. Terrified, she informed Bennoch that she had changed her mind. Hawthorne's preface would be acceptable. But Parker wanted no more to do with Miss Bacon. The weary Bennoch, undoubtedly encouraged by the incredibly patient Hawthorne, turned elsewhere for a publisher. Soon enough, and by rare good fortune, he found one in the smaller firm of Groombridge and Sons, who promptly took over the final printing and binding of the book.

Meanwhile, assured that her theory would soon be given the waiting world, Delia busied herself in Stratford with her last great enterprise. If she could now verify her writings with documentary evidence taken from Shakespeare's grave, her book would be a sensation and her life's work would be crowned with immortality. She began her "experiment" by making a preliminary visit to the Holy Trinity Church, hastily surveying Shakespeare's burial place in the chancel, and then asking a clerk of the church when fewest visitors and tourists were present. He advised her as to the best day, and a week later she returned at eight o'clock in the morning and hovered near the grave of the Bard, awaiting a moment when she might be alone to examine the flagstone over the coffin more closely. But there were at least twenty visitors during the day, and Delia had no time alone. She asked the clerk if she could return one evening after hours. The clerk had no objection.

At seven o'clock one evening, accompanied by Mrs. Terrett, in whom she had confided her daring purpose, Delia went back to the church. The clerk was waiting with key and candle. Delia and Mrs. Terrett went inside, though the elderly landlady was much frightened. "I told her I was not in the least afraid," Delia related to Hawthorne. "I only wanted her to help me a little. So I groped my way to the chancel, and she waited till the light was struck. I had a dark lantern like Guy Fawkes, and some other articles which might have been considered suspicious if the police had come upon us. The clerk was getting uneasy, and I found he had followed us. . . ." Delia persuaded the clerk to take Mrs. Terrett with him and to leave her alone. She was left alone only after she promised not to disturb the grave or do anything that might cost the clerk his job.

Now, for the first time, Delia was able to examine the flagstone over Shakespeare's coffin. She had been directed, by Lord Bacon, to search beneath "stones." She was worried lest there be another stone under the top lid. If so, there would be room for little else beyond the wooden coffin. She was alone for three hours, poking about in the crevices of the flagstone, judging its weight, peering up at Shakespeare's bust lost in the darkness. A creak of the floor told her that she was being watched. The worried clerk had reappeared. At last she confessed to this bewildered person what her real purpose was—and he, troubled, begged her to consult the church vicar.

The vicar proved most considerate. He did not blanch when he heard Delia's request. Solemnly he heard her out. When she was done he did not say No. "I cannot help fancying," said Hawthorne, "that her familiarity with the events of Shakspeare's life, and of his death and burial (of which she would speak as if she had been present at the edge of the grave), and all the history, literature and personalities of the Elizabethan age, together with the prevailing power of her own belief, and the eloquence with which she knew how to enforce it, had really gone some little way toward making a convert of the good clergyman." The vicar replied that he could not, under any circumstances, permit Delia to undertake the removal of the flagstone alone. However, it might be permitted in his presence, if she vowed not to touch the coffin itself. At any rate, he wanted time to think about it and to consult a Stratford lawyer who was a personal friend.

In a few days the vicar reported his decision to Delia. While he doubted that her experiment would prove successful, he saw no reason to prevent it. She could go ahead at once, and search beneath the flagstone in his presence if she guaranteed to leave no "trace of harm." Whether the vicar was merely humoring her, hoping she would withdraw her request, or whether he sincerely meant to give her the chance to prove her theory, we shall never know. For at the brink of discovery, at the moment of scholarly truth, she hesitated. Had Bacon's cryptic message meant that she would find her confirmation in this actor's tomb—or in his own? Or had he really meant that she look in Spenser's last resting-place?

"A doubt stole into her mind whether she might not have mistaken the depository and mode of concealment of those historic treasures," Hawthorne wrote. "And after once admitting the doubt, she was afraid to hazard the shock of uplifting the stone and finding nothing. She examined the surface of the gravestone, and endeavored, without stirring it, to estimate whether it were of such thickness as to be capable of containing the archives of the Elizabethan club. She went over anew the proofs, the clues, the enigmas, the pregnant sentences, which she had discovered in Bacon's letters and elsewhere, and now was frightened to perceive that they did not point so definitely to Shakspeare's tomb as she had heretofore supposed. . . ."

She did not go to the vicar again. Instead, she began to haunt the church by night. Lantern in hand, she would make her way down the aisle to the tomb and sit there staring. The age-worn curse leered up at her, and challenged her, but she did not accept its dare. She was afraid. And she was weary beyond all human weariness. Her mind was made up. Her frail hands need not move Shakespeare's bones. Her book would accomplish the task far better.

In the first week of April 1857 the book, the product of years of privation, obsession, and hope, appeared at last. It was entitled *The Philosophy of The Plays Of Shakspere Unfolded By Delia Bacon . . . with A Preface by Nathaniel Hawthorne, Author of "The Scarlet Letter," Etc.* The title page carried quotations credited to Lord Bacon, *Love's Labour's Lost*, and Prospero (the last reading: "Untie the spell"). One thousand copies of the huge volume—Delia devoted 100 pages to a statement of her general proposition

Very gratefully yours
Delia Bacon.

DELIA BACON

from a daguerreotype taken in May 1853

CAPTAIN JOHN CLEVES SYMMES

and 582 pages to her text—were printed. Half bore the imprint of Groombridge and Sons, Paternoster Row, London, and the other half, at Hawthorne's suggestion, the imprint of his American publisher, Ticknor and Fields, Boston, to be delivered for sale in the United States.

The preface by Hawthorne, to which Delia had so strenuously objected, was devoted largely to quotations from Delia's earlier writings. For the rest, Hawthorne's pen treated his charge with consideration and courtliness. "My object," he wrote, "has been merely to speak a few words, which might, perhaps, serve the purpose of placing my countrywoman upon a ground of amicable understanding with the public. She has a vast preliminary difficulty to encounter. The first feeling of every reader must be one of absolute repugnance towards a person who seeks to tear out of the Anglo-Saxon heart the name which for ages it has held dearest. . . . After listening to the author's interpretation of the Plays, and seeing how wide a scope she assigns to them, how high a purpose, and what richness of inner meaning, the thoughtful reader will hardly return again—not wholly, at all events—to the common view of them and of their author. It is for the public to say whether my countrywoman has proved her theory. In the worst event, if she has failed, her failure will be more honorable than most people's triumphs; since it must fling upon the old tombstone, at Stratford-on-Avon, the noblest tributary wreath that has ever lain there."

There followed then, in almost 700 labored pages, the unfolding of a theory that might have better been told in 100 pages. As Sophia Hawthorne remarked privately: "Miss Bacon cannot speak out fairly though there is neither the Tower, the scaffold, nor the pile of fagots to deter her." The first chapter was called "The Proposition," and in its opening lines Delia revealed her true purpose. "This work is designed to propose to the consideration not of the learned world only, but of all ingenuous and practical minds, a new development of that system of practical philosophy from which THE SCIENTIFIC ARTS of the Modern Ages proceed. . . ." In short, she was more concerned with the hidden meaning underlying Shakespeare's plays than with their actual authorship. "The question of the authorship of the great philosophic poems which are the legacy of the Elizabethan Age to us, is an incidental question in this inquiry, and is incidentally treated here." The secret philosophy beneath the surface of the so-called Shakespearean plays did not come of "unconscious spontaneity," but rather was the clever product of a "reflective deliberative, eminently deliberative, eminently conscious, designing mind." The mind was really several minds "under whose patronage and in whose service 'Will the Jester' first showed himself."

The round table of radicals concerned with the common welfare was led by Bacon and Raleigh, and included also Sir Philip Sidney, Lord Buckhurst, Lord Paget, and the Earl of Oxford. Edmund Spenser, though not highborn, was much admired by the others for *The Shepheardes Calender*, brought out in 1579, and was invited to join the group. According to Delia, one critic of the time, unnamed, who praised Spenser as well as Sidney and Raleigh, hinted at this "courtly company" and added mysteriously: "They have writ excellently well, if their doings could be found out and made public with the rest." It was Bacon who had the idea of employing popular plays as a medium of propagandizing the masses. "The Method of Progression, as set forth by Lord Bacon, requires that the new scientific truth shall be, not nakedly and flatly, but artistically exhibited; because, as he tells us, 'the great labour is with the people, and this people who knoweth not the law are cursed.' He will not have it exhibited in bare propositions, but translated into the people's dialect." Yes, the plays would be the medium, but their real meaning must not be too apparent and their authorship must not be known. "It was a time . . . when a '*nom de plume*' was required for other purposes than to serve as the refuge of an author's modesty, or vanity, or caprice. It was a time when puns, and charades, and enigmas, and anagrams, and monograms, and ciphers, and puzzles, were not good for sport and child's play merely. . . ." And when the plays were ready it was Ben Jonson who introduced the actor and theater-manager Shakespeare to this "courtly company" of authors.

In chapter after chapter, Delia reiterated and expanded her proposition, analyzing various Shakespeare plays and exposing the secrets they hid and yet propounded. Her dissection of *King Lear* was typical. "It is all one picture of social ignorance, and misery, and *frantic* misrule. It is a faithful exhibition of the degree of personal security which a man of honourable sentiments, and humane and noble intentions, could promise himself in such a time. . . . To appreciate fully the incidental and immediate political application of the piece, however, it is necessary to observe that notwithstanding that studious exhibition of lawless and outrageous power, which it involves, it is, after all, we are given to understand, by a quiet intimation here and there, *a limited monarchy* which is put upon the stage here. . . . It is a government which professes to be one of law, under which the atrocities of this piece are sheltered. And one may even note, in passing, that that high Judicial Court, in which poor Lear undertakes to get his cause tried, appears to have, somehow, an extremely modern air. . . ." This play, and all the plays, were part of a "great scientific enterprise," and "this enterprise was not the product of a single individual mind."

Delia's book was before the public. For even the most hearty reader it was a formidable package. Though it contained colorful writing, and wit, and sound literary criticism, the best of it was lost in a swamp of garrulous redundancy. The style was agitated and insistent. To be trapped in midpage was like being caught in an armed riot. The reader, cudgeled and bloodied by repetitive argument and phrase, staggered into long passages leading on and on into nowhere. The evaluation of Elizabethan writings was often profound, but the theory of joint authorship was lost in a maze of verbosity. The theory was there in print, nevertheless, and Shakespeare-scholars were outraged. They termed the book the product of a deranged mind, referring, of course, to its author's eventual lapse into insanity. To this, the indignant Ignatius Donnelly would reply that advocates of Shakespeare were as susceptible to lunacy as confirmed Baconians. Donnelly cited the example of George H. Townsend, who was the first to come to the defense of Shakespeare after the publication of Delia's book. Townsend, too, lost his mind, and eventually died by his own hand.

The Philosophy of the Plays of Shakspere Unfolded had been "the world's work," and it was now before the world for judgment. Hawthorne recorded the reaction to that "ponderous octavo volume, which fell with a dead thump at the feet of the public, and has never been picked up. A few persons turned over one or two of the leaves, as it lay there, and essayed to kick the volume deeper into the mud; for they were the hack critics of the minor periodical press in London. . . . From the scholars and critics of her own country, indeed, Miss Bacon might have looked for a worthier appreciation. . . . But they are not a courageous body of men; they dare not think a truth that has an odor of absurdity, lest they should feel themselves bound to speak it out. If any American ever wrote a word in her behalf, Miss Bacon never knew it, nor did I. Our journalists at once republished some of the most brutal vituperations of the English press, thus pelting their poor countrywoman with stolen mud, without even waiting to know whether the ignominy was deserved."

The book had this distinction: it was the first of its kind. Even that celebrity was quickly challenged. In 1856, while Delia's book was still on press, a cheerful, forty-four-year-old Englishman, William Henry Smith, offered to read to his debating society a paper advocating Bacon's authorship of Shakespeare's plays. Fellow members objected, but John Stuart Mill supported his right to be heard. Smith read his paper, which emphasized the parallel writings in Bacon and Shakespeare and argued that Bacon's known cultural background and creative talent made him a more likely candidate for authorship of the plays. Smith had this paper printed, and a copy sent to Lord Ellesmere, head of England's Shakespearean Society. A year later Smith expanded his paper into a modestly priced booklet entitled *Bacon and Shakespeare: An Enquiry Touching Players, Playhouses and Play-Writers in the Days of Elizabeth*. While this publication made a convert of Lord Palmerston, it made an enemy of Delia Bacon. She screamed plagiarism. She insisted that Smith had pirated her article in *Putnam's Monthly*. Hawthorne wrote Smith on Delia's behalf. Smith proved that his advocacy of Bacon was not plagiarism, but coincidence, and all hands were satisfied that Delia had been the first in the field.

Today, after a century, most American literary sources bestow upon Delia the title of pioneer. *American Authors* calls her the first Baconian. Van Wyck Brooks refers to her as "the originator of the 'Shakespeare-Bacon' movement." And the *Dictionary of American Biography* concludes: "To its author remains the credit, or discredit, of having first inaugurated the most absurd, and, in other hands, the most popular, of literary heresies."

Upon its publication, however, it seemed doubtful that it would pioneer anything, for it seemed doubtful that anyone had read it through. "I believe that it has been the fate of this remarkable book never to have had more than a single reader," said Hawthorne. "I myself am acquainted with it only in insulated chapters and scattered pages and paragraphs. But since my return to America a young man of genius and enthusiasm has assured me that he has positively read the book from beginning to end, and is completely a convert to its doctrines."

Of course, Hawthorne was being facetious. He knew the book had more than "a single reader," for his own wife, Sophia, had read it through before publication. The "single reader" referred to by Hawthorne, the "young man of genius and enthusiasm" who became Delia's first convert, was William Douglas O'Connor of Boston. O'Connor was a clever young journalist who was discharged by the *Saturday Evening Post* for too staunchly defending John Brown in print. He held several government jobs, notably with the Light House Board and the Life Saving Service. He was the first to champion Walt Whitman and to call him "the good gray poet," and in 1860 he was the first to champion Delia Bacon. In his novel, *Harrington: A Story of True Love*—a "fiery and eloquent novel," Whitman called it—O'Connor's abolitionist hero believed in Delia's theory. And at the end of the book O'Connor paid tribute to Delia's brilliance. Two more books, these devoted to factual arguments in favor of the Baconian theory, followed in the next nine years.

O'Connor was not the only person of note to read Delia's book and become converted to her views. The most famous of the others were Ignatius Donnelly and Mark Twain. When Donnelly was preparing his 998-page *The Great Cryptogram*, he wanted to include a portrait of Delia in it. Her family refused to submit a picture because, said Donnelly, "They do not *want her identified with the theory that Francis Bacon wrote the Shakespeare plays!*" Yet, Donnelly added, the entire Bacon family would be remembered in history only because of Delia's theory. Mark Twain admitted that he had read Delia's book the year after its publication while he was an apprentice pilot on the Mississippi, and he had become a convert at once. His pilot, George Ealer, worshipped Shakespeare and regarded Delia as a demon. "Did he have something to say—this Shakespeare-adoring Mississippi pilot—anent Delia Bacon's book?" asked Twain. "Yes. And he said it; said it all the time, for months—in the morning watch, the middle watch, the dog watch; and probably kept it going in his sleep."

If only a few read the book, they were enough. They read it and they argued about it, and the controversy grew and spread. One hundred years later Delia's heresy continued to persist, to fascinate, to excite, to anger, to amuse. Dozens who followed in her footsteps—writers, scholars, eccentrics—were unaware of her existence. Many others knew to whom they owed their ideas, but preferred to ignore that pioneer. Because she had died insane, Delia's memory became an embarrassment to the movement she inspired. But there can be little doubt that in the decades since Delia's death almost every new theory on the authorship of the Shakespeare plays has had its inception, directly or indirectly, in her sturdy, unreadable book.

Most who have challenged Shakespeare since 1856 have begun by following Delia's method of attacking the unworthiness of the "Old Player." Thus, in 1909, Mark Twain, still under Delia's spell, would point an accusing finger at Shakespeare's last will. "It was eminently and conspicuously a business man's will, not a poet's. It mentioned *not a single book.* Books were much more precious than swords and silver-gilt bowls and second-best beds in those days, and when a departing person owned one he gave it a high place in his will. The will mentioned *not a play, not a poem, not an unfinished literary work, not a scrap of manuscript of any kind.* Many poets have died poor, but this is the only one in history that has died *this* poor. . . ." Thus, in 1931, Bertram G. Theobald would ask readers in *Exit Shakspere*, as Delia had asked before him, many pointed questions about the Bard. If, as most Shakespeare scholars agree, he was little educated when he arrived in London at the age of twenty-three, when did he acquire the learning to write the poems and plays? Why did the theater-owner Philip Henslowe, whose diary alluded to most of the great dramatists of the day, never refer to Shakespeare? Why did Richard Burbage, the great actor, never mention Shakespeare as an author? How could Shakespeare have acquired so vast a legal background?

But to destroy Shakespeare was not enough, as Delia foresaw. It was necessary, by all logic, to discover the real author or authors. Only a few theorists supported her idea of group authorship. Of these the most prominent was Gilbert Slater who in 1931 published his *Seven Shakespeares*. This book contended that Bacon, Raleigh, Paget, Buckhurst, Marlowe, and the Countess of Pembroke, with Edward de Vere, Earl of Oxford, as their leader, had collaborated on the plays for which Shakespeare took credit. Slater based his case on the fact that the Earl of Oxford had received an annual pension of 1,000 pounds from a secret fund set up by Queen Elizabeth. This sum, he speculated, was used to pay the syndicate for creating propaganda favorable to the Queen—quite the reverse of Delia Bacon's contention that a similar syndicate had toiled, instead, to undermine the Queen.

The great majority of theorists, however, favored one pretender—and among all pretenders they most favored Sir Francis Bacon. Delia had, of course, made her strongest case for Bacon, and William Henry Smith had been right behind her. Now came the deluge. Few Baconians confined their assaults on Shakespeare to deduction and the laws of logic. One who did was Theobald, who in 1932 put forth Bacon as his choice on the grounds that the man was a genius who liked to call himself "a concealed poet." Further, Shakespeare was dead (and Bacon very much alive) when the First Folio came out with six absolutely new plays and with 193 lines in faultless style added to *Richard III*. Also, Bacon's private notebook of jottings—1,600 of them in all—was not published until long after Shakespeare's death, though the man who was Shakespeare used many of these jottings in the plays.

Most Baconians were less restrained. They chose to arm themselves with every freakish literary weapon available. Delia had scorned such weapons. "She never devoted herself to whims or fancies about capital letters," her nephew said, "or irregular pagination, or acrostics, or anagrams, as concealing yet expressing the great philosophy which the plays inclosed."

In 1888, just six years after having published a novel supporting Plato's story of the sunken Atlantis, the irrepressible Ignatius Donnelly, who was to be known as the "Apostle of Protest," brought out *The Great Cryptogram.* After a study of the First Folio, in which he found pages irregularly numbered, words unnaturally hyphenated, and abnormal columns of print, Donnelly became convinced that Bacon had been the true author of the plays. By tracking down key words like "volume" and "maske" in the Second Part of *Henry IV*, and by an ingenious method of word counting, Donnelly felt that he had proved the hidden authorship.

Six years later, a Detroit physician named Orville W. Owen carried the cipher method to an even greater extreme. By construction of a ponderous wooden deciphering machine, consisting of two wheels mounted five feet apart, to which were attached 1,000 feet of canvas bearing pages cut from Shakespeare's plays, Owen hunted out all occurrences of four guide-words: *honour*, *fortune*, *reputation*, and *nature*. By examining dialogue constructed around these four words, Owen discovered not only that Bacon had written Shakespeare but also that he had written the complete works of Marlowe, Spenser, Burton, and several others. Furthermore, Owen's remarkable contraption ground out titillating historic gossip: that Queen Elizabeth had secretly married Dudley, that Bacon was their son, that Bacon had murdered Shakespeare to put an end to the Bard's attempts at blackmail.

While the dazzling ingenuity of the Baconians was often much admired, industrious and outspoken skeptics were always ready to defend Jonson's "Star of Poets." On one occasion George Bernard Shaw took the time to invent a cipher by which he proved to the world that *he* had written all of Shakespeare's plays. On another occasion, when Albert Boni, the American publisher, was about to underwrite a Baconian cipher system that miraculously revealed the true authorship of the Shakespearean plays, an office boy in the firm applied the cipher to the *Daily Racing Form* and proved that Bacon had written that too.

However, Delia had offered claimants other than Bacon, and seven decades after the publication of her book many anti-Shakespeare theorists began to emulate her. Except for the strong support thrown behind the Earl of Oxford, whom Delia had included in her syndicate, most theorists backed Elizabethans whom Delia had ignored or overlooked. In 1912 Professor Celestin Demblon, of Belgium, suggested Roger Manners, fifteenth Earl of Rutland, for whom Shakespeare had a shield painted in 1613. In 1919 Professor Abel Lefranc, of France, suggested William Stanley, sixth Earl of Derby, who lived a quarter of a century after Shakespeare's death. In 1920 J. Thomas Looney, a schoolteacher, suggested Edward de Vere, seventeenth Earl of Oxford, who entered Cambridge before he was nine years old, helped fight the Spanish Armada, acted in plays at court, and published twenty-four lyric poems. In 1943 Alden Brooks suggested Sir Edward Dyer, who was a Rosicrucian, an alchemist, a favorite of Queen Elizabeth, and "our only Inglishe poett," according to Spenser. In 1955 Calvin Hoffman suggested (though his candidacy had been proposed before) Christopher Marlowe.

Against this continuing dissidence the true believers fought back with faith and logic. From the moment of Delia's original attack the defenders of the Bard rallied to preserve his name and credit. Most defenders felt that Delia and her converts persisted in overlooking Shakespeare's one major asset—his genius. As John Mackinnon Robertson wrote of the Baconians: "A kind of thesis which finds its motive in the assumed improbability of the possession of abnormal literary genius by an actor who had left school at 14, has accumulated through all its variants a mass of improbabilities not to be matched in speculative research on any other field."

Admitting that Shakespeare's birth was lowly, that his formal education was limited, that his background lacked nobility—were these facts enough to bar him from authorship of the plays? "This respect for the literary value of noble birth is impressive in its unanimity," remarked Marchette Chute, "but a little hard to explain logically, since the most learned of Elizabethan dramatists was a bricklayer, and the most poetic, next to Shakespeare, was the son of a cobbler." Too, had not Ben Jonson noted that Shakespeare knew at least "small Latin and less Greek"? If no English university recorded his attendance, neither did it record the attendance of Jonson himself, or Henry Chettle, or Thomas Kyd. If Shakespeare had no legal training to explain the knowledge of law displayed in his plays, neither did Jonson or George Chapman, who wrote several plays that exhibited far more knowledge of law.

In Shakespeare's lifetime fifteen plays appeared bearing his name. For most authors this would have been sufficient evidence of authorship. Why not for Shakespeare? During his lifetime, Francis Meres, Jonson, and others acknowledged his existence and praised his output. For most authors this would have been sufficient evidence of fame. Why not for Shakespeare? And shortly after his death, the Folio was published containing an engraving of him made by Martin Droeshout, while the parish church in his home village erected a bust created by Gerard Janssen, the son of a tomb maker. For most authors these would have been sufficient evidences of honor and tribute paid by friends and admirers. Why not for Shakespeare?

Frank Ernest Hill has summarized the pro-Shakespeare position admirably in *To Meet Will Shakespeare:* "The Shakespeare case is supported by many facts and specific comments. The evidence for it is direct, and it is great both in volume and in variety. In contrast, all other cases are 'if' cases. . . . Not one clear statement from a seventeenth-century writer or other person in a position to know says 'Oxford (or Bacon or Derby or Rutland) wrote the works supposed to be William Shakespeare's.' "

But in April 1857 the forty-six-year-old Delia Bacon could not know the literary stir her volume would one day provoke. In fact, she knew little of the reception it was accorded in the British press, or how poorly it sold in her own time. Ill, exhausted, inert, she dwelt now with a friendly shoemaker and his family in Stratford, paying them seven shillings a week and trying them sorely with her recurring hallucinations. To her brother, Leonard, with whom she had become reconciled, she wrote: "Having fulfilled my work as I thought . . . I have not cared to know the result. Since the day I heard it was published I have made no inquiry on the subject . . . I am calm and happy. I do not want to come back to America."

Two months after the publication of the book, Hawthorne received a short letter in Liverpool from David Rice, a physician who was also Mayor of Stratford. Rice wrote that he had attended Miss Bacon and was concerned. "She is in a very excited and unsatisfactory state, especially mentally, and I think there is much reason to fear that she will become decidedly insane."

Though Hawthorne had not been in touch with Delia since the disagreement over the preface—in almost her last letter to him she had said that he was "unworthy to meddle with her work"—he immediately undertook responsibility for her welfare. He advised Rice to care for her and to charge all expenses to him. He wrote to the Reverend Leonard Bacon, informing him of her condition and asking his advice. Bacon replied: "The crisis at which my sister's case has arrived, requires me to say, plainly, that in my opinion her mind has been 'verging on insanity' for the last six years. . . . My fear has been, all along, that whenever and wherever her book might be published, the disappointment of that long and confident expectation would be disastrous if not fatal to her." He agreed that Delia must be returned to her family in America at once. Immediately Hawthorne went ahead with preparations for her transportation home and for adequate care.

But it was too late. Delia's condition had worsened. She could not be moved. And Hawthorne, unfortunately, could no longer assist her. His consulship at Liverpool, which he had come to detest, was at an end by his own request, and soon he was off for a year and a half in the "poetic fairy precinct" of Italy. By December Delia's insanity had become sufficiently acute to necessitate her removal to a private insane asylum at Henley in Arden, eight miles outside Stratford. There, in the forest of Arden, she remained confined for over three months.

In March 1857, twenty-one-year-old George Bacon, one of the Reverend Leonard Bacon's sons, arrived in England on an American frigate after two years spent in and about China. He was hurrying back to America, but he remembered that he had an ailing aunt in Stratford and went to call upon her. When he learned that she had been removed to an insane asylum in Henley, he was shocked. Without consulting his elders, he determined to take Delia home, where she belonged. He delayed his passage one week, secured his aunt's release from the asylum, packed her onto a vessel, and, on April 13, 1858, led her down the gangplank in New York.

Her family placed her in a sanitarium called The Retreat, in Hartford, Connecticut. Her two brothers and two sisters and their children were in constant attendance upon her. She sank deeper and deeper into the distorted regions of unreality. But in a few last lucid moments she recognized the members of her family and spoke to them happily and warmly. Not once did she mention William Shakespeare.

On September 2, 1859, wrote the Reverend Leonard Bacon, "she died, clearly and calmly trusting in Christ, and thankful to escape from tribulation and enter into rest." She was buried in the old cemetery at New Haven, and over her grave was placed a brown cross inscribed with the words "So He bringeth them to their desired haven." This was decent, and it was kind, but it was not enough. There was one more thing to be said, and four years later, in his autobiographical volume *Our Old Home*, Nathaniel Hawthorne said it:

"No author had ever hoped so confidently as she; none ever failed more utterly. A superstitious fancy might suggest that the anathema on Shakespeare's tombstone had fallen heavily on her head, in requital of even the unaccomplished purpose of disturbing the dust beneath, and that the 'Old Player' had kept so quietly in his grave, on the night of her vigil, because he foresaw how soon and terribly he would be avenged. But if that benign spirit takes any care or cognizance of such things now, he has surely requited the injustice that she sought to do him—the high justice that she really did—by a tenderness of love and pity of which only he could be capable. What matters it though she called him by some other name? He had wrought a greater miracle on her than all the world besides. This bewildered enthusiast had recognized a depth in the man whom she decried, which scholars, critics, and learned societies devoted to the elucidation of his unrivalled scenes, had never imagined to exist there. She had paid him the loftiest honor that all these ages of renown have been able to accumulate upon his memory. And when, not many months after the outward failure of her lifelong object, she passed into the better world, I know not why we should hesitate to believe that the immortal poet may have met her on the threshold and led her in, reassuring her with friendly and comfortable words, and thanking her (yet with a smile of gentle humor in his eyes at the thought of certain mistaken speculations) for having interpreted him to mankind so well."

VII

The Explorer of the Hollow Earth

"I declare that the earth is hollow, habitable within. . . . I pledge my life in support of this truth, and am ready to explore the hollow if the world will support and aid me in the undertaking."

JOHN CLEVES SYMMES

By early 1823 the United States Congress, which had so faithfully served Monroe's second administration, was sorely in need of a rest. Problem after problem of national import had been met and successfully solved. A war against Algeria had been won. Florida had been purchased from Spain. A Missouri Compromise had been reached on the slavery question. The states of Mississippi, Illinois, and Alabama had been admitted to the Union. The newly established republics of Mexico, Colombia, Peru, and Chile had been recognized, paving the way for what was to be Monroe's famous Doctrine. With this activity behind it, Congress could reasonably expect few more difficult tasks during the duration of its term. Yet, quite suddenly, in January 1823, Representative Richard M. Johnson, of Kentucky, who was to become vice-president of the United States, rose in the House to present respectfully a petition requesting that Congress finance an expedition into the center of the earth—and at once Congress was again in an uproar.

To be sure, there had been rumor of such a projected expedition for five years, ever since a retired veteran of the War of 1812, Captain John Cleves Symmes, of New Jersey, Missouri, and Ohio, had conceived the daring idea that "the earth is hollow, habitable within. . . ." Armed with a prolific pen and oratorical zeal, Symmes had convinced thousands of excited Americans that the interior of the earth could be entered and explored through an opening at the North Pole 4,000 miles in diameter and an opening at the South Pole 6,000 miles in diameter.

On March 7, 1822, Symmes had personally induced Representative Johnson to ask his fellow congressmen to "equip and fit out for the expedition two vessels of two hundred and fifty or three hundred tons' burden." Johnson had passed the suggestion along to the House of Representatives, and had spoken briefly on its behalf, but the project had been ignored as unsound.

Instead of withdrawing the idea, Symmes remained undiscouraged. Realizing that while Congress might not readily accede to the request of one individual, it might be more receptive to public pressure, Symmes devoted the next ten months to building that pressure. By January 1823 Representative Johnson again had a petition, not from Symmes but from hundreds who believed that "the national honor and public interest might be promoted by the equipping of an exploring expedition for the purpose of penetrating the Polar region, beyond the limits already known, with a view not only of making new discoveries in geography, natural history and geology, but of opening new sources of trade and commerce." The man to lead this expedition, the petitioners further urged, was none other than "Captain John Cleves Symmes, late of the United States Army," who, "with scientific assistants," was prepared to descend into the earth's interior. Because the petition bore "many respectable signatures," Johnson felt obliged once again, more forcefully, to present it to his colleagues in the House of Representatives.

The exhausted congressmen, unprepared for lengthy and involved discussions of the earth's lithosphere, reacted with vocal dismay. Representative Farelly, of Pennsylvania, made a motion to table the new petition. In the short debate that ensued, Johnson reminded his colleagues that "respectable" voters were behind it. Moreover, if Symmes was right, a new race might be discovered within the earth, a discovery which would give all Americans clinging to the exterior world "great profit and honor." Johnson begged that the petition not be shelved. "Something useful might come of it," he said. In the roll call that followed, Johnson won. The petition was not shelved. But the problem still remained: what to do with it?

There was general agreement that the petition should be referred to committee, any committee, for further study and recommendation. Representative Arden moved that the petition go to the Committee on Commerce, as "the object of the memorialists is to establish a commerce with the interior inhabitants." The members of the House seemed confused by this motion, and when it was put to a roll call, it was voted down. In the days that followed, no further disposition could be agreed upon, and eventually the petition to send Symmes into the bowels of the planet died of inertia.

Hearing the unhappy news on a lecture tour, Symmes still refused to give up hope. He doubled his efforts to bludgeon Congress into offering federal aid. A month later, the House of Representatives was swamped by new petitions and memorials demanding support of Symmes. The longest petitions came from Charleston, South Carolina, and from Greenville, Ohio. No sooner were these shelved than Representative Ross, of Ohio, wearily appeared on the floor waving three more from his constituents. In the Senate the volume of requests was smaller, but they persisted. The most impressive list of signatures was offered by Senator Benjamin Ruggles, of Ohio, but his fellow senators remained unmoved.

In December 1823, shortly after President Monroe had

declared in his annual message that "the American continents . . . are henceforth not to be considered as subjects for future colonization by any European powers," the bombardment by Symmes and his followers was resumed. The members of the House of Representatives, realizing they could no longer avoid the issue, testily put the financing of a Symmes expedition to a vote. There remains no record of how large a majority of congressmen decided against it. But we do know that there were "twenty-five affirmative votes."

In defeat Symmes won a triumph. If his government would not help him sail through a polar cavity into the earth's inner shell, at least twenty-five congressmen had indicated approval of the plan. It was inspiration enough. Thereafter, Symmes was to make verification of his theory by private exploration his life's goal.

The furor in Washington, if it did nothing else, served to introduce to the less scientific-minded population one of the most diverting and persistent burrowers in world history. John Cleves Symmes was born in Sussex County, New Jersey, on November 5, 1780. His forebears were among the early Puritans. Except for an uncle, Judge John Symmes, who had been a delegate to the Continental Congress and had helped found the city of Cincinnati, his relatives were undistinguished. Symmes had a "common school education" and devoted much of his youth to reading scientific books.

In 1802, at the age of twenty-two, having determined upon a military career, he enlisted in the United States Army. After serving at several crude forts in the Midwest, he was promoted to the rank of ensign and stationed at a garrison just outside Natchez, Mississippi. There a fellow officer who disliked his brusque individuality remarked to friends that Symmes was not a gentleman. When this insult was repeated to Symmes, he was much offended. He followed his fellow officer to the parade grounds, and in full view of all "tweaked his nose . . . publicly" and challenged him to a duel. The affair of honor was promptly staged, and resulted in a Pyrrhic victory for Symmes. While he wounded the affronting fellow officer seriously, though not fatally, he himself sustained an injury that "stiffened his left wrist for life."

Soon enough he was able to redirect his aggressions toward more patriotic ends. In June 1812 Congress declared a war against Great Britain which was to produce the heroism of Captain Oliver Hazard Perry, the legend of *Old Ironsides*, the creation of "The Star Spangled Banner," the burning of the White House, the loss of 1,877 American lives, and the final capitulation of the British in 1815. It also resulted in a deserved promotion for Symmes. He was made regimental senior captain. At Lundy's Lane, in a night battle fought one mile from Niagara Falls, Symmes led a company—"with bravery, skill and gallantry," we are told—in one of the war's bloodiest and most confused clashes. At Bridgewater he commanded his company to unload seventy rounds of cartridges, and fought beside his men as they successfully repelled three British bayonet assaults. At Fort Erie, inside Canada, a garrison occupied by the United States Army for several months, he gathered a commando group and sallied forth to surprise and overwhelm an enemy battery and personally spike its cannon.

After the Treaty of Ghent was signed, Symmes retained his rank of captain and remained in the Army in the role of minor hero. For four years he was quartermaster at a military installation on the upper Mississippi. In 1816 he resigned from the service, obtained a government license to sell private supplies to troopers and Indians, and set up shop at the trading post of St. Louis in the Missouri Territory. At this settlement he met and fell in love with the young widow of another soldier. The fact that she had six children did not deter him. He married her and gave her four more children, one of whom he named Americus Vespucius Symmes, which would seem to indicate that he had already acquired more than a passing interest in exploration.

During these postwar years private enterprise and his expanding family interested him less and less. Most often he was found perusing his beloved books of science. His first interest, as later he would recall, was in the worlds of outer space. He purchased a telescope and gazed at Jupiter. He studied charts and drawings of Saturn, and concluded that the existence of rings around Saturn "establishes . . . that the principle of concentric spheres, or hollow planets, does exist," He decided that Sir Isaac Newton had been in error and that an atmosphere filled with an "aerial elastic fluid" or "microscopically invisible hollow spheres of ether" accounted for gravity: "the aerial fluid creates a *pushing* instead of a *pulling power* which is the real principle of gravity." He also decided that formless matter in rotation took the shape of spheres and "therefore a nebular mass in rotation, as our earth during its formation, will not assume the form of a solid sphere, but rather of a hollow one." The idea of hollow planets seemed perfectly logical to Symmes. Hadn't nature made the interior of animal bones, wheat stalks, and human hair completely hollow?

With growing confidence in his concept of the universe, Symmes at last came down to earth. He read the writings of a Professor Burnet, who believed that the earth had once been a small core covered with oil to which the fluid of the atmosphere had adhered, thus forming the earth crust. He read the writings of a Professor Woodward, who contended "that the earth is now formed of distinct strata, arranged in concentric layers, 'like the coats of an onion.' " He read the writings of Whiston, who believed that the earth had been conceived of a comet, and that a liquid abyss had formed on that comet and then been covered by a shell, so that in final appearance the earth resembled the yolk, albumen, and shell of an egg.

Symmes's vague conjectures gradually assembled themselves into a clear pattern. The earth, like the planets beyond, was hollow, and filled with concentric spheres—that is, with smaller globes placed one within the other and all possessing a common center. Excitedly he reached back into the past for any corroboration. He did not have to reach far. Throughout history there had been those who had supposed that the earth might be hollow and might contain smaller planets within itself. Plato had spoken of "huge subterranean streams" and "passages broad and narrow in the interior of the earth." In 1692 the eminent Dr. Edmund Halley, later astronomer royal and Oxford professor, who ten years earlier had observed the famous comet that was to be named after him, informed the Royal Society of London that beneath the earth's 500-mile crust lay a void through which three planets the size of Venus, Mars, and Mercury spun. Halley's theory was adopted by the great German mathematician Leonhard Euler, who modified the three inner planets to one, and gave that planet daylight and a prospering civilization.

In 1721 Cotton Mather spoke of an interior universe, and two decades later Baron Holberg wrote a novel in which his hero fell inside the earth and there discovered a sun and a solar system and himself became a whirling satellite for three days. In the early 1800's a Scottish mathematician and physicist, Sir John Leslie, renowned for his work in radiation, speculated on a hollow earth furnished with two blazing planets similar to the sun called Proserpina and Pluto.

These readings gave Symmes the courage to undertake his next step. He needed courage, for while others had spoken of concentric spheres within a hollow earth, Symmes's thinking had gone much further. He conceived, as no one had before him, of gaping holes at the North and South poles through which he and other bold spelunkers might sail to the five planets inside. In the spring of 1818 he acted. From his shop in the Missouri wilderness he mailed to leading scientific academies of Europe, to presidents and professors of American universities, and to members of the United States Congress five hundred copies of an announcement with the simple heading "Circular," and the motto "Light gives light to light discover ad infinitum." Addressed from St. Louis, Missouri Territory, North America, and dated April 10, 1818, the notice of discovery read:

I declare that the earth is hollow, habitable within; containing a number of solid concentrick spheres; one within the other, and that it is open at the pole twelve or sixteen degrees. I pledge my life in support of this truth, and am ready to explore the hollow if the world will support and aid me in the undertaking. John Cleves Symmes of Ohio, Late Captain of Infantry.

To this startling notice was attached another, an afterthought in the form of a postscript, which read:

N.B. I have ready for the press a treatise on the principles of Matter, wherein I show proofs of the above proposition, account for various phenomina, and disclose Dr. Darwin's "Golden Secret."

My terms are the patronage of this and the new world, I dedicate to my wife and her ten children.

I select Dr. S. L. Mitchel, Sir H. Davy and Baron Alexander Von Humbolt as my protectors. I ask one hundred brave companions, well equipped to start from Siberia, in the fall season, with reindeer and sledges, on the ice of the frozen sea; I engage we find a warm and rich land, stocked with thrifty vegetables and animals, if not men, on reaching one degree northward of latitude 82; we will return in the succeeding spring, J. C. S.

With these notices, we are told, Symmes enclosed a medical report testifying to his sanity. This last was wholly unnecessary. For though the French Academy regarded his discovery and proposal with dismay, other recipients were more tolerant. In England, scientists, remembering their own revered Dr. Halley, cautiously withheld criticism. In Russia, scientists were definitely impressed, and eventually, as we shall see, showed their willingness to co-operate. In the United States, scientists, whatever their personal reactions, were loath to poke fun at a war veteran. They withheld judgment, though soon enough large portions of the lay public would voice approval.

His initial circular having brought him no patronage—though it had established his priority as author of what he called his "Theory of Concentric Spheres"—Captain Symmes decided to appeal directly to the people of his native land. From his St. Louis trading post he issued two more circulars, and in less than a year, three more, one of which elaborated upon his original notion that there were holes at the North and South poles through which an explorer might enter the interior world. Soon these polar openings came to be commonly known as Symmes's Hole or Symmes's Cavity.

Obsessed by his theory and the need to prove it, Symmes moved his person, his books, and his large family to Newport, Kentucky. He read heavily, thought deeply, and then began to write numerous articles for the popular press, one of the earliest being a piece entitled "Light Between The Spheres," published in the *Cincinnati National Intelligencer* during August 1819. In Kentucky he gathered about him his first devoted disciples, citizens who would soon impress their local representative, Congressman Richard M. Johnson, with the necessity of presenting Symmes's case in Washington. In Kentucky, too, Symmes made the decision to stump the nation on behalf of his theory.

His first lecture was delivered before a large audience in Cincinnati during 1820. Shortly after, he addressed other large gatherings in Lexington, Frankfort, Zanesville, and Hamilton. One of our rare glimpses of Symmes as a human being is of him as a lecturer. "The arrangement of his subject was illogical, confused, and dry, and his delivery was poor," John W. Peck wrote in 1909. "However, his earnestness and the interesting novelty of his subject secured him attentive audiences wherever he spoke."

Of his physical aspect in those years we know nothing. We know only that his erudition surprised his skeptics, that his temper flared quickly in the face of ridicule, that his lack of patience did not permit him to co-ordinate his radical ideas into any organized and detailed form, that his old military companions still spoke of him as "zealous and faithful" and that an impressed college disciple thought him "a high-minded, honorable man." But if his personality made no impression on his time, his imaginative theory certainly did. Through his muddled writings and halting lectures Symmes doggedly spread the gospel of a new world underfoot. Soon few communities in America's Midwest or South did not have some knowledge of the Captain's stimulating ideas.

Once, when he attempted to enlighten both the student body and faculty of Union College in Kentucky with a series of scientific lectures, an undergraduate named P. Clark made "copious notes." It is to Clark that history owes the only record extant of Symmes declaiming his theory in public.

"The earth is globular, hollow, and open at the poles," said Symmes in his initial lecture. "The diameter of the northern opening is about two thousand miles, or four thousand miles from outside to outside. The south opening is somewhat larger. The planes of these openings are parallel to each other, but form an angle of 12° with the equator, so that the highest part of the north plane is directly opposite the lowest part of the south plane. The shell of the earth is about one thousand miles thick, and the edges of this shell at the openings are called verges, and measure, from the regular concavity within to the regular convexity without, about fifteen hundred miles."

The details of the projected expedition, by which Symmes hoped to prove his theory, were familiar to all who heard or read the discoverer's words. Symmes would lead "one hundred brave companions" in two ships equipped with reindeer and sleighs to Siberia, and thence to the hole or verge at the North Pole, which was 4,000 miles in diameter in contrast to the larger hole at the South Pole, which was 6,000 miles in diameter. The great opening would be reached by sailing through the Bering Strait. Every sign, argued Symmes, pointed to its existence. For one thing, explorers often spoke of the brilliant twilight of the Arctic regions. "This twilight coming from the north," said Symmes, "may be caused by the sun's rays thrown into the interior through the southern opening, which by two refractions, one at each opening, and two or three reflections from the inner concave surface, would pass out at the north over the verge, and produce there this strong twilight." Also, explorers often reported that mysterious warm air currents melted ice in the Arctic Sea. The best explanation for these currents would be that they rose out of the North Pole cavity. Finally, the curious migration of wild life—birds winging north into the cold regions, instead of south—was conclusive evidence "that there is a land beyond the frozen Arctic belt, wither some beasts, fowls and fish go at the approach of winter and whence they return in the spring sleek and fat."

Symmes was not certain that the members of his expedition would know at once when they entered the earth's interior. There was probably no dropping-off place. Rather, the curvature of the wide rim might be so gradual as to "not be apparent to the voyager, who might pass from the outer side of the earth over the rim and down the inner side a great distance before becoming aware of the fact at all." Once inside the earth, the travelers would not tumble off the concave inner shell. Aerial fluid would encompass them and press them safely to water and land.

Symmes did not think that the interior would be a world of darkness. While there would be no dazzling sunlight, there would be a softer, more congenial light, the reflection of the sun's rays as they slanted through the North Pole opening. The expedition would probably meet a new race of people, of what physique Symmes dared not guess, and it would come across lands that might "abound with animals, with organs only adapted to the medium which they are destined to inhabit."

Within this spacious earth interior would be five more earths, one inside the other, like the parts of some incredible Chinese puzzle. Each would have an opening "filled with a very light, subtile, elastic substance . . . of the nature of hydrogen gas," and this escaping gas would create earthquakes and form volcanic ranges. Ocean currents and marine life would gush through these openings, and the expedition, if not yet unnerved, might continue downward into the inferno from inner planet to inner planet until it reached the very core.

This was the theory. On its behalf, as one critic remarked caustically, "the master and his disciples have traversed the whole country, from south to north, and from west to east, so that all men, in all places, might be enlightened in the truth." That by now there were influential disciples, there is ample written evidence. The foremost of these was a wealthy resident of Hamilton, Ohio, James McBride, a trustee of Miami University who possessed a valuable library of six thousand volumes. It may have been McBride who encouraged Symmes to move to Hamilton in 1824. Or the move may have been inspired by Symmes's desire to dwell in a community that had been receptive to his lectures. At any rate, once Symmes was settled in Hamilton, McBride became his patron and collaborator.

Symmes being reluctant to assemble his notes into book form, McBride assumed the responsibility. In 1826 the firm of Morgan, Lodge and Fisher, in Cincinnati, published a slender volume entitled *Symmes' Theory of Concentric Spheres*, by James McBride. The disciple's prose was less fanatic than the master's:

"According to captain Symmes, the planet which has been designated the Earth, is composed of at least five hollow concentric spheres, with spaces between each, an atmosphere surrounding each; and habitable as well upon the concave as the convex surface. Each of these spheres are widely open at their poles. . . . Although the particular location of the places where the verges of the polar openings are believed to exist, may not have been ascertained with absolute certainty, yet they are believed to be nearly correct; their localities have been ascertained from appearances that exist in those regions; such as a belt or zone surrounding the globe where trees and other vegetation (except moss) do not grow; the tides of the ocean flowing in different directions, and appearing to meet; the existence of volcanoes; the *ground swells* in the sea being more frequent; the Aurora Borealis appearing to the southward. . . ."

In commenting upon this modest and restrained effort, the *Ohio Archaeological and Historical Quarterly* noted: "The author undertakes to set forth the theory without asserting its truth, disclaiming scientific ability to pass upon it, inviting criticism, but requesting any who assert its fallacy to furnish some other rational and satisfactory explanation of the facts advanced."

Another valuable disciple was the Union College student, P. Clark, who during 1826 and 1827 jotted notes on Symmes's speeches, but who was of too conservative a cast to publish them at once. As a matter of fact, it was not until 1873 that Clark paid belated tribute to his idol with an article in the *Atlantic Monthly* entitled "The Symmes Theory of the Earth." So constant was his faith, however, that even the passage of almost a half century (during which time many of Symmes's contentions had been discredited) had not dulled his defense:

"Since this theory was promulgated by its author, enough has come to light to prove that he was correct in his views of the existence of a warmer climate at the north, and of an open polar sea. And it is believed that, if his theory had been fully made public long ago, much hardship, suffering, and expense would or might have been avoided in the futile attempts to find a passage through the bleak and desolate regions around Baffin's Bay. That Behring's Straits offer the best route into the arctic regions admits of little or no doubt, and an expedition for this purpose from the Pacific coast is well worth the consideration of the government."

But if Symmes had his small coterie of partisans, as well as his larger following of adherents merely curious to see his eccentricity put to test, he also had his detractors. In fact and in fiction his ideas were disparaged and his person ridiculed. During 1820 the publishing house of J. Seymour, New York, issued a novel entitled *Symzonia; a Voyage of Discovery*, by Captain Adam Seaborn, obviously a pseudonym. This entertaining work of science fiction was a burlesque of Symmes, his theory, and his projected expedition. In the narrative, the author-narrator, inspired by Symmes, outfits an expedition to the polar regions, supposedly to hunt seal. Nearing the location of the "icy hoop" that leads into the interior world, the crew find the bones of a monster on an island. Before the crew can mutiny, the Captain allows his steamship to be drawn rapidly south by powerful currents. Soon they are inside the earth. A new continent stretches before them. The Captain names it Symzonia. In its metropolis the Captain and crew find an albino race of human beings, attired in snow-white garments and speaking a musical language. Symzonia, lit by two suns and two moons, is a socialist utopia. The albino people, ruled by a Best Man, possess prosperity, gold, and advanced inventions, such as dirigibles armed with flame throwers that spew burning gas for a half mile and more. Eager to maintain their utopia, the Symzonians force the Captain and his crew to return to the more avaricious outer world.

Most attacks on Symmes were more direct. In 1827 the *American Quarterly Review* dissected the hollow earth theory. "Captain Symmes not only believes the earth to be hollow," said the periodical, "but that it is inhabited on the inner surface. If it be so, the inhabitants must be placed in a most unstable position." The magazine deduced that men dwelling 150 miles inside the earth could weigh only eight ounces each on the average. Of course, "it would be one of the advantages of these inner men, that they might fly through the air, with great ease, by the aid of a lady's fan." Not only were Symmes's ideas unscientific, but his efforts to finance an expedition—"travelling, from place to place, and, like a second Peter the Hermit, zealously preaching up a crusade to this Holy Land"—were absurdity itself. "We are gravely told, that, to judge by the size of the seals, and bears . . . which come from the interior of the globe, it must be better suited for animal life than the portion which has fallen to our lot, so that by emigrating to this land of promise, we may probably be relieved from many of the evils to which mankind are subjected here above. . . . However, we fear that this desirable change can never be effected, and that we must be content to finish the journey of life, in the less comfortable condition of outside passengers." In conclusion, though Symmes "may be a gallant soldier and an estimable man," he remains a "very unsound philosopher."

Neither this type of criticism nor his repudiation by Congress disheartened Symmes. Determined as ever to explore the interior, he appeared as principal speaker at a benefit rally staged in the Cincinnati Theatre in Cincinnati during 1824. Though the rally was well attended, the curiosity of his audience did not open its pocketbooks. For lack of funds the expedition was deferred. But in 1825 Symmes learned that the Russian government, so receptive to his original circular, was preparing an expedition to northeastern Siberia. Only three years before, another expedition, under a Russian navy captain named Fabian Bellingshausen, had made the first discoveries of land south of the Antarctic Circle, and this had now encouraged the Tsar to support an exploration of the

Arctic. Because the destination of the new Russian expedition sounded reasonably close to his northern "verge," Symmes hastened to write its powerful leader, Count Romanozov, offering his services. The Russians, still impressed by his knowledge of the polar wastes, accepted his offer. Though excited by the high position offered him, Symmes was forced to withdraw at the eleventh hour. He did not have funds to cover his fare to St. Petersburg.

He would never have a similar opportunity to prove his theory, though it is thought that one of his disciples succeeded in making the grand effort months after Symmes's death. This disciple, Jeremiah N. Reynolds, a graduate of Ohio University, had been attracted to Symmes's theory during the earlier lectures. In 1828, when Symmes filled lecture engagements in Pennsylvania, New York, Massachusetts, Maine, and Canada, Reynolds accompanied him on part of the tour. Some time before they reached Canada, Reynolds took off on his own, paraphrased his teacher's lectures in many public appearances, and quickly raised a considerable sum of money. Then he went to Washington, and, through the good offices of Secretary of the Navy Samuel L. Southard, convinced President John Quincy Adams that a ship should be requisitioned to survey the South Pole and investigate Symmes's ideas. Adams apparently approved the plan, but before it could be executed, he was out of the White House and Andrew Jackson was in. Jackson considered the project nonsense and canceled it.

At this dark moment a wealthy New York physician named Watson, his mind filled with concentric circles, offered private financing. In October 1829 the brig *Annawan*, with Captain N. B. Palmer in charge, and the brig *Seraph*, under the command of Captain B. Pendleton, sailed out of New York harbor for the South Pole. Jeremiah N. Reynolds, aboard the *Annawan* as senior scientist, was the lone Symzonian to accompany the expedition. While the publicized purpose of the expedition was discovery, the announcements failed to mention what the explorers expected to discover. John W. Peck, who investigated the effort eighty years later, had no doubts: "It seems to me probable that the sending out of the private south polar exploring expedition of the 'Seraph and Annawan' was for the purpose of testing Symmes' theory—either incidentally or primarily."

There were eventually numerous reports on the findings and adventures of the expedition, no two of them agreeing. According to the most popular account, the vessels made a landing at latitude 82 degrees south, but the foot party lost its way and was rescued from starvation in the nick of time. A rebellious crew then forced the ships to head for home, mutinied off Chile, put Reynolds ashore, and went on to seek more profitable discoveries in piracy. Less spectacular accounts omit the suffering landing-party, though they mention a minor rebellion off Chile which was quickly suppressed. One account goes so far as to say that the J. N. Reynolds aboard the *Annawan* was not Symmes's follower, Jeremiah N., but a more conservative scientist named John N. All histories of the unlucky expedition agree on one point: the southern opening was not found, and the earth's interior was not visited.

Symmes was not to witness this fiasco. During his strenuous lecture tour of Canada in the winter of 1828, he had fallen seriously ill. He returned to the comforts of Hamilton, Ohio, where he died on May 29, 1829, aged forty-nine, and was buried with full military honors. His theory had greater longevity.

Four years after his passing, the twenty-four-year-old Edgar Allan Poe based his short story "Ms. Found in a Bottle" on Symmes's theory. In this purportedly unfinished piece the hero is aboard a 400-ton vessel drawn toward the South Pole by strong currents, entering a whirlpool, and sinking into the earth's interior—"we are plunging madly within the grasp of the whirlpool—and amid a roaring, and bellowing, and thundering of ocean and tempest, the ship is quivering—oh God! and—going down!"—at the narrative's conclusion. In "The

Unparalleled Adventure of One Hans Pfall" Poe described the North Pole as "becoming *not a little concave*," and in the "Narrative of A. Gordon Pym" he related the story of a voyage that was to have its destination in Symmes's inner world.

In 1864 Jules Verne published his widely read novel, *Journey to the Center of the Earth*, which owed its inspiration to the theory of Sir John Leslie and the ideas advanced by Symmes. Instead of entering an opening at one of the poles, Verne's Professor Von Hardwigg, his nephew, and a native guide lower themselves into the interior through the crater of an extinct volcano in Iceland known as Sneffels. Following a descending tunnel, they continue one hundred miles beneath the earth's crust. Soon they stumble upon the mammoth cavern that is the inner world. There are clouds above and there is a sea below. Constructing a raft, they sail this sea, observing a subterranean world still in an earlier stage of evolution. There are mushrooms towering forty feet; there is a boiling volcanic island; there are skeletons of early man; there is an ugly fight to the death between a giant, lizardlike plesiosaurus and an aquatic ichthyosaurus. In an effort to leave the inner world, the fictional children of Symmes attempt to use dynamite to clear a tunnel. The explosion starts an earthquake, and they are erupted to freedom through the crater of the volcano Stromboli in Italy.

In 1868 Professor W. F. Lyons brought out his book *A Hollow Globe*, which supported Symmes's theory of an interior earth, but did not mention Symmes by name. In 1878 one of Symmes's ten children, Americus Vespucius Symmes, sought to rectify this omission. Americus's filial tribute consisted of a collection of his father's writings, notes, and clippings, all gathered between hard covers under the title *The Symmes Theory of Concentric Spheres, Demonstrating that the Earth Is Hollow, Habitable Within, and Widely Open About the Poles*, and published by Bradley and Gilbert, of Louisville. Though Americus credited full authorship to his father, and listed himself only as an editor, he did make one creative contribution to the volume. Symmes had contended that there was a civilization underground. Americus could not resist elaborating. This civilization, he said, was none other than that of the Ten Lost Tribes of Israel, who had been located by others in areas as diverse as Mexico and Atlantis. As to the general content of the book, Americus remained confident. "Reason, common sense, and all the analogies in the natural universe," he concluded, "conspire to support and establish the theory."

In 1920 appeared a book, an enlargement of an earlier publication, entitled *Journey to the Earth's Interior* by Marshall B. Gardner, the employee of a corset company in Illinois. Though in his privately printed treatise Gardner spurned Symmes's inner planets, dismissed the master's researches as superficial, and regarded his predecessor as merely a "crank," he was not averse to adopting most of Symmes's original ideas. Gardner agreed that the earth could be entered at either pole, where there were openings 1,400 miles in width. Inside, beneath the 800-mile earth crust, but brilliantly illuminated by a single miniature sun, would be found a hollow world from which the Eskimos had ascended to the outer surface.

Beyond these literary monuments to his memory, only two tangible evidences of Symmes's eccentricity remained. One was a small wooden globe that Symmes had employed in his lectures. This eventually found its way into the Academy of Natural Sciences in Philadelphia. The other was a stone memorial erected by his son Americus in Hamilton, Ohio. The memorial, featuring a replica of Symmes's hollow world, bore inscriptions on two sides. On one side was engraved a story of his heroism: "John Cleves Symmes joined the Army of the U.S. as an Ensign in the year 1802. He afterward rose to the rank of Captain and performed daring feats of Bravery in the Battles of Lundy's Lane and Sortie from Fort Erie." On the opposite side was engraved a recognition of his genius: "Capt. John Cleves Symmes was a Philosopher, and the originator of 'Symmes Theory of Concentric Spheres and Polar voids.' He contended that the Earth was hollow and habitable within."

The tribute he most desired—an expedition into the earth's interior—he would never receive. For less than a century after his death men had already learned firsthand that Symmes's Hole existed neither in the Arctic nor in the Antarctic. If Peary's discovery of the North Pole by land in 1909 had not been evidence enough, then certainly the flights made by Admiral Richard E. Byrd over the North Pole in 1926 and the South Pole in 1929 would have severely taxed Symmes's faith. As a matter of fact, soon enough, men would know all they needed to know of the inner world without the use of polar openings. Instead of attempting physical exploration, the engineers and geologists of a new era would sink man-made wells deeper into the ground than the Grand Canyon—an oil well in Wyoming would penetrate 20,000 feet below the surface, and another in California would reach a depth of over 21,000 feet—and through these drillings, as well as by analysis of radioactive rock, heat measurements in mines, and earthquake waves, they would learn much about the unseen world below. Though their borings and instruments would not take geophysicists more than one quarter of one per cent of the distance toward the earth's center, they would know with some assurance that beneath the earth's thin granite crust, only thirty-seven miles thick, lay a zone of rock, then one of iron, and then the great core itself, the size of Mars, composed of iron and nickel in a molten, plastic stage.

In this hot, dense interior, Symmes would have found little room for his five concentric spheres, little comfort for his underworld citizenry. Fortunately he had died before the final disillusionment—or he might not have rested so easily in his hollow and happier earth.

VIII

The Editor Who Was a Common Scold

"*. . . let all pious Generals, Colonels and Commanders of our army and navy who make war upon old women beware.*"

ANNE ROYALL

Between the years 1825 and 1829 the president of the United States was John Quincy Adams, whose father had been a chief executive before him. Adams was a lonely introvert, learned, austere, honest, and of formal habits—except for one. It was his custom, during his single term, to rise before dawn, usually between four o'clock and six o'clock, dress, surreptitiously leave the White House, cross the expanse of front lawn that looked out upon the Potomac River, step behind a growth of shrubbery, remove his clothes, and then, quite naked, step into the water for a relaxing swim. Sometimes he would paddle about for an hour, then crawl up to the bank to dry himself with napkins, slowly dress again, and finally return to the White House fully refreshed and ready for his breakfast, his Bible, and his governmental chores.

We do not know when these presidential swims ceased to be relaxing, but we do know when they ceased to be private. They became a spectator sport on that early summer morning, toward the end of the President's term, when he emerged from the Potomac in his usual state of undress to find a rotund, unkempt, gray-haired woman casually seated on his underwear, shirt, and breeches. Startled, the President hastily retreated into the river, halting only when the water reached his chin.

When he found his wits he angrily ordered the lady to leave at once. In a rasping voice she replied that she had hunted down the President so that she might interview him about the controversy surrounding the Bank of the United States, and that she intended to remain until he made a statement. It must be understood that this was an age when the President did not give interviews to reporters or hold press conferences, and that to grant this request John Quincy Adams had to break a precedent of long standing. Yet, he knew that if he did not break precedent, he might remain in the Potomac for the remainder of his administration—for he knew the woman on the bank, and knew that if he was the immovable object, she was the irresistible force.

Her name was Anne Newport Royall. Raised on the Pennsylvania frontier, married to a wealthy and scholarly veteran of the Revolution, she had been deprived of her rightful inheritance and had come to Washington to obtain a widow's pension. Adams had first met and befriended her the year before he was elected to the presidency, while he was still Monroe's secretary of State. He had tolerated her obvious eccentricity, ignored her Masonic fanaticism, and promised to assist her in collecting the pension. He had also introduced her to his English-born wife, and had subscribed in advance to a book of travel she was planning to write. The book had since become five books, and her last three volumes, entitled *The Black Book, or a Continuation of Travels in the United States*, had shocked, irritated, and amused Washington and readers throughout the nation.

While other lady writers dipped their quills in gentility, Anne Royall more often dipped hers in venom. She, who would meet all fourteen presidents from Washington to Pierce, had already interviewed President Adams's eighty-nine-year-old father. "When I mentioned his son, the present President and Mrs. A the tear glittered in his eye; he attempted to reply but was overcome by emotion. Finding the subject too tender I dropped it as quickly as possible." She was less tender with other public figures. She found John Randolph of Roanoke pompous but gentlemanly. "He is said to be immensely rich but not charitable." A brigadier general, who was anti-Mason, was ridiculous: "He is in height not quite so tall as the Puppy-skin Parson, about five feet, I should think, and about the size of a full-grown raccoon, which he resembles in phiz." A New Haven attorney who ejected her from his office deserved only ridicule. "He generally wears a blue coat, short breeches and long boots; his body is large, his legs spindling; he wears powder in his hair; his face resembles a full moon in shape, and is as red as a fiery furnace, the effect of drinking pure water, no doubt."

Anne Royall was as frank and harsh in discussing the municipalities that she visited, the sectional customs that she observed, and the national issues that she heard debated. In the pages of *The Black Book* she made clear her distaste for the Bank of the United States. The bank, a powerful monopoly capitalized at $35,000,000, controlled the lion's share of government deposits. Its president, the socially eminent Nicholas Biddle, of Philadelphia, had once remarked: "As to mere power, I have been for years in the daily exercise of more personal authority than any President." Upon meeting Anne Royall in person after she had castigated him in print, Biddle warned her with a smile: "Ah, Mrs. Royall, I will have you tried for your life for killing my President."

To the relief of a majority of the population, the bank's charter was to expire in 1836. However, there was a rumor that Biddle might try to force the Congress and President Adams to forestall this expiration by granting a new fifteen-year monopoly. It was to clarify this burning question for a forthcoming book that Mrs. Royall, tugging at her worn shawl and waving her green umbrella, had stormed the White House in an effort to see President Adams. He had refused to admit her. Persistent as an angry bee, Mrs. Royall investigated the President's routine, learned of the morning swims, and soon managed to secrete herself on the White House grounds. When her prey was in the water she made her way to the riverbank and planted herself upon his clothes.

As the President impatiently remained immersed in the Potomac, Anne Royall shrilly reiterated her demand for an interview. Wearily, one may be sure, the President gave indication that he would co-operate. Mrs. Royall then asked him several pointed questions about the Bank of the United States. As she was a rabid Jacksonian who wanted the charter revoked, her questions were doubtless irritating. Nevertheless, the President answered them directly and fully. When the interview was done, Mrs. Royall rose, graciously thanked him, and triumphantly hobbled away. And Adams, having dispensed with the first executive press conference in American history, was free at last to wade out of the water and resume the dignity of full attire.

When someone at a later date asked Adams what he made of the remarkable Mrs. Royall, he ruefully replied: "Sir, she is a virago errant in enchanted armor." No man ever characterized her better.

She was born Anne Newport near Baltimore, Maryland, on June 11, 1769. Her father, William Newport, was an offspring of the aristocratic Calvert family, but illegitimate and an embarrassment. He was given the name Newport instead of Calvert, awarded a small annuity, and kept at a distance from the manor house. He married a farm girl, and, mindful of his noble ancestry, named the first of his two daughters after Queen Anne of England. When the colonies seethed with revolt, and men took sides, Newport refused to be linked with the patriotic rabble. He announced himself a Tory sympathetic to the British crown and worked for the Tory cause. When his neighbors made threats, and the Calverts ended his annuity by fleeing to England, Newport realized that Maryland had become uncomfortable.

In 1772, when Anne was three years old, Newport took his family for a brief stay with his wife's relatives in Virginia, and then joined a wagon train heading for the wilderness of Pennsylvania. In Westmoreland County, in the vicinity of present-day Pittsburgh, he built a narrow cabin, furnished it with a large bed and four crude stools, and tilled a small farm. He encouraged his wife to practice herb healing on the colonists, and he taught Anne the rudiments of reading by the phonetic method. On some unrecorded date Newport lost his life, probably in an Indian massacre. His widow and two daughters hastily moved to the safety of a fortified settlement known as Hannastown. Anne was twelve years old when her mother, desperately in need of support, married her second husband, a man named Butler. For Anne, the products of this new union were a measure of security and a half brother named James.

The Indians, attempting to stem the tide of white migration, were on the warpath. Life became a succession of alarms. So frequent were the hit and run attacks that eventually they became a bore. When redskins approached one cabin outside the fort, as Anne recalled later, the housewife refused to take flight until she had dusted the furniture. "I can't go off and leave such a looking house," she said. But the party of savages that advanced on the thirty to forty cabins of Hannastown on July 13, 1782, was larger and more formidable than usual. Anne and her family fled to the protection of one of the three nearby forts. A large crowd of guests, including the settlement founder's family, attending a wedding celebration at Miller's Station in the vicinity, did not flee. The Indians fell upon them, slaughtered the men, took sixty women and children captive, put all of Hannastown to the torch, and left.

Despite the horror of this attack, most of the survivors remained in the area. Anne stayed on only three years more. By 1785, when she was sixteen, her stepfather had died, her younger sister had married, and she, her half brother, and her mother were again destitute. Mrs. Butler decided to leave the frontier and seek help from relations in Virginia. Upon arriving in Staunton, Virginia, Mrs. Butler fell ill of blood poisoning. She was advised to visit the nearby health resort at Old Sweet Springs, located in a valley of Monroe County. Though the cure worked, it did not replenish the family purse. Mrs. Butler would have been reduced to beggary had not the richest man in the county, Captain William Royall, heard of her lot. He immediately hired her as "his washwoman and menial," an eccentricity frowned upon by his fellow landowners, who felt that such tasks assigned to a white woman instead of a slave would cause general loss of face. In hiring Mrs. Butler, Captain Royall also undertook the responsibility of providing for her children. And thus it was, in the most unashamedly romantic tradition, that Anne entered the great house on the slope of Sweet Springs Mountain and first laid eyes upon her future husband.

Captain Royall had served America well during the revolution. In 1777, at the age of twenty-seven, he had personally raised and financed Virginia's first company of militia. He claimed that Patrick Henry had served under him. He and his militia raided a ship on which the British Governor, Lord Dunmore, guarded a vast store of ammunition. He spent, Anne later stated, "a fortune in the war. He was rich and generous. He brought the troops from Virginia and North Carolina, after Gates' defeat, at his own expense to Guilford Courthouse, N.C. Entitled to ten rations a day, he never drew a dollar. He was Judge-Advocate to the Brigade, Judge-Advocate to the regiment." He was an aide to Lafayette, and belonged to the same Masonic Lodge as his friend George Washington. He left the Army not a general, as Anne liked to think, but a captain, and in lieu of back salary accepted the acreage at Sweet Springs Mountain.

Because he was the wealthiest landowner in the area, his eccentricities were tolerated. He released slaves and would not buy new ones. He allowed his livestock to run wild. He would not permit "unnatural" cattle such as geldings and steers in his herds. He was obsessed with the virtues of Freemasonry. He was devoted to Thomas Paine and Voltaire, and his enormous library, filled with books by democratic authors and French philosophers, was generally regarded as radical. He was aristocratic and bookish, yet friendly and kind. He was uninterested in his many property holdings, and he disliked his many relatives. He lived the life of a puttering, scholarly recluse until he became interested in Anne.

For twelve years Anne lived under the Captain's keen eye, first as a somewhat spindly, energetic assistant to her mother in household chores, then as a slender, darkly attractive assistant to her employer in managing minor affairs of his estate, and finally, as her master's pretty and maturing protégée. After the passage of a few years Captain Royall learned, to his utter astonishment, that Anne possessed an intelligence beyond what he had expected in a menial. She wanted to become as educated as he was himself. She hungered to know what he knew. Only her semiliteracy held her back. The Captain's astonishment turned to delight. He made Anne his project and his Galatea. After teaching her to read and to write, he fed her book after book off his shelves, all of Jefferson, all of Voltaire, all of Masonic history. He poured his entire library into her until, as one contemporary reported, "she became the most learned woman in all the county." For almost twelve years he molded her in his image. Then he fell in love with his creation.

What happened next happened with almost Biblical simplicity. It was a warm autumn day in 1797. Anne was working in the fields. "The dogwood was in bloom," she remembered, "and I was out sowing seeds when the messenger came with a saddle-horse for me to go and get married." It was proposal, betrothal, and wedding all in one afternoon. When Anne returned to the house, the Reverend William Martin and the Captain were waiting. The marriage took place at once. The certificate gave the date as November 18, 1797.

The marriage lasted sixteen years. Despite the disparity in their ages—on their wedding day Royall was forty-seven years old, Anne twenty-eight—and despite the Captain's reticence about declaring his love, their union was a happy one. Though Royall's neighbors frowned upon this elevation of serving wench to mistress of the manor, and though Royall's relatives were shocked to see their inheritance diverted to a comparative stranger, Royall was contented with his choice of mate. By conventional standards the marriage may have seemed bleak. It produced no children, no gay parties, no exciting trips, and, from all indications, no moments of high passion. But there was always, as Anne often professed, the deeply satisfying and peaceful pleasure of intellectual affinity.

Actually Anne's relationship to the husband whom she worshipped remained that of student to mentor. Persistently he instructed her in the precepts of Voltaire and the values of Freemasonry. Month after month, Anne and her Captain undertook challenging reading projects and discussed what they had read. Together, on foot and on horseback, they managed the estate. Occasionally, when there was a holiday, Royall permitted relaxation from the routine and encouraged Anne to direct festivities in the area. At such times, he presented her with gifts of valuable property holdings. In 1813, when he was sixty-three and Anne forty-four, Captain Royall took to his bed with a painful illness. After long weeks of suffering, he died. With him to the grave went the last peace and security Anne was to know.

Yet in the first days of widowhood it appeared that Anne would be independently wealthy. Her husband's last will and testament, written five years before, gave her every protection against want. "In the name of God, AMEN. I, William Royall, of Monroe County, do make and ordain this, my last Will and Testament in manner and form following viz: I give unto my wife, Ann, the use of all my Estate, both Real and Personal, (except one tract of land) during her widowhood. . . ." Excepting the one tract of land left to a niece, nothing was bequeathed to Royall's large and indignant clan of relatives. Everything belonged to Anne as long as she did not marry again.

Immediately Royall's relatives banded together to fight this unequal distribution of his wealth. Led by one of Royall's nephews, William R. Roane, an attorney who needed the money—and was "a great fool," said Anne—they filed suit to have the will declared invalid. Their charges were threefold: that Anne had never legally married Royall, that Anne had influenced him to sign the will while he was senile, that Anne had entertained a succession of lovers, among them a young barrister with whom she frequently corresponded.

Without her husband to protect her, and with malicious slander against her on all tongues, Anne decided that she wanted to get as far away from Virginia as possible. As her estate was in the hands of the court, Anne liquidated her personal holdings to pay for her travels. She sold a house and real estate in Charlestown, both earlier gifts of her husband's, and with this money and a small allowance granted by the court, she started south accompanied by three colored slaves and a courier.

She traveled constantly and in state for six years. Except as she was disturbed by word of the interminable judicial wrangling at home, she found the inns and sights and people of Savannah, Charleston, and New Orleans relaxing and stimulating. "Hitherto, I have only learned mankind in theory," she wrote, "but I am now studying him in practice. One learns more in a day by mixing with mankind than he can in an age shut up in a closet." While she returned several times to Monroe County to give depositions in the legal marathon, she now leased a house in Huntsville, Alabama, and made it her home. There, early in 1823, she learned that the Virginia courts had handed down their final decision, and that she was disinherited. The Royall relatives had won the battle, and overnight she became penniless.

She viewed the defeat with incredulity. She could not explain it. Actually, there was an explanation. Her absence from the courts, which permitted all scandal attached to her name to go unrefuted, had helped to weigh the final judgment against her. She was fifty-four years old and as impoverished as she had been at sixteen when first she entered Royall's household as a servant. Dazed and soon depressed, she was rendered temporarily immobile. But if the mentally disturbed can rarely help themselves, Anne Royall was an exception to the rule. From some deep reservoir of character she found the strength to stir herself to action. While her next movements may have drawn her closer to eccentricity, they certainly helped her escape insanity.

Her destination was Washington, D.C. Her late husband had been a gallant veteran of the Revolution. As his widow, she deserved a pension. She would attend to her just claim in person. And along the way she would gather material for a book. For, like millions of amateurs at writing before and since, Anne had long been commended for the style of her private letters. It was encouragement enough. The pension would support her and the writing would occupy her mind. To avoid further depressive moods, she said, "I resolved to note everything during my journey worthy of remark and commit it to writing."

She began the two-week journey on horseback, then transferred to a public stagecoach. She had money for three days' food and lodgings. When this was gone she found her food in the garbage behind tavern kitchens and slept in the open. Then, remembering that her husband, a prominent Mason, had often assured her that Masons were the kindest folk on earth, she began to call upon members of the order in each community. They were indeed generous, and not one refused to provide her with funds for necessities and travel fare. In Alexandria, Virginia, again reduced to pauperism, Anne called upon M. E. Clagget, a Mason who owned the City Hotel. "At ten o'clock, one cold December night, I arrived at his house without one cent in my pocket, a single change of raiment and badly dressed. I had not a friend on earth. Mr.

Clagget took me in and from the 15th of December to the 6th of April following kept me—not in a style according to my appearance, but furnished me with an elegant parlor and bed-chamber and gave me a servant to wait on me the whole winter."

Refreshed, she resumed her journey to the capital. But first she wanted to visit Richmond, to search out evidence of her husband's war record in support of her pension claim. By the time she dragged herself into Richmond she was again destitute. Unable to ferret out Masons, she accosted ordinary citizens on the street. First she asked for loans and was refused. Then she begged for money and was ignored. Finally, she tried to soften the hardhearted with passages quoted from the Bible, again to no avail. At last she obtained some small sums, and embittered by the lack of Southern hospitality, took boat and stage for Washington.

She arrived in the capital on the morning of July 24, 1824. Too poor to rent lodgings, she selected a house at random and told her story, simply and directly, to the occupants, who were named Dorret. They sympathized with her, gave her a room and meals for six months "without fee or reward," and even supplied her with fresh garments. During this period Anne enlisted the aid of John Quincy Adams on behalf of her pension claim. But because her husband's military record had been lost in the Richmond fire, and because the legality of her marriage had once been challenged, she was faced with the double burden of proving that Royall had served his country and that their wedding had not been irregular. For years she busily gathered affidavits backing her claim. And Adams, as secretary of State, as president, and as congressman, faithfully presented her tireless petitions. With monotonous regularity they were rejected, and Anne Royall would not see a dollar of her pension until almost a quarter of a century after her first application.

Suddenly the book she had planned to write as therapy became a financial necessity. With five-dollar subscriptions collected in advance from people as diverse as John Quincy Adams and Joseph Bonaparte, she continued her researches through New England. And all the while she wrote. In 1826 the result of all this desperation and energy was issued from a press in New Haven. The book was entitled *Sketches of History, Life and Manners in the United States, by a Traveller.* Its sharp delineation of personalities and conditions encountered in her travels caused an immediate sensation. It was widely commented upon, and it sold well. The most balanced review was published in the *Boston Commercial:*

"Sometimes she lets fall more truths than the interested reader would wish to hear, and at others overwhelms her friends with a flattery still more appalling. At any rate, hit or miss, the sentiments she gives are undoubtedly her own; nor will it be denied that she has given some very good outlines of character. Her book is more amusing than any novel we have read for years."

The next year, encouraged by this reception, Anne made her first—and, happily, her last—sally into fiction, a romance entitled *The Tennesseean, a Novel Founded on Facts.* It related the painful adventures of one Burlington, a Princeton student who was forced to make his own way after his wealthy parent had been defrauded in business. Burlington attempted merchandising in Nashville, then chased riches in Mexico, at last fell into the hands of brigands and pirates, and finally escaped to freedom—poorer, but richer in having won a Spanish bride. The novel was not a success, and it might have ended Anne's creative career at once had not a dramatic political occurrence brought her unexpected literary patronage.

The setting for the dramatic political occurrence was Batavia, New York, where resided in 1826 a dissolute bricklayer and Royal Arch Mason named William Morgan. When citizens of the community decided to form a Grand Lodge, they excluded Morgan because of his reputation as a drunkard. In angry retaliation, Morgan composed a book, *Illustrations of Masonry*, which was intended to expose the secret ritual of the order. When he prevailed upon a local editor to publish it, the Masons of Batavia became worried. Somehow they contrived to have Morgan arrested on charges of bad debts and petty theft and removed to the Canandaigua jail. On the night of September 11, 1826, two men appeared at the jail, announced that they were Morgan's friends and offered to bail him out. Only the jailer's wife was on hand. The offer seemed reasonable, and she complied. But the moment Morgan was led outside she heard him shout: "Murder!" She rushed to the door in time to see Morgan in the hands of four abductors, struggling to free himself. Shoved into a carriage, he was spirited away. He was never seen or heard of again.

News of the incident spread across the land, and with it the rumor that Morgan had been murdered and dumped into the Niagara River or strapped to a canoe and sent over the falls. Even as those suspicious of Freemasonry began to agitate, Governor De Witt Clinton of New York, himself a Mason of note, sought to smother the hysteria by offering a reward of $1,500 for information leading to the arrest of the kidnappers. The offer of reward came too late. Already opportunistic politicians, led by Thaddeus Stevens, had seized upon the affair and kept hatred burning. The Masonic Grand Lodge, roared Stevens, was "a chartered iniquity, within whose jaws are crushed the bones of immortal men, and whose mouth is continually reeking with human blood."

The agitation might have died of natural causes—Morgan's widow had gone off to become one of Joseph Smith's multiple Mormon wives—had not an anti-Mason political party, dedicated to suppressing the order, come into being. At last the Masons realized the danger and rallied to save their discredited order. It was then that their leaders remembered Anne Royall. She had long been one of their staunchest supporters. Her first book had proved that her pen was a rapier. And excepting one girl who had become a first-degree Mason at Newmarket, Ireland, in 1713 (after having overheard the ritual in her father's house), no woman was better informed as to the purposes of the order. Why not actively enlist her in the service of Freemasonry?

In 1827 the Masons made their bargains with Anne. They would finance an immediate tour of Pennsylvania, New York, and all of New England. She would be at liberty to research her books—and write as she pleased, though a good word for the order would not be amiss—if at the same time she would propagandize for the Masonic cause. Anne was satisfied. This unexpected backing from men she admired helped her to visit, during the next three years, almost every section of the United States and to produce four books in nine volumes that would make her name a national scandal and her person a national curiosity.

In pursuit of her research Anne was never unmindful of her benefactors. Wherever she went she crusaded for the cause of Freemasonry. Sometimes she met impatience. In Burlington, Vermont, where anti-Masonic sentiment was feverish, she cornered a shopkeeper named Hecock and chastised him for his intolerance. Hecock, a man of few words, did not bother to debate the issues. He merely reached out, picked Anne off the floor, and heaved her down a long flight of stairs to the street below. More than her pride was injured. She repaired a fractured leg herself, and for several years walked with a limp.

But it was in her writings that she repaid the Masons for value received. "Was not General Washington a good man?" she asked in her books. "He was a Mason. Was not Dr. Franklin a good man? He was a Mason. Was not De Witt Clinton a good man? He was a Mason. These are enough. Now all of these are not only the best, but the greatest men in the world." The anti-Masons "might as well attempt to pluck the sun and moon out of the heavens, as to destroy Masonry—old as the deluge. And, to give my opinion of it in a few words,—if it were not for Masonry the world would become a herd of savages." As for the martyred Morgan, the story of his violent death was only "a vile speculation to make money, and not only to make money, but further designed as a political engine."

If she served the Masons well in her relentless travels, she served her reading public better. Despite the repetition of her personal prejudices and injuries that marred her objectivity, the three volumes of *The Black Book*, the two volumes of *Pennsylvania*, the *Letters from Alabama*, and the three volumes of *A Southern Tour* gave a more accurate representation of the American scene than was to be produced by the equally mobile Mrs. Trollope. On foot and on horseback, by stage and by water, Anne ranged the primitive land from Delaware to Missouri and from Illinois to Louisiana. She wrote precisely what she saw, which was almost everything.

In Pennsylvania she liked the smoke of Pittsburgh, but thought Philadelphia "a den of British Tories, domestic traitors, missionaries and Sunday Schoolism." In South Carolina she regarded Charleston as "the receptacle for the refuse of all nations on earth—the only reputable people there are the Jews." In Maryland she saw Baltimore as "illiterate, proud and ignorant." In Virginia she found that the "roads were as bad as its schools." In North Carolina the ladies took snuff, and in the District of Columbia they did not know how to dress. In Louisiana there was true graciousness, but this very graciousness might lead to disaster. "Their slaves, in the end, instead of being a benefit, has proved a very serious injury. . . . They have secured nothing to their children but poverty, whilst they have reared those children up, not to industry, but to high notions."

Her curiosity was infinite. She tried everything once. She visited the lunatics in a Maine asylum. She smoked a peace pipe with the Cherokee Indians. She boarded a steamer in Virginia to examine the boilers. She forded a river that George Washington had once crossed. She searched for Jefferson relics at Monticello. She stayed at a female seminary in Pennsylvania, and approved, and frequented a barroom in the same state, and disapproved. "There is too much whiskey everywhere," she decided.

Relentlessly she hunted down the celebrated. She interviewed Governor Clinton of New York, found him corpulent and strongly silent, yet "a man of great size, great soul, great mind and a great heart." She hiked a great distance to meet Dolly Madison, and was delighted when Dolly polished her dusty shoes. "Her face is not handsome nor does it ever appear to have been so. It is suffused with a slight tinge of red and is rather wide in the middle. But her power to please —the irresistible grace of her every movement—sheds such a charm over all she says and does that it is impossible not to admire her."

Besides anti-Masons, only one national group incurred her constant displeasure. She despised all Evangelicals, not only the clergymen who preached the Calvinistic faith, but also their followers. In print she referred to male members of the church as Hallelujah Holdforths, and she called their women Miss Dismals. She accused their missionaries of contaminating the Indians, their lobbyists of trying to control the federal government.

Anne's books, at least her earliest books, were well circulated. Her invective was admired and feared, and for a brief period she exulted in a new sense of power. But her persistent attacks on Evangelicalism brought her powerful enemies. They were determined to silence her, and in 1829, when they thought they had their ammunition, they struck. In the Court of the District of Columbia, a unique complaint was filed against her. According to Anne, "there were three counts in the indictment: 1. A public nuisance. 2. A common brawler. 3. A common scold. The first two charges were dismissed. The third was sustained."

The actual charges against Anne Royall had been instigated by members of a Presbyterian congregation that met regularly in an engine house near her dwelling. Their peddling of tracts and their singing of hymns irritated Anne. When youngsters of the congregation were encouraged to stone her residence, and when the church's most prominent member, John Coyle, ostentatiously prayed for her conversion under her window, she became furious. She was especially furious, she said, because this same John Coyle had given her maid a bastard child. At once Anne let the congregation and the entire neighborhood know what she thought of them. Publicly she berated Coyle, or Holy Willie, as she nicknamed him, for being "a damned old bald-headed son of a bitch." She called a friend of his Simon Sulphur, and yet another male member of the church Love Lady, because she vowed that he had once been observed in Capital Park trying to convert a pretty colored girl while both were "in a state of nature." The Presbyterians had had enough. They consulted an attorney. He consulted his legal sources, and he came up with something that they might call her. So they called her a Common Scold, had her arrested, and brought her to trial.

After one delay on technical grounds, Anne was arraigned before the three judges of the Circuit Court in May 1829. There was wide interest in the trial because the charge of being a scold, a hang-over from early English law, had never before been tried in America, and because the punishment involved tying the accused to a ducking stool and dousing her in a body of water. The case of the United States versus Royall was played before a packed and noisy courtroom. The prosecution presented twelve witnesses, among them Coyle and Henry Watterson, the chief librarian of Congress (whom she had insulted in one of her books). The witnesses swore that Anne had cursed and berated them in the streets, and in general had made a nuisance of herself. Anne hotly denied the charges. She was followed to the stand by a variety of friends who vouched for her good character. The most prominent of these was Senator John Eaton, of Tennessee. As secretary of War, Eaton would gain notoriety by marrying his former mistress, Peggy O'Neale Timberlake, a lively innkeeper's daughter, in defense of whose virtue President Jackson was to fire his entire cabinet. Now on the stand in Anne Royall's behalf, Senator Eaton acquitted himself gallantly. His testimony, said Anne, "was clear and unequivocal and directly opposed to that of the prosecution." Despite this defense, the judges found Anne guilty as charged.

When the moment came to mete out punishment, the judges sent for an actual ducking stool that had been constructed in the Alexandria navy yard and held in readiness. The moment it was displayed they realized that they could not enforce so barbaric a penalty. Instead, they fined Anne ten dollars for being a scold and demanded fifty dollars' security against her committing the same crime again. The money was supplied by two friendly newspapermen, and Anne was free. In her way she had made history. She was the first woman ever found guilty of being a scold in America—and there would not be another until 1947, when three sisters in Pittsburgh were similarly tried and variously sentenced to from three to twenty-three months in jail.

The rigors of the trial and the humiliations suffered as a result of its outcome brought an end to Anne Royall's career as author. After one more trip to the South she was too exhausted to travel. Moreover, her books were being taken less seriously and their sales were on the decline. She had no choice but to make Washington her permanent home and to invest her small savings in a business. Obviously the business would have to be one in which she could make use of her only talent: the ability to observe, to express herself, and to maintain an original point of view. And so, at the age of sixty-three, Anne Royall became the publisher and editor of her own weekly newspaper.

The first issue of *Paul Pry* appeared in the streets of Washington on December 3, 1831. Its four pages carried advertising, local news, jokes, excerpts from fiction, political comment, and a vigorous editorial from the pen of the proprietor:

"Let it be understood that we are of no party. We will

neither oppose nor advocate any man for the Presidency. The welfare and happiness of our country is our politics. To promote this we shall oppose and expose all and every species of political evil, and religious frauds without fear, favor or affection. . . . As for those cannibals, the Anti-Masons . . . we shall meet them upon their own ground, that of extermination. For the rest, let all pious Generals, Colonels and Commanders of our army and navy who make war upon old women beware. Let all pious Postmasters who cheat the Government by franking pious tracts beware. Let all pious booksellers who take pious bribes beware. Let all pious young ladies who hawk pious tracts into young gentlemen's rooms beware, and let all old bachelors and old maids be married as soon as possible."

The headquarters for this journal of opinion was a small two-story brick building behind a tumble-down house in the shadow of the Capitol dome. Anne pulled the plumbing and fixtures out of the kitchen and replaced them with a decrepit and unpredictable Ramage printing press and several fonts of uneven type. Her staff consisted of a printer, two youngsters from a Catholic orphanage, a porter, and a young editorial assistant named Sarah Stack. Mrs. Stack, whom Anne called Sally, was a serious, unimaginative widow who supported five orphan children.

There was no circulation department. Anne, usually accompanied by Sally, would make the rounds of Washington, selling individual copies of the paper and soliciting subscriptions at two dollars and fifty cents a year. As the two women trudged to private residences and businesses, through the halls of the Senate and the House, and into the offices of government buildings, they made a remarkable picture. Anne, her alert face wrinkled and toothy, her voice loud and insistent, was short and dumpy in her shabby shawl and green calash dress. She would disarm potential subscribers with jokes and gossip, then excitedly waving her thickly mittened hands, would admonish them to buy her periodical. Most often harried customers would submit to enlightenment, and would either present her with one dollar as down payment against the full subscription price or merely agree to buy a copy of the paper. Then Sally, lanky, thin, and somber, would emerge from the background with her armful of papers.

Most of Washington officialdom—from congressmen to government clerks—was bullied into reading *Paul Pry*. Within a year, agents were soliciting subscriptions in every major American city. Those readers who purchased the paper but forgot to pay the balance of the subscription fee were reminded of their delinquency in print, their names and debts being detailed in the paper under the heading "Black List."

Actually, few who read *Paul Pry* did not want to read it again. In its five turbulent years of existence the journal, while not the most physically attractive newspaper in America—the pulp was cheap, the printing an eyesore, the proofing an adventure in myopia—was certainly one of the liveliest in the land. As in her books, Anne continued to assail anti-Masons, Evangelicalism, political corruption, birth control, flogging in the Navy, and the Bank of the United States. She advocated free speech, open immigration, improved labor conditions, justice to the Indians, territorial expansion, nondenominational public schools, sound money, states' rights, Andrew Jackson—and her own pension.

There were items of scandal, but they were always carefully researched and edited before publication. As Anne explained in one editorial: "We have received a shocking story of abuse toward an unprotected female by a prominent man who is a Presbyterian. But we must refuse to print it for several reasons: It came in too late. It is too personal. It bore no signature. It is against *a private man*. Public men are fair game." There were other diversions for the light-minded: excerpts from *The Pickwick Papers*, capsule biographies of well-known women, progress reports on Sally's erratic health, and execrable verse.

In 1836, when Anne was sixty-seven and *Paul Pry* in the

last year of its life, she had a fascinating visitor in the person of the youthful Phineas T. Barnum. The gaudy entrepreneur had been in show business only one year—having sponsored a wizened colored woman named Joyce Heth, who was, he claimed, 161 years old and George Washington's former nurse (she had just died and been found to be eighty years old and therefore not George Washington's former nurse)—and his great years with Tom Thumb, Jenny Lind, and Jumbo the Elephant were still ahead of him. Barnum, accused of hoax and faced with failure, was grateful for stories Anne had published in his defense. He came to pay his respects, and left to record in his diary a striking portrait of this "celebrated personage . . . the most garrulous old woman I ever saw."

According to Barnum, Anne mistook him for Congressman Claiborne of Mississippi. When his identity was straightened out, Anne explained that she had been expecting several members of the House of Representatives.

"All the congressmen call on me," she said with pride. "They do not dare do otherwise. Enemies and friends all alike, they have to come to me. And why should they not? I made them—every devil of them. You see how I look, ragged and poor, but thank God I am saucy and independent. The whole government is afraid of me, and well they may be. I know them all, from top to toe—I can fathom their rascality, through all its ins and outs, from the beginning to the end. By the way, Barnum, whom do you support for president and vice-president?"

Cheerfully Barnum replied that he thought he would vote for Martin Van Buren and Richard M. Johnson. Anne turned purple. "I have seen some fearful things in my day—some awful explosions of tempestuous passion," Barnum recalled later, "but never have I witnessed such another terrible tempest of fury as burst from Mrs. Anne Royall."

Sputtering, she fell upon him. "My God! my God! is it possible? Will you support such a monkey, such a scoundrel, such a villain, such a knave, such an enemy to his country, as

Martin Van Buren! Barnum, you are a scoundrel, a traitor, a rascal, a hypocrite! You are a spy, an electioneering fool, and I hope the next vessel you put foot on will sink with you."

Bewildered by the terrible onslaught, Barnum forced an uneasy laugh, as if to tell her she was teasing him. But she was not teasing him.

"Oh, you villain! laugh, will you? when your country is in danger! Oh, you don't believe it, but let me tell you, the conspirators know too much to let you foolish Yankees into their secret. Remember, I was once with them, and I know all about it."

"Why, Anne, you must acknowledge there are some good people in our ranks."

"No, I don't. There's not one devil of you who cares a cent for his country. You would not give a farthing to save it from destruction. See how I live! see how I work to save my country! I am at work every moment—see my house—see, I have no bed to lie on—no anything—and then *you* tell about loving your country! Oh, you deserve to be lynched, every devil of you!"

After a half hour more of similar harangue, through which Barnum sat benumbed, Anne finally ran out of breath and invective. Her voice reduced to a mere shout, she studied Barnum a moment, and then suddenly apologized.

"Well, Barnum," she said, "you are a good fellow, and I am really glad to see you. How sorry I am that we mentioned politics, for I am so nervous. Now, I want a real good talk with you. . . . Come, Barnum, go with me into the printing office, and there we can talk and work together."

In the printing office, where a man and a boy were at the press, a large pile of wrapped newspapers lay in the middle of the floor. Anne commanded Barnum to sit with her and help sort them. "Anne then seated herself upon the dirty floor, and as there was no chair in the room, I sat down beside her, not daring even to spread my handkerchief or in any way remove the dust, lest she should construe it into an insult." For a half hour more they assorted papers as Anne rattled on, recounting various incidents of her long life. When he could get in a word, Barnum wondered if he might sponsor her on a lecture tour through the East. She was not interested. When he left, she extracted his promise to call again. But thereafter, still shaken, he gave her a wide berth and admitted that he "never again met the eccentric old lady."

In November 1836, inexplicably, *Paul Pry*—which, said *The New England Religious Weekly*, "contains all the scum, billingsgate and filth extant"—ceased publication, only to be supplanted a month later by a more conservative weekly called *The Huntress*. This new conservatism, intended to increase circulation by a decrease in muckracking, did not extend to the treatment of anti-Masons or Evangelicals. The smaller pages did little to confine the editor's temper. Nor did her advancing years and growing infirmity mellow her opinion. When there was protest against Catholic immigration, Anne saw at once that the real threat lay in the tyranny of the overpatriotic, and she cried out against them in *The Huntress:* "A Catholic foreigner discovered America, Catholic foreigners first settled it. . . . When the colonies were about to be enslaved, foreigners rescued it. . . . At present, we verily believe, that the liberty of this country is in more danger from this native combination than from foreigners."

For more than a decade she continued to occupy herself with *The Huntress*. Circulation was small, and she barely made ends meet. Once, she wrote a three-act play, *The Cabinet: or, Large Parties in Washington*, and Joseph Jefferson's father agreed to produce it. On opening night, with tickets already sold, the show was canceled because of pressure brought to bear by church groups and anti-Masons. Though Masons came to her rescue, and gave the play one performance in their hall, it proved a financial disappointment. Above all, Anne persisted in her pension fight. When, at last, acting on an affidavit supplied by Lafayette, Congress conceded that Captain Royall had served the Revolution and that Anne had indeed been his wife, the petition was rejected because Anne had been married in 1797 and the law provided benefits only to widows who had been married before 1794. But in 1848 Congress liberalized the statute of limitations, and Anne's excruciating, twenty-four-year struggle was capped by victory. She was offered the choice of a $480 annuity for life or a total payment of $1,200. As she was seventy-nine years old, ill, and in debt, she took the lump sum of $1,200. It was a mistake. She would live six years more. When her obligations were met and a new printing press installed, she was left with three dollars.

In 1854, aged eighty-five, she was still on the job. When she wanted to interview President Pierce, she was invited to the White House. She may have reflected on how the times had changed. It was a quarter of a century since she had been obliged to trap another president in the nude to obtain her story. Pierce was friendly, and her account of the visit in *The Huntress* was kind:

"He looked stout and healthy but rather pale. His countenance used to be gay and full of vivacity when he was a Senator in Congress several years ago, but now it wears a calm and dignified composure, tinctured with a pleasing melancholy. . . . We could not refrain from dropping a tear when he spoke to us of his lady, after whose health we inquired. The sad bereavement she met with in the sudden loss of her only and beloved boy has shadowed the bright walks which surround the Presidential Mansion."

It was her last major story. On Sunday morning, October 1, 1854, she died in her sleep. "To the hour of her death," noted the *Washington Star*, "she preserved all the peculiarities of thought, temper, and manners, which at one time rendered her so famous throughout the land." She was laid to rest in the Congressional Cemetery. There was no money for a gravestone. Her total legacy amounted to thirty-one cents.

IX
The First in the East

"I wans to make my Enemys grin in time Lik A Cat over A hot pudding and goue Away and hang there heads Doun Like A Dogg. . . ."

TIMOTHY DEXTER

The year 1802 was a lusterless one in American literature. In that twelve-month period no novel or work of non-fiction gained widespread popularity or gave promise of any degree of permanence. Two years earlier, in 1800, Mason Weems, a traveling bookseller and part-time preacher nick-named the Parson, had produced a success with his *Life of George Washington; with Curious Anecdotes, Equally Honourable to Himself, and Exemplary to His Young Countrymen.* In 1809, two volumes of *A History of New York*, by Washington Irving, were printed in New York, and were given a friendly reception and attained a moderate sale. But between these years lay 1802, a reproach to Yankee creativity and a barren island for book lovers.

Yet there are people well versed in curiosa who will dispute the last, who will insist that in the year 1802 American literature had one of its finest hours. And perhaps, after all, they are right. Certainly 1802 provided a volume that may still be regarded as one of the most unusual ever published in the United States.

It was not a best seller—though its author had "thousands" of copies printed and distributed free of charge with his compliments. This distribution, as well as the curiosity of the book's content, stimulated wide interest. Public demand for the volume grew until a market price of one dollar a copy was established. Through the years that followed, there were at least eight new printings of the work.

It was not, it might be added, a book of enduring literary quality—though a century and a half later, erudite readers might find their discussions enlivened by the tome's futuristic approach, and groups of select bibliophiles might continue to chuckle over its oddity.

The first edition was brought off the presses in Salem, Massachusetts, and doled out to all takers from a vast Georgian mansion in Newburyport whose grounds were decorated with forty life-sized wooden statues of such celebrities as Horatio Nelson, Adam and Eve, George Washington, Louis XIV, and the author himself. The book measured four inches by six. Its twenty-four pages of prose were bound in soft covers. The title page was conservative enough:

A Pickle for the Knowing Ones: or Plain Truths in a Homespun Dress by Timothy Dexter, Esq . . . Salem: Printed For The Author. 1802.

It must be remarked at once that of freak books in literature there has been no end. Their quaint procession has been well documented by Holbrook Jackson and Walter Hart Blumenthal. In the two centuries before Timothy Dexter's publication, and in the years since, literature has been exhilarated often, and debased infrequently, by eccentricity in the print shop or the author's study. In France once appeared a book entitled *Nothing*, by Mathelá, which contained, appropriately, two hundred blank pages. Less amusing, as Carlyle would have it, was the appearance of the second edition of Jean Jacques Rousseau's *Social Contract*, supposedly bound with the skins of French aristocrats who had laughed at his first edition. In England, in 1634, appeared *The Feminin Monarchi, or the Histori of Bees*, by Charles Butler, all set down in phonetic spelling, and, in 1866, an edition of *Pilgrim's Progress* written and printed in Pitman's shorthand. In America the reading public was astounded, in 1835, by Francis Glass's *Washington Vita*, a biography entirely in Latin, and no less astounded five years later by the publication, in New York, of *Dentologia: A Poem on the Diseases of the Teeth. In Five Cantos*, by Solyman Brown. By 1881 the reading public hardly lifted its collective brow when the book shops advertised a science-fiction novel entitled *! ! !*, by George Hepworth. But before all these, in America at least, came *A Pickle for the Knowing Ones*, by Timothy Dexter. His assault on credulity was the first—and perhaps the very best.

When the well-read New Englander of 1802 opened his copy of *A Pickle for the Knowing Ones*, he found that the entire book was one long sentence or, rather, no sentence at all. Not a single comma, semicolon, quotation mark, apostrophe, exclamation point, or period marred its half-coherent text. Grammatically, it was without beginning or end. Thought melted into thought without stop. Like the universe, like time itself, it emerged from infinity and receded into infinity. Its organization was nonexistent. It was chaotic. Dexter literally wrote what came into his head, and what he put to paper antedated automatic writing and free-association techniques.

However, if the author ignored punctuation completely, he was lavish with capital letters. Words were capitalized throughout, even if they were the wrong words. The names of men and places were often demoted to lower case. A conglomeration of adverbs, adjectives, and verbs was elevated to upper case. Only one word was consistently capitalized—sensibly enough, the pronoun *I*. As to spelling, it might be better to draw a veil over the entire subject. Dexter's spelling was entirely by ear, by mood, by whim. Sometimes it was accomplished phonetically, more often by Divine Right.

"I Command pease and the gratest brotherly Love," said Dexter, supporting his plan for a United States of the World. He suggested that "nasions" all "be Linked to gether with that best of troue Love so as to govern all nasions on the fass of the gloub not to tiranize over them but to put them to order if any Despout shall A Rise . . ." In the jungle of Dexter's orthography the reader met strange, half-familiar creatures like "Jorge washeton," who was once George Washington, and "mr bourr," who had been better known as Aaron Burr; he came across rarely seen sites like "plimeth," which had been Plymouth and "Nouebry Port," which had resemblance to Newburyport; he saw—but not before passing a hand over his eyes—"a toue Leged Creter," which was only a two-legged creature, "A Scoyer," who was merely an "onnest" squire, and several "Rougs," who proved to be harmless rogues, all this before sitting down to partake of "Loovs & Littel fishes," which could be better digested when known to be loaves and little fish. This was the style and the form of *A Pickle for the Knowing Ones*. It might have given pause even to Jean François Champollion, conqueror of the Rosetta stone.

Timothy Dexter realized his mistake at once. A book without punctuation was hardly a book at all. He sought to correct this lapse. By some means—possibly in a second printing now lost, or in a separate pamphlet, or in a letter to the editor of the local newspaper—Dexter added one more page to his book. This page was bound in all printings after 1838. The addition, which appeared at the very end of his philosophical autobiography, secured Dexter his literary immortality. It read as follows:

> fourder mister printer the Nowing ones complane of my book the fust edition had no stops I put in A nuf here and thay may peper and solt it as they please
>
> ,,,
>
> ,,,
>
> ,,,
>
> ;;;
>
> ;;;
>
> :::

....
.............!!!!!!!!!!!!!!!!!...................
..............!!!!!!!!!!!!!.....................
................!!!!!!!!!.......................
........................!........................
,,,
............????????????????......................

With this generous offering of punctuation, Timothy Dexter anticipated the vogue of do-it-yourself in the mid-twentieth century. It was a stroke of genius, this offering to the restless and overenergized reader an opportunity for therapy, a chance to work with his hands and his wits by peppering and salting the virginal book with punctuation. Surely, too, though he could not know it, and though he had no literary pretensions, Dexter anticipated, perhaps pioneered, an entire new school of writing. Imitators and converts followed in abundance. Just thirteen years after *A Pickle for the Knowing Ones* appeared, there was published in England a two-volume work called *The Elements of Geometry* by the Reverend J. Dobson. The Reverend's hand faltered only at the end of paragraphs, when he laid down periods. Otherwise, his mathematical prose was as denuded of punctuation as Dexter's. It was not until another age—with the emergence of Knowing Ones like Gertrude Stein, James Joyce, and E. E. Cummings—that Dexter's advanced method, his lack of stops, his erratic capitalizations, his abstract approach, his stream-of-consciousness style, came into full flower and found wide acceptance.

In Dexter's own time his avant-garde effort was less appreciated. While his little book amused, even charmed, a few of the more tolerant and discriminating readers in America, its general tone provoked only irritation, especially in his own community. Those neighbors who had thought him a lunatic for earlier indiscretions were now positive of it mainly because *A Pickle for the Knowing Ones* was an egotistical, opinionated, coarse defense of Dexter, by Dexter, against all "Enemys" who were anti-Dexter.

The book opened with a flat declaration by its author of his own importance and his right to be heard. "Ime the first Lord in the younited States of A mercary Now of Newburyport it is the voise of the peopel and I cant Help it and so Let it goue Now as I must be Lord there will foller many more Lords pretty soune for it dont hurt A Cat Nor the mouse Nor the son Nor the water Nor the Eare . . ."

Before the befuddled reader could recover, the author hurriedly outlined his plan for a great "Dexters mouseum." The museum, already begun, would feature wooden replicas of the most famous figures in history—not only the author himself, but "mister pitt" and "the king of grat britton" and even "Loues the 16" of France. It would, Dexter promised, be one of the "grate Wonders of the world."

Now the book became more autobiographical. "How Did Dexter make his money ye says . . ." He told how he made it—by shipping warming pans to the West Indies, among other speculative follies. He told how much money he made. He gloated over the percentages of his profits. Next he discussed improvements that he contemplated on his house. Then he digressed on one "Bonne partey the grat," who turned out to be Bonaparte the Great. There followed a discussion of the tomb the author had built for himself, with a list of its peculiar furnishings, some invective against politicians, priests, the devil, and college men, and an indignant recital of how a lawyer once tried to beat him up. After that, there was a learned discourse on the three bridges spanning the Merrimack, some angry words on why the author had separated from his wife and come to regard her as a ghost—"I have bin in hell 35 years in this world with the gost"—and an announcement that his house would soon be for sale. There was a modest hint that the author might make a good Emperor of the United States, a reminiscence of his youth, a suggestion for the names of his pallbearers, and, for a change of pace, the inclusion of two funny stories.

LORD TIMOTHY DEXTER

engraved from life in 1805 by James Akin

What did contemporary critics, and those who followed, think of all this?

Samuel Lorenzo Knapp, who knew Dexter and became his Boswell, thought that *A Pickle for the Knowing Ones* preserved "all the *saws*, *shreds* and *patches* that ever entered the head of a 'motley fool.'" An anonymous critic for the *National Aegis* was even less kind. "For what purpose are riches given to some men," he wondered, "unless to display in more glowing colours the disgusting deformities of their Characters? . . . In his '*Pickle* for the knowing ones' he had effectually *preserved the full grown fruits* of his nonsense." After the author's death the *Newburyport Impartial Herald*, which had once praised the book, did an about-face. Dexter's "ruling passion appeared to be popularity, and one would suppose he rather chose to render his name 'infamously famous than not famous at all.' His writings stand as a monument of the truth of this remark; for those who have read his 'Pickle for the Knowing Ones,' a jumble of letters promiscuously gathered together, find it difficult to determine whether most to laugh at the consummate folly, or despise the vulgarity and profanity of the writer." Mrs. E. Vale Smith, preparing her *History of Newburyport* for publication in 1854, discussed Dexter and his book with many persons who had met him. Of the book she could only think that it was "a final effort for posthumous fame," and of the author she could only remark that his "vices were profanity, a want of veracity, and irreverence, while his execrable taste led him into such vicious displays as were calculated to have an injurious effect, especially upon the young."

But reaction was not all one-sided. In 1802 the *Newburyport Impartial Herald* had thought that Dexter's book would "be a valuable acquisition to the lovers of knowledge and polite literature." The passage of years brought others into the fold. Oliver Wendell Holmes was charmed by the "famous little book." He wrote of Dexter: "As an inventor of a new American style, he goes far beyond Mr. Whitman, who, to be sure, cares little for the dictionary . . . I am afraid that Mr. Emerson and Mr. Whitman must yield the claim of declaring American literary independence to Lord Timothy Dexter, who not only taught his countrymen that they need not go to the Herald's College to authenticate their titles of nobility, but also that they were at perfect liberty to spell just as they liked, and to write without troubling themselves about stops of any kind." In 1925 J. P. Marquand became a proselyte. "In all seriousness," he said, "this bold Dexterian effort actually possesses a style of its own, which all its faults combine to give it, a strength and characteristic vivacity that many more accomplished penmen and spellers have tried in vain to achieve. Every page, every line has an utter naturalness that is refreshing to a jaded taste."

Unfortunately, *A Pickle for the Knowing Ones* outlived its author. Few encyclopedias and biographical dictionaries remembered him. One that did called him that "Machiavellian *parvenu* and avowed toper" who became "an incomparable literary figure." Parvenu he was, and toper and literary figure, too. But he was considerably more. He dwelt in an age of much eccentricity among the great, but few great eccentrics. The earliest days of the republic were serious days. Men were strait-laced and dedicated and often humorless. There was little time or patience for the nonconformist. It surprised no one that Thomas Paine called his second book *Common Sense*. Men like John Randolph, Israel Putnam, and William Franklin were individuals in their ideas and in their habits, but they were not eccentrics. They conformed to the ways of colonial society. They went along. Timothy Dexter did not go along. He was his own planet and his own civilization. Or, more accurately, when a new nation was formed, he did not join it. If the flag of the infant republic had thirteen stars, one had surely been omitted. For Timothy Dexter was the fourteenth.

In the *New England Historical and Genealogical Register* it is recorded that "Nathan Dexter of Malden & Esther

Brintnall of Chelsea" were married in the latter part of June 1744. There had been Dexters in Malden, Massachusetts, since the first Dexter had emigrated from Ireland almost a century before. With the marriage of Nathan and Esther Dexter, the family line would remain unbroken. Nine months and two weeks after their wedding, they produced a son, Nathan, followed two years later by a second son, Timothy, and two years after that by a daughter named Esther.

Timothy Dexter's birth was auspicious—or so he always insisted. He was born on the morning of January 22, 1747, while a snowstorm raged outdoors. The constellations were so situated in the heavens on that day that young Dexter later became convinced he was "to be one grat man." Nothing is known of his father's occupation except that it brought little income. It is thought that young Dexter was exposed to a limited amount of schooling.

In May 1755, when he was eight years old, Timothy Dexter was sent to work on a farm in Malden. This move not only lightened the burden on the impoverished Dexter family, but also gave the second-born adequate board and keep as well as instruction in a means of livelihood. Timothy Dexter remained a farm laborer for six and a half years. Then, aged fourteen, eager to acquire a trade that held more promise of profit, he left the farm forever and traveled to Charleston, South Carolina, to become an apprentice leather-dresser. In "Chalston," he recalled, "I stayed Leven months at Dressin of skins for briches & glovs—then went to boston there stayed till I was free . . ."

In Boston, a bustling metropolis of 17,000 persons, Dexter resumed his apprenticeship. Leather-dressing was a popular craft in those times, and much in demand, but the work was harsh and exhausting. For seven years Dexter toiled amid the stench of hides and tannin, sleeping and living in a cramped hovel and eating his employer's leftover food, until at last his servitude was ended. His employer bestowed the traditional freedom-suit upon him, as a mark of his graduation and his maturity. The garment was, apparently, a splendid one, for Dexter always remembered it as made of "guinea Cloth" worth five shillings sterling a yard.

The moment Dexter was on his own, he disposed of the suit. He was ambitious, and he needed ready cash. He offered the suit to a Boston vendor, who disagreed with him sharply about its value. "I was angry," admitted Dexter, but in the end he sold the suit for "Eight Dolors & 20 sents." This modest sum, he was confident, would lay the foundation for his fortune.

His goal was the thriving community of Newburyport, Massachusetts. Only six years earlier Newburyport had become an incorporated town after 206 of its "water-side people" petitioned to be "set off from Newbury." By 1769 its population was upwards of 2,300. The extensive shipbuilding activity in the one-square-mile seaport, encouraged by the British, provided employment for carpenters, blacksmiths, painters, and rope-makers. Warehouses were stuffed with local farm produce, cheaply made gold-plated beads, and rum, which would be exchanged for English calico, cutlery, and sugar. The general prosperity made retail shops in the community flourish. Individual fortunes were being amassed quickly, and the Yankee inhabitants were beginning to dwell in the splendor which they had so long admired in their English betters. Here, if any, was the place for a strong young enterprising leather-dresser. In the two weeks that elapsed between the time Dexter left his apprenticeship and the time he arrived in Newburyport, his confidence grew. "I had faith by reading A book," he said. "I was to have this world's goods and be Come grate and be Amonkest grat men in the East . . ."

The forty miles from Boston to Newburyport by way of Salem and Rowley took Dexter a day or two, on foot, "with A bondel in my hand" and what remained of eight dollars and twenty cents in his pocket.

Within a year after setting foot in Newburyport he had

acquired property, a wife, a family, and a business, in the order named. Land records of the period indicate that by early 1770 he was dealing in Salem real estate, and, with a partner named Mulliken, had acquired mortgaged property in Chester. Where he obtained the capital for these transactions in so short a time, we do not know. He had little means. In referring to Dexter's first Newburyport year, when he was but twenty-three, William C. Todd wrote: "I remember a few years ago an old gentleman told me that his father was associated with Dexter, and related anecdotes of him when poor, and living in an humble way as a leather dresser in one of the poor sections of town."

Though Dexter possessed few assets beyond a trade and some mortgaged property, and though he yet displayed little business acumen, one person in the town saw a good prospect in him. This was the widow Frothingham. She had been the daughter of Deacon John Lord, of Exeter, New Hampshire, when she married a Newbury glazier named Benjamin Frothingham. In June 1769 the glazier, aged fifty-two, died. His departure, it might be noted, coincided closely with Dexter's arrival in the community. Elizabeth Frothingham, aged thirty-one, was left in "good circumstances" with her house on the Merrimack River and her four children. In May 1770, after eleven months of widowhood, Mrs. Frothingham was wedded to Timothy Dexter, nine years her junior.

In acquiring a bride, Dexter also acquired a residence. He had a place for business at last. Immediately he decorated the entrance to the house with a glove carved of wood and opened his leather-dressing shop in the basement. He produced gloves, breeches, and morocco leather, and he sold hides. Upstairs, the thrifty and industrious Mrs. Dexter took in mending and conducted a huckster's store. However, all activity in the residence was not of a commercial nature. In 1772 the Dexters had a son named Samuel, and in 1776 a daughter named Nancy.

The shot fired at Lexington in April 1775 and heard round

the world was heard by all but Timothy Dexter. When, through 1776, the Revolutionary War sparked and sputtered near and about him, Timothy Dexter was above the battle. Though the great homes of Newburyport were soon over-furnished with the loot won by hastily commissioned privateers who preyed upon British shipping, Timothy Dexter confined his ambitions and his labors to his basement shop. In April 1776 he was calmly advertising "Good Deer Sheep and Moose skins. Likewise Deer Sheep and Moose Skin Breeches, and a quantity of good Blubber."

In that same year Dexter was elected to his first and last municipal post by popular plebiscite. He was made Informer of Deer. Though still a nonentity, he may have been elevated to the august seat because of the shortage of manpower. Possibly, too, the office may have been an expression of gratefulness by fellow patriots for modest donations he had made to the town's welfare. Or, it could have been a joke perpetrated by many who already suspected that their leather-dresser had comic qualities. Certainly there was an element of irony in electing a leather-dresser, whose livelihood was won by preserving deerskins, to the task of seeing that deers kept their skins.

The elective post that Dexter held for years made few demands on his energies—and fortunately so. By the time Cornwallis had surrendered his sword to Washington at Yorktown, Dexter had saved "several thousand dollars" and was busily casting about for a speculation that might make him his fortune. He found it soon enough.

The peace that followed the successful Revolution was an uneasy one. While the thirteen states wrangled over ratification of the new constitution, their citizens suffered from a growing economic depression. In Massachusetts exports dropped 75 per cent. Not only was trade stagnant, but also the torn young government was buckling under war debts. One of the most immediate problems for the average man was the depreciation of state securities and federal currency.

It was in this monetary travail that the phrase "not worth a Continental" originated.

The legend on a federal bill gave promise of sound, solvent government: "Continental Currency. Twenty Dollars. This Bill entitles the Bearer to receive Twenty Spanish milled Dollars, or the Value thereof in Gold or Silver, according to the Resolutions of the Congress, held at Philadelphia, the 10th of May, 1775." In less than a decade this scrip was hardly worth the paper it was printed on. With inflation it required five of these Continental twenty-dollar bills to purchase a single cheap calico dress, and bales of the currency to purchase goods or property of real value. Veterans of Valley Forge and Bunker Hill had been paid off in this now almost worthless money. Ordinary citizens had patriotically invested much of their earnings in now depreciated state bonds. Inhabitants of Newburyport were among the hardest hit. Many had invested in Massachusetts securities, which rapidly lost value until they were worth only "about two shillings and sixpence on the pound."

This crisis inspired Timothy Dexter's most decisive gamble. Gathering together all the hard cash he could lay his hands upon, his savings of years and his protesting wife's assets, he began to buy up the seemingly worthless Continental currency and state securities. With good money, he bought bad. He gave one gold dollar for perhaps five or ten or twenty Continental dollars. In cash he was soon poor. In paper, and on paper, he was wealthy beyond his wildest fancies. Yet, what he had bargained for, and now possessed, was truly not worth a Continental. Why had this perspiring tanner, this frugal caretaker of six dependents, this solid and stable Informer of Deer, taken so mad a risk?

Most historians pay lip service to the judgment of Samuel Lorenzo Knapp, who had simply maintained that Dexter was a lucky fool. Knapp's knowledge of Dexter was such that few who wrote after him dared to contradict him. For Samuel Knapp knew Dexter personally. As a matter of fact, Knapp was born in Newburyport shortly before the Continental gamble. Though he had been educated at Dartmouth, had studied in France, and had practiced law in Boston, he spent much of his time in Newburyport. Once he even went to jail there for debt. It was in jail that Knapp seriously undertook a literary career. He wrote the first biography of Daniel Webster. He wrote lives of General Lafayette, De Witt Clinton, and Aaron Burr. Finally, in the very last year of his life, he put to paper the story of Timothy Dexter. His *Life of Timothy Dexter* appeared thirty years after its subject's death. In it Knapp revealed that he had spoken to Dexter frequently and that his book was based on "memoranda made many years ago." According to Knapp's memoranda, Dexter, in his currency investments, had idiotically and blindly aped the investments of others, unaware that they had been motivated by philanthropy rather than profit.

"Two benevolent gentlemen in Boston, John Hancock, governor of the commonwealth at the time, who had formerly been president of the continental congress, and Thomas Russel, the most eminent merchant then in America, to keep up the public confidence and to oblige a friend would make purchases of these securities until the amount was considerable," recorded Knapp. "This had the desired effect in some measure, and a few other purchasers were found, but hard money was so scarce that not much was done in this brokerage. Dexter, finding his great neighbors, Hancock and Russel, doing something in stocks, took all his own cash with what his wife had, and in imitation purchased likewise. He probably made better bargains than the magnates did. He bought in smaller quantities, and had better opportunities to make his purchases than they had. He felt he could live on his industry, and ventured all on the chance of these securities ever being paid."

Not until 1887 did anyone challenge Knapp's assertion that Dexter had blundered into his riches by "imitation" of "two benevolent gentlemen in Boston." In that year William C.

Todd, writing in the *New England Historical and Genealogical Register*, cast a stern eye on the "patriotism" of Hancock and Russell. He implied, though he did not state, that Hancock, Russell, and a number of other members of Congress were attempting to profiteer on inside information that the government would soon assume state debts, redeem state bonds, and stabilize wartime currency. Todd made it plain that Dexter had as much knowledge or foresight as Hancock and Russell and as much daring, in attempting to make "money out of the depreciated securities of the government and state."

"The Dexter . . . of Knapp's Life and of common belief, the fool who made his money by senseless speculations that always turned out well, is a fiction," Todd contended. "The real Dexter, with all of his folly, acquired his property as other people do—by prudence, industry and business sagacity, which gave him a fortune for that period." Todd readily admitted that Dexter was "a vain, uneducated, weak, coarse, drunken, cunning man, low in his tastes and habits, constantly striving for foolish display and attention." But he reiterated that Dexter, for all his foolishness, was possessed of a "business shrewdness, to which, and not to luck, he owed his success."

When Dexter at last possessed his huge hoarding of paper currency, he waited nervously for news that it might be redeemed at par. It was a suspenseful and painful interlude, inasmuch as Dexter was constantly scolded by his wife and chided by his neighbors for his stupidity. In this harrowing period Dexter had eyes and ears for only one name and one man. His entire future was staked on the political talents and persuasiveness of brilliant, handsome, young Alexander Hamilton, Washington's first secretary of the Treasury.

Hamilton, who championed big government, big industry, big cities, and big banks, was strongly opposed by Washington's secretary of State, Thomas Jefferson, who visualized America as a more temperate agrarian nation. Timothy Dexter's hopes rode on Hamilton's vast funding plan, which Jefferson's Southern friends disliked. Hamilton advocated a Bank of the United States to issue paper money and to keep it stable, and he wanted the $18,000,000 in bonds that had been printed and sold by the various states and the $52,000,000 worth of bonds that had been issued by the federal government to be funded at full face value. He insisted that this was a matter of honor and good business. The House of Representatives voted the measure down.

Undiscouraged by the rebuff, Hamilton met Jefferson over dinner and proposed a horse trade. If Jefferson would encourage Virginia legislators to back the assumption bill, Hamilton would find New York legislators to support the establishment of the national capital on the Potomac River, a step that Jefferson much desired. Jefferson agreed to the deal, to his subsequent regret. In a short time Hamilton's assumption bill was pushed through Congress. Hamilton's friends and colleagues, as well as speculators, made $40,000,000 profit by cashing in the securities and currency that had so recently been called trash. And overnight Timothy Dexter, of Newburyport, was a wealthy man.

His first reaction to sudden riches was a belief that they made him the equal of all other men with money, no matter what their ancestry or station. He felt that he belonged in the dazzling world of the Hancocks and Russells. It is thought that he tried to enter Boston society, but without success. Next he attempted to mingle with the older families of Salem, and again was snubbed. Finally he returned to Newburyport, fully confident that he would be accepted in its better social circles. There were, indeed, people worth cultivating in the seaport town. John Quincy Adams, after he became president, often recalled his days as a law student in Newburyport and always thought its society better than that of Washington.

"Most of the leading families were but one generation removed from the plough or the forecastle," Samuel Eliot Morison has pointed out, "but they had acquired wealth before the Revolution, and conducted social matters with the grace and dignity of an old regime. . . . We read of weekly balls and routs, of wedding coaches drawn by six white horses with liveried footmen, in this town of less than eight thousand inhabitants." This was the society Dexter longed to join. True, he had made his thousands *after* the Revolution, and by means which many of his fellows resented, but nevertheless he was rich. However, mere riches were not enough. His social superiors neither answered his cordial invitations nor offered invitations of their own. Once more Dexter was ignored.

This time he decided to fight back. Gold evidently was not enough. One needed tradition and roots. But could these be bought? Dexter thought that they could. It was still a period of depression, and real estate was cheap. One of the very best houses in Newburyport, in all New England in fact, the large brick mansion on State Street owned by the famous Nathaniel Tracy, was on the market at a price far below its value. Dexter snatched at the bargain. Within two days the great Tracy was out and the appalling Dexter was in and all Newburyport society was struck speechless.

To appreciate the dumfounded silence with which this move was met, one must know the man who had been replaced by a half-literate leather-dresser. Nathaniel Tracy, two years younger than Dexter, had been born to wealth, had been graduated from Harvard at the age of twenty, and had returned to Newburyport to become a merchant as his father had been before him. Forming a partnership with the clever and genteel Jonathan Jackson, young Tracy had employed a fleet of sailing ships for exporting and importing. With the revolt against the British at its height in 1775, Tracy applied to the General Court of Massachusetts for license to convert his merchant ships into privateers. The British were caught unprepared by this legalized piracy, and Tracy's flotilla captured 120 English vessels and almost $4,000,000 worth of cargo. The profits were staggering. Tracy built the magnificent square brick-house on State Street, furnished the interior with carved banisters, gilded mirrors, liveried Negro servants, and a fully stocked wine cellar. He entertained with dignity and elegance. "He was," remarked a neighbor, "a gentleman of polished manners and fine taste." But the day of reckoning came soon.

George III commanded his finest frigates and heavy-gunned vessels to the colonial war. The Yankee privateers were swept from the seas. Of the 24 privateers owned by Tracy and Jackson, 23 fell into enemy hands. Of the 110 merchant ships they owned, 97 were captured or destroyed by the British. At least $3,000,000 in cargoes was lost. And though Tracy had lent his embattled government $160,000, and had sold the Army clothing and supplies on credit, he could obtain none of his investment back at war's end. Soon he could no longer support the house. He retired to a rented farm in the country, while Timothy Dexter moved into State Street and a new era was ushered in for Newburyport.

With quiet desperation, Dexter tried to emulate Tracy. He spared no expense in furnishing the house. He attired himself in the manner befitting a gentleman of means. He rode through town in a splendid coach drawn by two horses. He rode through town and he rode back again. There was no one of importance to see. No one of importance came to see him. He discovered Tracy's wine cellar, stocked it with the choicest European imports, as well as with the locally made Laird's ale and porter and the best whiskeys and rum produced by Newburyport's many distilleries. Amid his bottles he languished in high spirits, and when he emerged he was a new man. No longer would he try to be Tracy. Henceforth he would be himself—and one day, yet, he would make his neighbors "hang there heads Doun Like A Dogg."

Hides and tannin were things of the past. He aspired higher. Salem land records still give evidence of Timothy Dexter's rise. The earliest conveyances identify him as a "leather dresser." Later, he is a "trader," then a "merchant," and finally, at retirement, a "gentleman." After his acquisition of the brick house, Dexter directed his energies toward the world of commerce. In 1790 he built the 171-ton brig *Mehitabel*, and two years later the 153-ton *Congress*. He exported goods to Europe and the Indies, West and East, and his wealth multiplied and his fame grew. But the Dexter legend was not created by the profits he made. It was created, rather, out of the means he employed to make these profits.

Timothy Dexter sent coals to Newcastle. He sent warming pans and woolen mittens to the semitropical West Indies. He sent English Bibles, opium, and live cats to foreign lands, and glutted his warehouse with whalebone. And, most incredibly, on each of these transactions he made a profit. He boasted, afterwards, that on the whalebone alone he had earned "one tun and halfe of silver on hand and over . . ."

How could anyone not go bankrupt on such merchandising eccentricity? It might be instructive to know the dizzying details as set down, quite frankly, by the master himself in *A Pickle for the Knowing Ones.*

"How Did Dexter Make His Money ye says bying whale bone for staing for ships in grosing three houndred & 40 tons —bort all in boston salum and all in Noue york under Cover oppenly told them for my ships they all laffed so I had at my oan pris I had four Counning men for Rounners thay found the horne as I told them to act the fool . . . all that time the Creaters more or less laffing it spread very fast here is the Rub—in fifty days they smelt a Rat—found where it was gone to Nouebry Port—spekkelaters swarmed like hell houns—to be short with it I made seventy five per sent . . ."

In less Chaucerian prose, Dexter had employed cunning runners or agents, men who would act naïve, to purchase 340 tons of whalebone in Boston, Salem, and New York to be used for "stay stuff" on his ships. Those who sold the excessive quantity of whalebone laughed at the idiocy of the purchase. Dexter had the last laugh. He made 75 per cent profit on his investment.

Yet Dexter's version must never be accepted as definitive, as, to irritate his enemies and defend himself, he often related only half of any story. Actually, Dexter overheard a refitter on one of his vessels remark one day that it was almost impossible to buy enough "stay stuff." The refitter meant ship's rigging. But Dexter misunderstood. He thought the refitter was referring to corset stays, a small amount of which was manufactured from whalebone. At once Dexter set out to corner the whalebone market. He said that he was "full of Cash I had nine tun of silver on hand at that time . . ." This would have been about $60,000. The 342 tons of whalebone verged on folly. For by dictates of the styles than in vogue, corset stays were not sufficiently in demand to absorb Dexter's whalebone. But then something happened. A vessel from France arrived with the latest Paris fashions. These included broad skirts with larger corsets that required yards of whalebone. And who had a monopoly on whalebone? The genius of Newburyport, of course. Was his adventure in merchandising fool luck? Or did he alone among businessmen understand and foresee the fluctuations of high fashion?

Emboldened by his success in "stay stuff," Dexter embarked on even more spectacular risks. There were his shipments to the West Indies, an influx of oddity that dazed and delighted the merchants of Havana. "I Dreamed," he wrote, "of worming pans three nites that thay would doue in the west inges I got no more than fortey two thousand—put them in nine vessels for difrent ports that tuck good hold I cleared sevinty nine per sent the pans thay made yous of them for Coucking . . ."

Long before central heating and electric blankets, warming pans were devices employed by New Englanders to heat their glacial beds. These covered pans were filled with hot coals and placed between the bed sheets. They were, needless to say, designed for climes of low Fahrenheit. Dexter's purchase of 42,000 of them for export to the West Indies began as a crude joke. Some merchants' clerks goaded him into the investment. The Captain, under charter to Dexter, must have been shaken by the ruinous cargo he had been hired to transport to the tropics. But once again economic history adjusted itself to Dexter's innovations. The arrival of the warming pans in the Indies coincided with a production war between two giant molasses-makers. Each was in need of any utensil that might speed his output. At once, Dexter's Captain saw the light. Or perhaps the light he saw was only a reflection of Dexter's shining creativity. According to Knapp, the Captain contemplated his unlikely cargo, then being "a young and ingenious man," he "took off the covers, and had handsome handles put to them, and called them skimmers, and the pan part ladles. He then had them introduced into a large sugar-making establishment, and they were much approved of, as the best machinery of their kind invented." The warming pans in the disguise of ladles sold at 79 per cent profit, and were used in the Indies mainly for skimming the scum off cane syrup as it boiled in huge vats. Some of the reconverted pans found their way to private families, who used them to fry fish over open fires. It is thought that Dexter made $6,000 in this venture.

Assured that the West Indies were a soft touch, Dexter next bombarded the native population with Bibles. "I bort twelve per sent under halfe pris they Cost fortey one sents Each bibbel—twenty one thousand," he admitted. "I put them into twentey one vessels for the west inges and sent a text that all of them must have one bibel in every familey or if not thay would goue to hell . . ." Whether or not this deluge of Good Books, with the accompanying text promising hell and fire to reluctant customers, was bought up entirely in the West Indies or distributed elsewhere is not known. We have only Dexter's word that he profited by 100 per cent—or the sum of $47,000—by his missionary zeal.

If the Bibles were wholly a speculative whim, the woolen mittens probably were not. There was much hilarity in certain Newburyport quarters when Dexter shipped his mittens to the sweltering Indies, though veteran merchants thought it anything but strange. For this was a time when a four-way trade existed among America, Russia, China, and India, with the West Indies serving as the exchange counter. Vessels out of St. Petersburg brought canvas hemp, iron, and linen to the Indies, where New Englanders accepted them in trade for rum, tobacco, coffee, and flour. Dexter's mittens did not remain long in the heat of a Caribbean warehouse. They were bought up by a merchantman headed for the cold Baltic regions, where they were disposed of in Russia.

Perhaps Dexter's most profitable deal with the Indies, in terms of percentage rather than of gross receipts, was his less-publicized feline transaction. Newburyport abounded in stray cats. Dexter learned that sailors often took them aboard ship as pets or to chase rats and then disposed of them for cash in the Caribbean islands, where a shortage of cats existed. Immediately Dexter began to collect and crate them. He sent his squealing cargo to the Indies, where large warehouse owners purchased them—some for as much as five dollars a head—to ward off destructive vermin.

Dexter's only recorded transaction of an unusual nature with the Old World resulted in his most memorable achievement. A practical joker, it is said, gravely suggested to him that there was a need for coal in Newcastle, England. Dexter was neither widely read nor widely learned. He could not know that Newcastle was a leading coal center of the world, and he could not have heard that familiar phrase of ridicule, "like carrying coals to Newcastle." With childish innocence, Dexter acted. He ordered immense quantities of Virginia soft coal loaded on his ships and carried off to Newcastle. Under any normal circumstances, the reaction of the Newcastle citizenry at the moment of the cargo's arrival might have made an unforgettable picture. But Dexter's coal arrived at the precise moment when Newcastle was paralyzed by a coal strike. The mines were empty, the miners unemployed, and all production was at a standstill. Not only Newcastle, but also all the vicinity surrounding, was suffering a shortage of fuel. Bids for Dexter's cargo were enormous. His profits added vastly to his "tuns" of silver.

When he wrote his little book, a tome not noteworthy for its modesty, Dexter allowed himself to appear humble only once. "I found," he wrote, "I was very luckky in spekkelation . . ." History blindly accepted this autobiographical verdict. But again, as in the case of the Continental currency, was it all luck?

William C. Todd, the great dissenter, felt that Dexter exaggerated, possibly even invented, the more incredible of his commercial transactions to promote the legend of luck and thus irritate his neighbors. Todd, contending that many of the Newburyport eccentric's ventures could only have been "lies or jokes," revealed that 342 tons of whalebone might have cost Dexter anywhere between $60,000 and $2,000,000, depending on the year the purchase occurred. Todd did not think that Dexter had that kind of money and said that if he did, the demand for corset stays would not have absorbed his whalebone, for very few women dressed in the height of Parisian fashion.

Todd regarded the warming-pan episode as even more improbable. "No hardware was made in this country until a little more than half a century ago [or about 1830] and all the warming pans in use came from Great Britain. The amount named would have cost $150,000, to be paid for in hard money. . . . Is it possible, rating his intelligence very low, that, if he had attempted such a speculation, he would not have been persuaded of its folly long before he could have executed it?" Furthermore, Todd thought the warming pans ill adapted to straining molasses. "Did any visitor to the West Indies ever see or hear of one of those 42,000 warming pans?"

Todd assailed the supposed Bible exportation with even more fervor. Obviously the Bibles had been printed in English. Who would buy them in lands where only Spanish was read? Besides, weren't the West Indies Roman Catholic, and didn't they have enough Holy Books of their own? Next, Dexter's shipment of mittens came under scholarly assault. Why would Russians need American mittens? They could buy their own home product more cheaply, for both wool and labor were cheaper in Russia than in America. As to the business of the cats and the coals to Newcastle, these Todd discreetly ignored.

While Todd's argument against Dexter's veracity is often devastating, other contemporary evidence supports the merchant-jester. Knapp remembered and recorded the incident of the warming pans. It is unlikely that he would have done so if the transaction had not occurred. An anonymous clergyman, writing Dexter's obituary in the *Newburyport Impartial Herald* a few days after his death, admitted: "The fortunate and singular manner of his speculations, by which he became possessed of a handsome property, are well known, and his selling a cargo of warming-pans to the W. Indies, where they were converted into molasses-ladles, and sold to a good profit, is but one of the most peculiar." Even Mrs. E. Vale Smith, who had no affection for her recent neighbor, conceded the occurrence of the incidents of the warming pans and the woolen mittens. Nor did she credit his success to luck. "We see no evidence of folly, but rather shrewd management, and cunning reticence to cover it; as it cannot possibly be supposed, that with vessels constantly arriving at Newburyport from the West Indies, and with cargoes from the North of Europe, he did not *know* that the one was a warm country and the other cold. No doubt, he knew the use to which his warming-pans were to be applied, before they left the wharf. . . ."

Though strange, unlettered, ostentatious, Dexter was not unintelligent. His craftiness and trickery were well known. He was the well-informed fool. He always learned the true value of an article and the possibilities of its use before speculating in it. Then he moved swiftly and audaciously, often trying to monopolize a single product, though, toward the end, his competitors resisted selling to him for fear his endorsement would put the product in demand. At the peak of his commercial career he frequented his wine cellar more and more often, quaffing deeply of rum and brandy. But he made it a policy to terminate all his buying and selling before the noon hour. This was because he never drank in the morning when he did business, and he never did business in the afternoon when he drank. The Dexter fortune was founded on sobriety and a hang-over.

Much of his business activity was less eccentric than the warming pans or Bibles, but certainly as profitable as they. He invested heavily in real estate. He backed homesteading in frontier Ohio, rented his stables for construction of carding machines to be used in the first woolen mill in America, and planned (possibly even erected) factories to manufacture cheap clay pipes of his own design.

One of Dexter's most conservative business acts, but one which was to play a great role in encouraging his future eccentricity, was his investment in the Essex Merrimack or Deer Island Bridge. Until 1793 travelers and farmers from the north entered Newburyport by crossing the Merrimack River on ferryboats. But the ferries were overcrowded. A company was formed to construct a toll bridge over the river at the point where a small island, called Deer Island, stood. A stock offering was made public. Sixty-three citizens bought stocks in the enterprise. With one hundred shares in his name, Dexter was the largest single stockholder.

On the Fourth of July holiday of that year, when many gathered at a tavern on Deer Island to celebrate the newly opened bridge overhead, Dexter appeared, accompanied by family and exuding good cheer. Inspired, perhaps, by the proximity of beverages and a few well-wishers, he mounted a tavern table to deliver an impromptu address. "Ladies and gentlemen," he said, "this day, the eighteenth year of our glorious independence commences. Justice, order, commerce, agriculture, the sciences and tranquillity reign triumphant in these united and happy states. America is the asylum for the afflicted, persecuted, tormented sons and daughters of Europe. Our progress towards the glorious point of perfection is unparalleled in the annals of mankind. Permit me, then, my wife and jolly souls, to congratulate you on this joyful occasion. Let our deportment be suitable for the joyful purpose for which we are assembled. Let good nature, breeding, concord, benevolence, piety, understanding, wit, humor, punch and wine grace, bless, adorn and crown us henceforth and forever. Amen."

This happy speech and the festive occasion that prompted it might serve to lull the unsuspecting student of Dexter's life. For the times were not happy times for Dexter, and the two years that followed were not festive. Though by enterprise and daring he had gained much wealth and solidified his financial position, he had made no inroads upon Newburyport society. To the oldest inhabitant, he was still an irksome, odd intruder. For one thing, he drank too much, and when he drank he talked too much, and when he talked he boasted of his merchandising feats. For another thing, in a community of excessive piety, he was confusingly irreligious.

In 1775, when still a leather-dresser, he had been converted by a housekeeper in his hire. This was his own admission. To what he had been converted he did not reveal. When he was advanced in years, he turned on the clergy. They were "gokbey handed preasts Deakens gruntters whimers"—that is to say, jockey-handed priests, deacons, grunters, whiners. Furthermore, "mankind and woman kind is in posed upon all over the world more or less hy preast craf o for shame o for shame I pittey them . . ." Occasionally he relented. He gave Saint Paul's Church one hundred pounds for improvements and he gave the Second Presbyterian Society a magnificent bell upon which was engraved: "The gift of Timothy Dexter Esq." Sometimes he even received members of the clergy. Once, when a clergyman visited him and offered up a prayer,

Dexter solemnly heard it out, then turned to his son and said: "Sam, wasn't that a damned good prayer?"

Periodically Dexter tried to win the affection of his fellows by means of donations to the community. Besides his church gifts, he repaired roads that were properly the responsibility of the government, and he willed $2,000 to Newburyport "for the benefit of such of the poor of the town, as are most necessitous." Incidentally, the interest earned by the $2,000 was, at least until very recently, being used to aid the indigent. But even in his charity Dexter somehow managed to antagonize. He offered to pave all of High Street, a work sorely required and involving great expense, if the town would change the name of the thoroughfare to Dexter Street. The city fathers said nay. Again, Dexter offered to build a large brick market-house in the center of town if it would bear the name Dexter Hall. Once more the city fathers said nay, but this time with anger.

Deeply affronted, Dexter withdrew to the bosom of his family. Here, too, there was lack of hospitality. At his hearth he found small solace and certainly no peace. His wife, Elizabeth, of uneven temper and unending verbosity, was a thorn in his flesh. From the day of his first absurd speculation in depreciated currency, she had opposed his gambles. That he was proved right and she wrong made matters no better. Resenting his manner of investments, his mode of living, his grandiose schemes, his predilection for pretty young wenches, and, eventually, his affection for the improbable servants and friends who were to enrich his later years, she descended into the role of senior nag.

From the day of their invasion of the Tracy residence, the Dexters were permanently embattled. Dexter stood his wife's insults so long, and then stood them no more. Did he leave her or divorce her or eliminate her by violence, as any normal man might have done? No, for Dexter possessed a creative turn of mind. On the day of decision he simply turned Elizabeth Frothingham Dexter, mate, into a ghost. Henceforth, for the most part, he would ignore her acutal existence as a person and treat her as an apparition. To strangers he would refer to her as "Mrs. Dexter, the ghost that was my wife." It must be remarked that the wraithlike Mrs. Dexter was the most vocal shade in the annals of the supernatural and possibly the most vigorous in a long line of ghosts, for she continued to haunt her husband's residences until he passed into the phantom world to which he had relegated her. With unblushing heartiness, she managed to outlive him by three years.

Dexter's male heir, Samuel, was no less disappointing. But Dexter never gave up on his son, who was generously permitted to retain his corporeal existence. As a youngster pampered and spoiled, Samuel tried to buy the friendship and protection of schoolmates with favors. Exposed to education at home and abroad, he remained ignorant. His head, according to one who observed him, was "stored with nothing that was useful or ornamental." In maturity he was possessed of impressive physique, but little wit. He spent money with reckless abandon, and after he discovered the pleasures of the bottle, his life became one lingering dissipation. The fault was not his, of course, as Knapp has sternly pointed out. "If he had been fortunate enough to have a sober and discreet father . . . feeble as he was, something might have been made of him."

Dexter made one effort to introduce his son to the world of commerce. He charged Samuel with the transport and disposal of a shipment to Europe. Upon arrival at his port of call Samuel indulged in drink and games of chance and was forced to give up the entire shipment to pay his debts. This was the end of Samuel's business career. Thereafter he was confined to quarters in Newburyport and spent much of his time keeping his father company in the wine cellar. Once, a year or two before Dexter's death, when father, son, and the ghost that was Mrs. Dexter lived in a finer home in Newburyport, the two men emerged from an alcoholic bout to find a tourist on the street staring up at their residence. Usually Dexter had no objections to voyeurism. But on this occasion, possibly, he had drunk too much and was in an ugly mood. He grabbed a musket, shoved it at Samuel, and ordered his son to prove himself. Samuel for once displayed good sense: he objected. His father darkly threatened him. Still Samuel refused to play sniper. In a rage Dexter took back the rifle, aimed it shakily, and fired. The bullet missed. The tourist, more furious than frightened, sped off to the Ipswich jail some twelve miles distant, and summoned the law. Dexter and son were brought before a magistrate. While Samuel was exonerated of attempted murder, Dexter was heavily fined. He refused to pay the fine. He was immediately clapped into the Ipswich jail. There he sat brooding for two months, martyred and stubborn, while his heir had the wine cellar to himself. When martyrdom wore thin, Dexter paid his fine and rejoined his son.

If Samuel was Dexter's pride only in conviviality, his younger daughter Nancy was his fondest hope in every way. She was comely, docile, and mentally retarded. "She blossomed for a while, a pretty but entirely vapid child with none of the mental adornments one anticipates in a nice young lady," wrote Knapp. She was the apple of Dexter's eye and his one domestic comfort. He dreaded the day she would depart his house for one of her own. For she was much courted. Young gentlemen came calling regularly, no doubt attracted by her beauty as well as by her father's widely advertised wealth. But suitors rarely returned for a second look. Her good prospects apparently could not overcome her lack of intellect. Dexter was not dissatisfied. The disembodied Mrs. Dexter, however, was much annoyed. She wanted a good match. Nancy wanted nothing. She was Still Life incarnate.

Then a more persistent visitor came calling. He attended Nancy once, and then a second time, and then again and again, until he asked for her hand. His name was Abraham

Bishop. He was a university graduate, a Connecticut judge, a cosmopolite who had visited the Far East, and a Mason. Dexter has left us a picture of Abraham Bishop—or A b, as he was wont to call him—a picture that may be highly colored by a father's distaste. "A b is the beast or Creater two leged Conekett boull—short Neck boull head thik hare big sholders black Corlley hare he wants to be A god . . ." But the beastly, bullish, hairy, and self-assured Bishop presented a more attractive visage to vacant Nancy. Awed by his scholarship and glib tongue, prodded by her mother, she was eager to marry him. Only her father objected. Dexter suspected that Bishop was less interested in his "babey" than in his "tuns" of silver. "He being A fox and A old fox, he was after the graps . . ."

In the end the ladies won. But the marriage was a disaster. "I have bin in hell all the time—more so sence Abraham bishup got in to my house . . ." the wretched Dexter wrote. Bishop took his bride to New Haven to live. His income was such that he required his father-in-law's help. After two years Dexter complained that Bishop, as well as son Samuel and "my wife that *was*," had cost him $10,000. Bishop, impatient with his wife's feeble mentality, cuffed her about continually. Once, while brutally beating her, he so injured her side that she was compelled to wear plasters on her body for three years. In despair, she began to drink, and finally lost her reason. She bore Bishop a child. When she had given way fully to alcoholism and insanity Bishop demanded a divorce. He obtained it, but not until he had cost his angry father-in-law "one tun of silver." Pitiful Nancy, bruised, addicted to "likker," and "Crasey," returned with her offspring to Newburyport and became the charge of her distressed parent for the rest of his life.

It is not inconceivable that Timothy Dexter, so beset, might have gone "Crasey," too, had he not at this moment in his life found an outlet for his troubled brain. He was almost fifty when he took up his pen in earnest and became an author.

Of course, motives other than mere escape brought him into literature. He still sought the respect of Newburyport society and thought to dazzle its members by his creative outpourings. More important, he had cast his eye, at last, on immortality. "Nearly every act of his apparent folly may be traced to one overpowering passion, uncontrolled by any natural or cultivated taste, though combined with considerable shrewdness: this passion was vanity," Mrs. E. Vale Smith has stated.

In earlier years, Dexter had enlightened Newburyport with an occasional letter to the editor. But by now he had lived much and suffered deeply, and he had wisdom in excess to impart. It is unfortunate that his style, original and uninhibited from the first, was marred in the beginning by the vandals who edited the *Newburyport Impartial Herald* and other journals. Actually the *Impartial Herald* was published for a time by a friend and admirer, Edmund Blunt, who had raised its circulation from 70 to 700 in two years. Perhaps veneration for his forty-dollar printing press, which had once served Benjamin Franklin, convinced Blunt that he must punctuate and rewrite Dexter's earliest ungrammatical effusions. Perhaps, too, Blunt did not wish to make an old friend appear the object of ridicule in the community—though later, in Salem, Blunt would agree to print Dexter's "unimitated and inimitable" master work, *A Pickle for the Knowing Ones*, without tampering with the text.

There was some reticence in Dexter's first offering to the *Impartial Herald*. "Mr. Printers, I hope my weak brothers won't be disturbed about my scratching a little in the newspaper. I do it to learn myself to write and spell which I never knew how; I am now at leisure and a man of pleasure. I mean no hurt—I let you know what I know without reading—what I know only by experience—Clear Nature has been my schoolmaster." At various times Dexter discoursed on brotherly love, the human soul, a seven-foot African lion he was displaying in his back yard, the perfidy of Abraham Bishop, the wisdom of appointing Dexter the Emperor of the United

States, female fashions, and the folly of entrusting public offices to men without means.

Then suddenly, without warning, like a bolt from the blue, was published in the *Impartial Herald* what appeared to be Timothy Dexter's valedictory to Newburyport:

"It costs eight hundred dollars a year to support a watch in this town, and yet gentlemen's windows are broken, fences pulled down and Cellars broken open, and much other misdemeanors done at night. Are the watch asleep, or are they afraid to detect those who are guilty of such practices? Boast not of it, if you call this Liberty and Equality. . . .

"Now fellow citizens is it wisdom, is it policy, to use a man or men so shocking bad as to oblige them to leave the town where they paid one Dollar a day to support government?

"A friend to good order, honor to whom it belongs, to great men a friend—to all good citizens and honest men good bye."

Timothy Dexter was leaving Newburyport at last. He had been provoked to move, he said, by unrestrained youths, thieves, and ruffians who were disturbing his peace and destroying his property. He did not announce, though it was plainly evident, that he was tired of being ostracized by polite society and hurt by the rejection of his offer to pave the town's main street. He had decided to go to a community where his originality and liberality might be appreciated and where his worldly goods would be protected. He purchased a vast country-estate in Chester, New Hampshire. He then disposed of the Tracy house at a profit. Early in 1796 he departed Newburyport for Chester. Early in 1797 he returned—to stay. The year of absence had not been without its advantages. For the Dexter who returned was a nobler Dexter, far better equipped to fend off the disapproval of his Newburyport neighbors.

What happened in Chester to alter Dexter's outlook? Somehow, in his new location, the leather-dresser and man of commerce acquired nobility. One day he was the plebeian Dexter, the republican Dexter, the everyman's Dexter—and the next he was Lord Timothy Dexter of Chester. The origin of his title remains a mystery. Had he knighted himself? Or had he been knighted by the circle of sycophants who courted a man of wealth? The facts are not known. All that is known is that soon, in the public prints, Dexter was referring to himself as "the first Lord in Americake the first Lord Dexter made by the voice of hamsher state my brave fellows Affirmed it they gave me the titel & so let it goue for as much as it will fetch it wonte give me Any breade but take from me . . ." Evidently Lord Dexter was realistic about his peerage. It would give him no bread. On the contrary, the high station would be costly. But he would not shirk the responsibility. After all, the "voise of the peopel and I cant Help it" had elevated him.

Yet even his rapid ascent to the peerage could not make him unaware of his antipathy toward Chester. A Baptist preacher in the new community directed a sermon and the threat of fire and brimstone at Dexter. Angered, Dexter walked out of the church. The tax collectors of New Hampshire, more persistent than those of Massachusetts, exacted one dollar a week from him for road improvements and twenty-four dollars for use of his carriages, and tried mightily to get their share of his "two Hundred wate of Silver." The specter that was Mrs. Dexter was more visible and more verbal than ever. Her activity may be attributed to the knowledge that Dexter was having visitations from more earthly females. It is with difficulty that one pictures Dexter as Casanova. But there is evidence that during his New Hampshire year he reserved much of his wit, and some of his wealth, for unattached females. At Hampton Beach he once became romantically involved with an attached female, much to his regret. Her boy friend belabored Dexter with more than words. Finally, there was the unhappy altercation Dexter had with a member of the bar. According to Dexter, a lawyer-fellow waylaid him and did him great violence. "I was beaten almost to Death . . . three men saw the Axon of the blodey seene without massay and carried sade Dexter in to the house sun fainting or Neare to it se and behold the olful site bleading and blind of one Eye . . ." The motive for this assault on His Lordship is not clear. Dexter said his debtors had uncharitably sent the lawyer to quarrel with him. Dexter also said that his attacker had objected to certain writings and had resented his victim's title. Although Dexter did not say that a woman was involved in the case, the possibility must not be dismissed lightly.

In September 1796, while still nursing his wounds, Dexter published an open letter to the citizens of Chester outlining, blow by blow, the recent combat and its ramifications. He gave his readers an ultimatum. They could keep either him and his wealth or the lawyer in the town. "Chouse for yourselves my frinds and felow mortals . . ." Apparently a choice was made, for six months later, Lord Timothy Dexter was back in Newburyport for the last, and most bizarre, phase of his existence.

When Dexter had dwelt in the Nathaniel Tracy house he had been a commoner, and the residence had been sufficient for his needs. But now he was a peer of the realm and he knew that more was expected of him. His gaze fell upon the three-story white Georgian mansion, located on a rise near the center of town, that had been constructed by Tracy's one-time business partner, Jonathan Jackson, and was now owned by a retired privateer named Captain Thomas Thomas, who was eager to sell.

"It was a princely chateau," wrote Knapp, "standing on the height of land about a quarter of a mile from the river, commanding a most beautiful and extensive view of the sea, the Isle-of-Shoals and the far surrounding country. The grounds had been laid out in the most approved European fashion by intelligent artists from England and France. The house was capacious and well finished and the outhouses tasteful and commodious. A lovelier spot or a more airy mansion Lucullus could not have wished."

Jackson had built the colonial house a quarter of a century before to celebrate his marriage to his partner's sister. He had been forced to sell to one of his employees, who, in turn, had fallen upon hard times. Dexter needed no urging to buy. In short weeks the deal was consummated and Dexter and his brood were comfortably situated in the square wooden palace overlooking the Merrimack River. Though renovation was not necessary, Dexter proceeded to make the house his own. For his living room he imported furniture and brocades and works of art from France. For his study he bargained for libraries of leather-bound, gold-tooled volumes he rarely had the patience to open. For his bedroom he acquired a counterpane that had once been the property of Marie Antoinette.

It was for the exterior, however, that Dexter reserved his personal touch. A large gold eagle was perched at the summit of the cupola. The eagle, much to its owner's delight, "turns with the wind." About the roof of the house Dexter placed minarets, and atop these, gilded balls, until the architecture resembled something that could have been described only by Scheherazade. The expanses of lawn, front and back were planted with 150 fruit-trees and a greater number of shrubs, many imported from distant lands.

In Dexter's stables stood his white horses and his ornamented coach, its sides decorated with coat of arms recently borrowed from a European book of heraldry. Nearby rose his greatest glory. "An elegant new Tomb," he described it, "on the top of which is erected the Temple of Reason, 12 feet square, 11 feet high, with 158 squares of glass in it." Inside the tomb rested Dexter's mahogany coffin lined with white lead, trimmed about with green and brass, and bearing eight silver handles. Also in the tomb, ready to accompany

Dexter on any hurried journey, lay a supply of fireworks, a speaking trumpet, pipes and tobacco, and "a bibel to read and sum good songs."

The most curious and best-remembered addition to his landscape was yet to come. In 1801 Dexter conceived and announced his outdoor museum. It was to be dedicated to the late George Washington and to his equals from the earliest dawn of history. It was to take the form of a series of statues of great personalities and symbolic figures, all carved of marble and life-sized. These representations would be distributed at the mansion's entrance, on the front lawns, in the rear gardens, so that all who wished might see them plainly and appreciate being a part of the human family. "I will shoue the world one of the Grate Wonders of the world, in 15 months," Dexter announced in the press, "if No man murders me in Dors or out of Dors." No man murdered Dexter, and he proceeded with his plans. There would be, he said, "The 3 presidents, Doctor Franklin, John hen Cock, and Mr Hamilton and Rouffous King and John Jea, and 2 granedears on the top of the hous, 4 Lions below, 1 Eagel, is on the Coupulow, one Lamb to lay down with one of the Lions,—One Yonnecorne, one Dogg, Addam and Eave in the garden, —one horse. The houll is not concluded on as yet—Dexter's Mouseum."

To execute the grand design Dexter hired an admirable artist and new friend, Joseph Wilson, who had carved figureheads and other decorations on sailing ships before arriving in Newburyport. Dexter had previously tested Wilson with the development of the gold eagle that turned on the cupola. The result had satisfied him, and he regarded Wilson "A fine fellow." However, Dexter did not let sentiment cloud his business sense. Knapp has it that Wilson received $15,000 for the task, but later research proves that the sum was $4,000. An architect, Ebenezer Clifford, was retained to assist the ship-carver.

As the project neared preparation there was only one major

change in its conception. Dexter had wanted marble, but Wilson insisted upon wood. Wilson argued that wood was more permanent. It was probably also much cheaper. In the end Dexter told his artist to go ahead with wood.

The outdoor museum was completed in little more than a year. There were forty wooden images in all, and their diversity indicated that their patron was a man of catholic tastes. Scattered throughout the property, mostly on pedestals and pillars, stood, among others, Louis XVI, Venus, an anonymous preacher, Governor Gilman of New Hampshire, two grenadiers, Motherly Love, four lions and a lamb, John Hancock, Moses, one dog, Adam and Eve, George III, Horatio Nelson, Governor Strong of Massachusetts, Aaron Burr, an Indian chief, Napoleon Bonaparte, the Emperor of China, William Pitt, Toussaint L'Ouverture, and Benjamin Franklin.

The four lions, symbols of international peace, guarded Dexter's door. Above them rose an arch, supported by two columns, on which stood George Washington—"father gorge with his hat on"—flanked by John Adams, carrying a cane and facing the father of his country "as if thay was on sum politicks," and President Thomas Jefferson, the "grat felosfer" grasping a scroll labeled "Constitution." For the position at the head of his walk, near the fence and facing the street, Dexter reserved Wilson's finest work of art. It was a life-sized statue of Timothy Dexter himself, mounted high on a pedestal and bearing the engraved inscription: "I am the first in the East, the first in the West, and the greatest philosopher in the Western World."

After the forty figures had been garishly painted, the Dexter mansion appeared less a residence than a rainbow. From the day the museum was completed, High Street was crowded with visitors from all New England, and eventually from all the East. The popular theory has it that Dexter erected this carnival with profit in mind. To reach his residence many tourists had to pay toll to cross the Essex Merrimack Bridge, in which Dexter was the largest shareholder, so they were contributing to his wealth. While Dexter was thus enriched, of course, money could not have been his primary motive. He was a sad and lonely man who wanted company and approval. The museum brought him company in excess. Whether it brought him approval is debatable.

Though spectacular, the forty wooden figures that graced Dexter's landscape were not the most interesting personalities to inhabit his royal domain. Inside the great house there was a more animate and more colorful ménage. Even the ghost that was Mrs. Dexter, and the drunken Samuel and the drunken Nancy, were pallid when compared with the retainers Dexter had gathered under one roof.

If King Arthur had his Merlin, Lord Dexter had his Madam Hooper. This crone, with a double set of teeth and a chicken for a companion, had sailed to America as the mistress of a British officer. With him she had gone through the privations of the Indian wars, and from him she had learned to fire a musket and brandish a broadsword. Finally abandoned, she had made her way to Newburyport. She had been fairly well educated, and so took up the profession of teaching. But few in Newburyport wanted to be taught. In desperation, she turned to fortunetelling. This was better, but ignominious, as many in the community thought her a witch. One day, by propitious chance, Dexter requested that she locate the thieves who were depleting his melon patch. It was the supreme test. Madam Hooper was ready for it. Muttering among her dream books and crude horoscopes—and perhaps putting her ear to the ground in a district from which many vandals had been graduated—she came up with the name of the culprit, thus endearing herself to Dexter for life. Promptly, accompanied by her chicken and her sorcery, she went to live in the great mansion as adviser to the master.

When Madam Hooper died she was succeeded by Mary McCauley, a leathery, husky, brusque woman who had done laundry for her keep until she became a prominent fortuneteller in the vicinity of Lynn. Mrs. McCauley's place in American history, as it turned out, would exceed even her employer's. At sixteen Mary, or Molly, as she was known, married a young barber named John Hays. When he was called to serve the revolutionary cause she followed. At Monmouth, when Lee retreated before the redcoats and Mad Anthony Wayne fought back with fury, Molly left the safety of the other wives to invade the battlefield and relieve the American wounded with pitchers of water. Thereafter she was always Molly Pitcher. At Monmouth, too, when her husband was hit and gunners were scarce, she manned a cannon. After the war and Hays's death, she married one George McCauley, who would not support her. She left him to support herself. Her fame as a seer was growing when Dexter made his offer. She moved into his dwelling, where, puffing a pipe and cussing like the veteran she was, she cheered him with her readings of astrology.

Another in the household was William Burley, whom Dexter called The Dwarf. He was a thimble-brained jester, towering six feet seven inches in height. For a housekeeper Dexter employed a vast and aggressive Negro, Lucy Lancaster, daughter of an African prince. She became Dexter's mainstay. She humored him, protected him, and understood him. During long periods she curbed his drinking and eccentricities. To visitors she was his apologist, insisting always that he was honest and good and that his follies were inspired by unemployment and a nervous temperament.

But the most improbable of those who served Lord Dexter was Jonathan Plummer, a local fishmonger turned book peddler. Plummer, a stocky, bowlegged, eloquent creature, had tried to make his way as a preacher, pawnbroker, and eligible bachelor (he courted, successively, nine "vigorous and antiquated virgins"), before concentrating on the retailing of halibut. Eventually he found that banned books and pamphlets dealing with pornography, murder, scandal, miracles, and atheism were in more demand than fish as food for the brain.

Hiding these lurid works under fish and straw in a wheelbarrow, he made his way about Newburyport. Gradually, as he had difficulty supplying the demand for lively reading, he began to produce writings of his own. Though murderers and sex monsters were occasionally his subjects, he soon saw in Timothy Dexter a better subject.

He penned a pamphlet in prose praising Dexter's commercial abilities. This was not enough. In the winged words of poetry, perhaps, he could express his innermost feelings and touch the sensibilities of one so rich and remote. When Dexter returned from New Hampshire, Jonathan Plummer had "a congratulatory ode" waiting for him. Of the eleven stirring stanzas, the first two will suffice:

Your Lordship's welcome back again—
Fair nymphs with sighs have mourn'd your staying
So long from them and me your swain,
And wonder'd at such long delaying;
But now you bless again our eyes,
Our melting sorrow droops and dies.

The town of Chester to a Lord
Must seem a desert dull and foggy,
A gloomy place—upon my word
I think it dirty, wet and boggy:
Far different from your Kingly seat,
In good saint James his famous street.

Understandably, Dexter could not resist. With the lure of a small regular salary, use of his premises and table, and a new red suit, Dexter acquired Plummer as his full-time poet laureate. Plummer enjoyed his new post and was inspired to excessive productivity. Only one thing rankled. The red suit had not been delivered. Plummer blamed this lapse on the fact that Dexter was suffering from the gout. "The painful disease, in a great measure, destroyed his Lordship's relish for poetry," Plummer noted. Eventually the gout was overcome, and Plummer had his suit. It was not red as he wished, but something far more imaginative, as his patron wished. The cocked hat, cloak, frock suit, and buckled shoes were black, but sprinkled with silver stars that sparkled and danced. In this silk-lined uniform, with a parsley on his hat and a gold-headed cane in his hand, Plummer went out to hawk his most grateful and airy poesy. This time the rhyme was fifteen stanzas, but a generous sampling will convey its tone:

Lord Dexter is a man of fame;
Most celebrated is his name;
More precious far than gold that's pure,
Lord Dexter shine forever more.

His noble house, it shines more bright
Than Lebanon's most pleasing height;
Never was one who stepped therein
Who wanted to come out again.

Lord Dexter, thou, whose name alone
Shines brighter than king George's throne;
Thy name shall stand in books of fame,
And princes shall thy name proclaim.

His mighty deeds they are so great,
He's honor'd both in church and state,
And when he comes all must give way,
To let Lord Dexter bear the sway.

When Dexter dies all things shall droop,
Lord East, Lord West, Lord North shall stoop,
And then Lord South with pomp shall come,
And bear his body to the tomb.

In heaven may he always reign,
For there's no sorrow, sin, nor pain;
Unto the world I leave the rest
For to pronounced Lord Dexter blest.

What made Dexter take up his pen again on his own behalf was not his lack of faith in the immortality of Plummer's verse, but simply that he was bored. In a few weeks, unhampered by stops, he scratched out the twenty-four pages of *A Pickle for the Knowing Ones.* When he wanted a printer, there was only one he could trust. Edmund Blunt had been the editor of the *Newburyport Impartial Herald* when Dexter had been a contributor, and now Blunt owned a prosperous printing-shop in Salem. Blunt still visited his favorite author. As late as 1853 he remembered, in a letter to Mrs. Smith, his friend Dexter, "with whom, in his own summer-house, on his coffin, decorated with decanters, &c., I have taken many a glass of wine, with a company of cavalry to which I then belonged." Undoubtedly, they discussed the book. In the spring of 1802 Blunt brought it forth.

Despite a mixed press, Dexter maintained sturdy confidence in his brain child to the very end. It was, he told an editor, "A Littel mousement to mankind at Large . . . I—I—me T Dexter of N Port Desires Any man or men on the gloube to Exseede me as to what I have Rote in my Littel book . . ."

None was tempted by his challenge. In literature, in originality, no man exceeded him.

With the book, his museum, and his retainers he reached his peak. There was little time left. He would have to stand by what he had accomplished. He was fifty-five years of age. The only surviving portrait of him, "engraved from the life" by James Akin, of Newburyport, was done in this period. It was said to be a startling likeness. In it Dexter is seen strolling with a small, hairless black dog, something that might be a cross between dachshund and chihuahua. His Lordship wears a broad, tasseled cocked hat, a white tie and shirt, a wrinkled waistcoat, a long, blue topcoat, breeches secured just above the ankles with ribbons, and comfortable-looking black shoes. He is carrying a gold-headed cane. His graying hair hangs below his ears, and his brows are bushy. His eyes seem large, alert, mischievous. The nose is long and thin, as is the upper lip, which is cast downward in the manner of the cynic. The jaw is determined. The arms are long, and the hands seem the hands of an artist rather than those of a laborer. The feet are large.

His work was done and the days were long. Daily, followed by his porcine dog, he took his constitutional within the boundaries of his estate. Often he paused to banter with his workmen. Sometimes he halted to contemplate the oddities of his museum, and when the spirit moved him, he eradicated the name of some celebrity and replaced it with another. Occasionally he invited visitors to share the fruits of his garden and enjoy his wooden images. When the visitors were pretty damsels they were soon damsels in distress, for Dexter was frequently inflamed and attempted "improper liberties with his female visitors." In recounting these instances, Knapp added: "When disappointed of his prey, he would rave about his house and curse his family for joining in league against him. How wretched is the life of a dotard, in the pursuit of what he calls pleasure!"

More often, as he suffered the gout and other assorted ills, he spent his days indoors. He addressed the local press and the papers in Boston with offers to sell his mansion and museum, which he estimated to be worth $25,000, at a bargain price. In 1806 the Probate Court determined the value at $12,000. He supervised and added to his collection of watches, clocks, and their works. The timepieces ticked and clattered in every roon of the great house. Dexter regarded his clocks as living shadows, railed against them when they ran down, and often wished mankind could be wound up like them. Many visitors desired to see his house and converse with its illustrious owner. Dexter preferred the company of old friends who drank with him, though he was not averse to receiving youths who addressed him as Lord or to entertaining foreign newcomers who professed to be noblemen. In one case, a peace advocate of Portsmouth named Ladd, eager to see Dexter in his natural habitat, pretended that he was a peer recently arrived from England. Dexter was most gracious. He was concerned about only one thing. What had the King of England been saying about him recently?

It was very late. Perhaps he had a premonition, or perhaps it was only the all-too-human desire to know what others would say about him after he was gone, that inspired his last eccentric gesture. He announced a "mock founnel." As it turned out, the mock funeral was staged with full cast and accessories. It lacked only the leading man. Dexter sent invitations to friends and acquaintances throughout the state. He tried to obtain the services of a minister. Failing in that, he hired a Dr. Strong to officiate and deliver a eulogy. Learning that a Lord North was in the vicinity, Dexter invited him to serve as a pallbearer, then christened his other "grand pall-holders" Lord South, Lord East, and Lord West.

Half of Newburyport, three thousand persons by Dexter's estimate, lined the thoroughfares to watch the funeral procession. At the sight of the vacant coffin, Dexter was moved to report, "there was much Cring." Would it be disrespectful to suggest that there was much crying because the coffin was vacant? As the procession marched to his tomb, there to deposit the empty casket, Dexter watched from an upstairs window. The solemnities over, the mourners poured into the residence to partake of a grand feast and wine. The resurrected host did not appear at once. Loud screams and wails from a far quarter of the house revealed Lady Dexter in agony. Her Lord stood over her, severely caning her for having failed to shed a tear at the funeral.

In the autumn of 1806, in his fifty-ninth year, Timothy Dexter became very ill. For forty-eight hours he was semiconscious and incoherent, and on October 26, 1806, he was dead.

His will, written seven years before, was generous and

sensible. His estate amounted to $35,027, still considerable after the inroads made upon it by Samuel Dexter, Abraham Bishop, and the museum. Out of this sum he provided for his family and relatives. To a friend who was a teacher he left two shares of Essex Merrimack Bridge stock, as well as silver spoons and gold buttons. To Malden, whence he had come, and to Newburyport, where he had risen to greatness, he left liberal donations for the impoverished. His last request was that he be buried in the beloved tomb in his garden.

All of his requests were granted save the last. The Newburyport board of health determined that such a burial might be unsanitary. He was laid to rest in the attractive Old Hill Burying Ground. A plain stone was placed at his grave. Upon it was chiseled a reticent inscription:

In memory of Timothy Dexter who died Oct. 26, 1806,
Ætatis 60.
He gave liberal Donations
For the support of the Gospel;
For the benefit of the Poor,
And for other benevolent purposes.

Was this recital all that was to be remembered? Surely his closest ones would perpetuate his name. But two of them did not survive him long, and the third was hopelessly out of touch with reality. Samuel Dexter died on July 20, 1807, Elizabeth Dexter on July 3, 1809. Nancy Dexter lived on in the great house alone even after it had been rented out as a hotel and tavern, until her merciful passing in 1851. Her daughter by Bishop, Dexter's only grandchild, grew to maturity, married well, but died in her youth. She was the last of the Dexter line.

What else was left? The graven images? Their lives were all too brief. In the terrible tempest of 1815 that swept across Newburyport, most of the forty wooden statues were toppled to the ground, many of them disfigured by the storm. With what consent Nancy could give, they were placed on public auction. A number of them brought, sad to relate, only a "few dollars," and the others were consigned to a bonfire, among them the majestic representation of Lord Dexter himself, which had not brought a single offer.

All that remained, and these only until 1850, were Adams, Washington, and Jefferson, weatherbeaten under the royal arch. With Nancy's death, the mansion was sold to Dr. E. G. Kelley, a man of conservative if inartistic tastes, who removed the three presidents and fed them to "the flames." He, in turn, sold the residence to George H. Corliss, who restored it to the respectability it had known under Jonathan Jackson in pre-Dexterian days. Later, the residence was converted into a public library. Its varied proprietors had sentiment enough to leave untouched one last symbol of Dexter's glory. In a federal guidebook to Massachusetts, published in 1937, there is brief mention of the Jackson-Dexter house at 201 High Street. It gives passing notice to Dexter's greatness: "The ornate wood-encased chimneys, the watch-tower surmounted by a gilded eagle, the columns flanking the door, give an aspect of eccentric charm to this old dwelling. . . ." It was the golden eagle alone, the brave bird that had once soared as high as Dexter, that survived the depredations of the pedestrian-minded.

Of Dexter's personal friends only one remained true to his memory. Jonathan Plummer, in his star-spangled livery, followed his patron's death with a broadside entitled *Something New*. In it he concluded that Dexter's kindness and charity outweighed his faults and that in another world he would rest beside "the glorious company of Abraham, Isaac and Jacob." Soon even Plummer had to forsake Dexter. For within a year he was peddling a work, of which he was the author, entitled *Parson Pidgin: or, Holy Kissing . . . Occasioned by a Report that Parson Pidgin Had Kissed a Young Woman*. Thirteen years later, suffering a loss of his mental powers, the poet laureate went on a hunger strike and expired.

All the magnificence of Lord Timothy Dexter was gone except the "Littel book." Perhaps it was enough.

A NOTE ON

Principal Sources

ALMOST all of the American eccentrics in this book were prolific writers. And, with the exception of Norton, who limited his literary contributions to the daily press, and Symmes, whose articles were not compiled until after his death, all of them wrote books. The total product of their uninhibited, fanciful, and highly original pens would certainly make one of the most bizarre libraries in existence. For here, on a single shelf, might be found a slender volume in defense of suicide, another entirely devoid of punctuation, another castigating anti-Masons, and yet another proclaiming Shakespeare an imposter and an idiot.

Yet, without this library of oddity, it would have been difficult for me to have undertaken the research and writing of this book. For my best source of information on American eccentrics remained the creative works of the eccentrics themselves. These works are too many to list in detail, but I should like at least to mention the handful that was most illuminating in helping me portray their authors: *The Philosophy of the Plays of Shakspere Unfolded*, by Delia Bacon, London, 1857; *Euthanasia*, by James A. Harden-Hickey, New York, 1894; *Our Writers*, by James A. Harden-Hickey, Paris, 1887; *The Symmes Theory of Concentric Spheres*, by John Cleves Symmes, Louisville, 1878; *An American Merchant in Europe, Asia and Australia*, by George Francis Train, New York, 1857; *My Life in Many States and in Foreign Lands*, by George Francis Train, New York, 1902.

Besides reading the writings of the eccentrics, I spent delightful and amazed hours and days, over a period of twelve years, in the libraries of Los Angeles, New York, London, and Paris, reading letters, diaries, and various published material written by those who had known the eccentrics in person or had previously studied them.

Contemporary newspapers served me well. Though the news and feature stories were often biased and inaccurate, and much care had to be taken in evaluating them, the wealth of firsthand, living, breathing detail in each account gave reality to characters who sometimes seemed almost fictional. The newspapers I consulted ranged from *Le Triboulet* in Paris (files from 1878 to 1883) to the *Tribune* in New York (files from 1893 to 1898).

Articles in popular and scholarly periodicals were equally helpful. Of the great number that I examined, I found the following particularly useful: an article by W. E. Woodward, *The American Mercury*, New York, September 1927; an anonymous book review, *American Quarterly Review*, Philadelphia, March and June 1827; an article by P. Clark, *The Atlantic Monthly*, Boston, April 1873; an article by Robert Ernest Cowan, *California Historical Society Quarterly*, October 1923; articles by Wilbur Glenn Voliva, *Leaves of Healing*, Zion City, May 1930; an article by John Weld Peck, *Ohio Archaeological and Historical Quarterly*, Volume 18, 1909; an article by David Warren Ryder, *Plain Talk Magazine*, Washington, D.C., January 1928; articles by William Cleaves Todd, *New England Historical and Genealogical Register*, Boston, Volumes XL and XLI, 1886, and Volume XLIV, 1890; an article by Harold Frederic, *The Saturday Review*, August 3, 1895.

While the literature of American eccentricity is extremely limited, I did manage to find several hundred books that discussed—a few fully, but most in passing—the unusual personalities who interested me. Of these books, a small number proved especially valuable. To their authors and publishers, my grateful thanks: *Delia Bacon*, by Theodore Bacon, Boston, 1888; *Pilgrims Through Space and Time*, by J. O. Bailey, New York, 1947; *Real Soldiers of Fortune*, by Richard Harding Davis, New York, 1912; *The Great Cryptogram*, by Ignatius Donnelly, Chicago, 1888; *Recollections of Seventy Years*, by Mrs. John Farrar, Boston, 1866; *Jewish Pioneers and Patriots*, by Lee M. Friedman, New York, 1943; *Our Old Home*, by Nathaniel Hawthorne, New York, 1907; *Uncommon Scold*, by George Stuyvesant Jackson, Boston, 1937; *Emperor Norton*, by Allen Stanley Lane, Caldwell, Idaho, 1939; *Lord Timothy Dexter*, by J. P. Marquand, New York, 1925; *Books in Red and Black*, by Edmund Lester Pearson, New York,

1923; *The Life and Times of Anne Royall*, by Sarah Harvey Porter, Cedar Rapids, Iowa, 1909; *The Terrible Siren*, by Emanie Sachs, New York, 1928; *Uncommon Americans*, by Don C. Seitz, Indianapolis, 1925; *The English Eccentrics*, by Edith Sitwell, Stockholm, 1947; *History of Newburyport*, by Mrs. E. Vale Smith, Boston, 1854; *The Nine Lives of Citizen Train*, by Willis Thornton, New York, 1948; *Mr. Shakespeare of the Globe*, by Frayne Williams, New York, 1941.

Index

Academy of Natural Sciences (Philadelphia), 241
Academy of Sciences (San Francisco), 166
"An Account of Mrs. Woodhull," 129
Adams, John, 244, 254, 303, 312
Adams, John Quincy, 238, 243–6, 253, 282
Adams, Mrs. John Quincy, 245
Advancement of Learning, The, 187
Akin, James, engraver, 308
Alabama controversy, 98
Aldington, Richard, *quoted*, 14
Algoa Bay (South Africa), 150
Alta California, newspaper, 158, 165
Alwato (forerunner of Esperanto), 112
American Association of Spiritualists, 135
American Authors, 213
American Quarterly Review, 236–7
Ames, Oakes, Massachusetts congressman, 84–5
Andrews, Stephen Pearl, Negro scholar, 112–13, 120, 132, 143
Anglo-American Association, 146
Annawan (brig), 238–9
Anne, Queen, 246
Anthony, Susan B., 96, 116, 118, 132; *quoted*, 131
Apollo Hall (New York City), 119, 131–3
"Apostle of Protest," *see* Donnelly, Ignatius
Around the World in Eighty Days, 63–5
Ashe, Elizabeth, 14
Aspley, William, editor, 168
Atlantic and Great Western Railroad, 76
Atlantic Monthly, 235
Atlantis (continent), 25
Aubrey, John, 185
Ayesha, 15
Bacon, Alice Parks, mother of Delia Bacon, 176–7
Bacon, David, father of Delia Bacon, 176–7
Bacon, Delia Salter (168–222): 23; disputes authorship of Shakespeare plays, 173; to England, 175; birth and early life, 176–7; teaching career, 178; early writings, 179–80; meets McWhorter, 182; McWhorter trial, 184; proposes Groupist theory, 187–8; meets Carlyle, 189; to St. Albans, 190; her article published in *Putnam's Monthly*, 192; helped by Hawthorne, 197; to Stratford, 203; her book published, 208; committed to asylum, 221; death, 221; *quoted*, 168, 171, 188–93, 196–7, 204, 206, 209–11, 220
Bacon, Sir Francis, 171–2, 174–5, 187, 189–90, 194, 198, 200, 207–8, 210, 212–13, 216–18, 220
Bacon, George, nephew of Delia Bacon, 221
Bacon, Leonard, brother of Delia Bacon, 178, 182–4, 201; *quoted*, 202, 220–1
Bacon, Theodore, nephew of Delia Bacon, 178, 181; *quoted*, 180–2, 216
Bacon and Shakespeare: An Enquiry Touching Players, Playhouses and Play-Writers in the Days of Elizabeth, 213
Barbier, policeman, 165
Barnum, Phineas T., 89, 263–5
Barracouta (warship), 51
Bath (England), 16
Baudelaire, Charles, 12, 31
Beaconsfield, Lord, *see* Disraeli
Beckford, William, orientologist, 15–17, 20
Beecher, Catharine, sister of Harriet Beecher Stowe, 135, 177–8, 184

Beecher, Eunice Bullard, wife of Henry Ward Beecher, 125
Beecher, Henry Ward, 94, 123–9, 136–9, 144
Bellanger, Marguerite, 29
Bellingshausen, Fabian, explorer, 237
Bemis, George P., secretary of George Francis Train, 91
Bennett, James Gordon, 74
Bennoch, editor, 204–6
Bentley, Richard, publisher, 16
Bernhardt, Sarah, 29
Bible Myths, 42
Bible Plagiarisms, 38, 41
Biddle, Nicholas, banker, 245
Bishop, Abraham, husband of Nancy Dexter, 295–7, 311
Bishop, Nancy Dexter, *see* Dexter, Nancy
Bismarck, 162
Black, James, Prohibition Party candidate, 87–8
Black Book, or a Continuation of Travels in the United States, The, 244–5, 257
Black Friday (1869), 105–6
Blake, Grinfill, 118–19
Blake, Katherine D., *quoted*, 118–19
Blake, Lillie Devereux, 118–19, 134
Blatvatsky, Madame Helena P., spiritualist, 36–8
Blood, Colonel James Harvey, spiritualist and promoter, 103, 110–13, 120–1, 129, 133–4, 136, 139–40, 143
Blount, Edward, editor, 168
Blumenthal, Walter Hart, 268
Blunt, Edmund, publisher, 297, 308
Bly, Nellie, reporter, 64, 92–3
Bonaparte, Joseph, 254
Bonaparte, Louis-Napoleon (Napoleon III), 30, 33, 45, 61, 69, 74, 161, 165
Bonaparte, Napoleon (Napoleon I), 30, 155, 272, 303
Boni, Albert, publisher, 217
Boston Commercial, 254
Boston Daily News, 32
Boston Journal, 136
Bowen, Henry, publisher, 127
Bradley and Gilbert, publishers, 240
Bradshaw, Martha, deaconess, 127
Brazil, 26–7, 51–2, 57, 148, 150–1
Bredon's Norton College, 146
Bridgewater, 227
Bride of Fort Edward: A Dramatic Story, The, 180
British Museum, 144, 174, 190
Brooklyn Eagle, 145
Brooks, Alden, 218
Brooks, Van Wyck, 213
Brown, John, 162, 214
Brown, Solyman, 269
Browning, Elizabeth Barrett, 201
Brummell, Beau, 13–14
Bryant, William Cullen, 109
Bryce, James, historian, 20
Buchanan, James, 195
Buckhurst, Lord, 187, 210, 216
Bull Run, battle of, 79, 80
Bullard, Mrs., mother-in-law of Henry Ward Beecher, 127
Bullard, Eunice, *see* Beecher, Eunice Bullard
Bulwer-Lytton, Sir Edward, 190
Burbage, Richard, actor, 215
Burgoyne, General, 179
Burley, William, 305
Burnet, Professor, 228
Burr, Aaron, 270, 280, 303
Burton, 217
Butler, congressman, 138
Butler, stepfather of Anne Royall, 247
Butler, Mrs., mother of Anne Royall, 247–8
Butler, General Benjamin Franklin, 115–17
Butler, Charles, 175, 268
Butler, James, half-brother of Anne Royall, 247
Byrd, Admiral Richard E., 242
Byrd Expedition, 7
Byrnes, Thomas, police inspector, 145
Byron, Lady, 135
Byron, Lord, 15, 135

Cabinet: or, Large Parties in Washington, The, 265
California State Assembly, 164
Calvert, William, *see* Newport, William
Calvinism, 20, 258

Index

Carlotta, Empress of Mexico, 30
Carlyle, Jane, 189
Carlyle, Thomas, 68, 114, 174–5, 188, 195–6, 199, 205, 268; *quoted,* 189–91, 204
Carroll, Lewis, 99
Carter, Ohio judge, 133
Cary, Henry, editor, 55
Casanova, 15
Castiglione, Contessa Nicchia de, 29
Cato, *quoted,* 44
Cecil, Lord David, *quoted,* 13–14
Central Pacific Railroad, 162, 165
Chambord, Count Henri de, 33, 36
Champollion, Jean François, 270
Chapman, George, 219
Chester (New Hampshire), 298–300, 306
Chettle, Henry, 219
Chicago Times, 130
Christian Apostolic Church, 6
Christian Union, 135
Chute, Marchette, *quoted,* 219
Cincinnati National Intelligencer, 231
Citizens' Party, 87
Civil War (United States), 78–9
Claflin, Buckman, *see* Claflin, Reuben Buckman
Claflin, Reuben Buckman, father of Victoria Woodhull and Tennessee Claflin, 102, 107–8
Claflin, Roxanna, mother of Victoria Woodhull and Tennessee Claflin, 107–8, 121; *quoted,* 120
Claflin, Tennessee Celeste, 94, 102–3, 110–11, 114–15, 119, 133, 136–8, 140–2, 146–7; *quoted,* 104, 121
Clagget, M. E., Mason, 252–3
Claiborne, congressman, 263
Clark, P., student, 232; *quoted,* 235–6
Clemens, Samuel, *see* Twain, Mark
Cleveland Leader, 82, 121
Clifford, Ebenezer, architect, 302
Clinton, De Witt, governor, 255–6, 258, 280
Cluseret, General Gustave Paul, 90, 92
Coates, Robert, actor, 17–18, 20
Coffroth, James, Sr., 163
Cogswell, Anna, actress, 109
Coleridge, Samuel Taylor, 171; *quoted,* 170
Columbian Exposition (Chicago, 1893), 6, 96
Columbus, Christopher, 5, 8
Committee on Claims, 164
Common Sense, 274
Commonplace Book, 169
Communist Manifesto, 114
Comstock, Anthony, 25, 94, 137–8
conformity, American, 20–4
Congregational Ministerial Association, 184
Congress (ship), 285
Continental currency, 279–80, 289
Cook, Francis, husband of Tennessee Claflin, 146–7
Cook, Mrs. Francis, *see* Claflin, Tennessee Celeste
Cooper, James Fenimore, 109
Corliss, George H., 312
Cornbury, Lord, *see* Hyde, Edward
Cornwallis, Lord, 278
Cozzen's Hotel, 96
Coyle, John, 259
Crédit Foncier, 83
Crédit Mobilier, 83
Crédit Mobilier of America, 83–6
Cummings, E. E., 271

Daily Racing Form, 218
Darwin, Dr., 230
Daudet, Alphonse, 28
Davis, Jefferson, 69, 81, 162, 164
Davis, Paulina Wright, 116–17
Davis, Richard Harding, 47; *quoted,* 41–2, 46, 56
Davy, Sir H., 230
Deer Island Bridge, *see* Essex Merrimack Bridge
Delmonico, Charles, 114–15
Demblon, Celestin, professor, 218
Demosthenes, 100–1, 111, 113, 140–1
Dentologia: A Poem on the Diseases of the Teeth, 269
Derby, William Stanley, 6th earl of, 218, 220
de Vere, Edward, *see* Oxford, . . . 17th earl of
Dexter, Elizabeth Frothingham, wife of Timothy Dexter, 277, 293–6, 299, 304, 310–11

Dexter, Esther, sister of Timothy Dexter, 275
Dexter, Esther Brintnall, mother of Timothy Dexter, 274–5
Dexter, Nancy, daughter of Timothy Dexter, 277, 295–6, 304, 311–12
Dexter, Nathan, father of Timothy Dexter, 274
Dexter, Nathan, Jr., brother of Timothy Dexter, 275
Dexter, Samuel, son of Timothy Dexter, 277, 293–6, 304, 311
Dexter, Timothy (267–312): 23; *A Pickle for the Knowing Ones*, 268; birth and childhood, 274–5; to Newburyport, 276; Continental currency investment, 279–82; buys Tracy house, 283; business ventures, 285–8; Essex Merrimack Bridge, 291; children, 295–6; buys Jackson house, 300–3; *A Pickle for the Knowing Ones*, 308; mock funeral, 310; death, 310; *quoted*, 267, 269–70, 272, 275–6, 285–7, 291–2, 297–300, 302
Díaz, 166
Dickens, Charles, 13
Dictionary of American Biography, 213
Disraeli, Benjamin, 12, 166, 171; *quoted*, 170
Dobson, J., mathematician, 271
Dodge, Granville M., 84
Donnelly, Ignatius, Minnesota congressman, 25, 184, 195, 212, 214, 217
Dorret family, 253
Doubleday, Abner, 37
Dougles, Norman, 19
Douglass, Frederick, author, 133–4
Dowie, John Alexander, faith healer, 6
Dred Scott case, 154
Drew, Daniel, 105
Droeshout, Martin, engraver, 219
Du Bois, Henri Pene, reporter, *quoted*, 54–5
Dudley, 217
Dumas, Alexandre, 29, 91
Dunmore, Lord, 248
Durant, Thomas Clark, railroad builder, 84
Dyer, Sir Edward, 218

Ealer, George, 214
Eaton, John, senator, 259–60
Eaton, Peggy O'Neale Timberlake, 259–60
eccentric, definition of, 10–11
eccentricity, English, 13–20
Echo de Paris, 64
Edison, Thomas Alva, 37, 96
Elements of Geometry, The, 271
Elizabeth, Queen, 187–8, 216–18
Ellsmere, Lord, 213
Emerson, Ralph Waldo, 12, 68, 175, 188–92, 195, 273–4; *quoted*, 12, 173–4, 193–4
Emerson, William, brother of Ralph Waldo Emerson, 194
Emperor Norton, 161
Equal Rights Party, 87, 132, 134
Erie Railroad, 76, 105
Esperanto, 112
Essays, 198
Essex Merrimack Bridge, 291, 303–4, 311
Eugénie, Empress, 30, 69, 75, 158
Euler, Leonhard, mathematician, 229
Eureka Lodging House, 158
Euthanasia; the Aesthetics of Suicide, 42, 60
Euthanasia Society, 42
Evans, Thomas W., 34
Everleigh sisters, of Chicago, 105
Exit Shakspere, 215

Faerie Queene, The, 188
faith healing, *see* Dowie, James Alexander, and Claflin, Tennessee
Farelly, congressman from Pennsylvania, 225
Farquhar, John, munitions dealer, 16
Farrar, Eliza, author, 172, 181, 199, 203–4; *quoted*, 172, 202
Feminin Monarchi, or the Histori of Bees, The, 268
Fenian Insurrection (Ireland), 90
Feroe, Caroline, 15

Index

Fierpepin's Metamorphosis, 32
First Folio, 169, 171, 216–17
Fish, Hamilton, Secretary of State, 148
Fisher, Alexander M., teacher, 177
Flagler, Anna, *see* Harden-Hickey, Anna Flagler
Flagler, John Haldane, father of Anna Flagler, 57–8; *quoted*, 47, 59
Flaubert, 29
Flying Cloud (clipper ship), 68
Fogg, Phileas, 63–6, 89, 92, 94, 97
Fort Erie, 227, 241
Fort Sumter, 78
Fox, Katherine and Margaret, spiritualists, 109
Franco-Prussian War, 61, 162
Franklin, Benjamin, 256, 297, 302–3
Franklin, William, 274
Fraser's Magazine, 190, 204
Frederick the Great, 188
French Revolution, 188
Frothingham, Benjamin, first husband of Elizabeth Frothingham Dexter, 277
Fruits of Conceit and Flowers of Nonsense, 16
Fugitive Slave Law, 173
Fuller, Margaret, author, 180, 196
funding plan, 281–2

Gambetta, Leon, 61–2, 90–2
Gardner, Marshall B., author, 241
Garnett, Richard, author, 16
Garrick, David, actor, 17, 169
George III, King, 150, 165, 284, 303
Gibson, Charles Dana, 56
Gilman, governor of New Hampshire, 303
Glass, Francis, 269
Golden Age, 123
Golden Age Tract, 129
Goldsmith, Oliver, 12
Gompers, Samuel, *quoted*, 101, 115
Goncourts, 29
Grant, Jesse R., 110
Grant, Ulysses S., 86–8, 91, 106, 110, 139, 149, 162
Great American Crank, *see* Train, George Francis
Great Britain, 51–2, 57
Great Cryptogram, The, 214, 217
Great Republic (ship), 89
Great Tower, *see* Beckford, William
Greeley, Horace, editor, 87–8, 109, 125, 135; *quoted*, 121
Greeley, Mrs. Horace, 121
Green, H. E., 73
Green, Hetty, 22, 74
Groombridge and Sons, publishers, 206, 209

Halley, Edmund, astronomer, 229, 230
Hamilton, Alexander, 281–2, 302
Hamilton, Lady Emma, 16
Hancock, John, 280–2, 302–3
Hannastown, 247
Harden, Antoine de, 28
Harden, Jacques de, 28
Harrington: A Story of True Love, 214
Harris, H. E., stamp firm, 50
Hart, Joseph C., author, *quoted*, 170–1
Harte, Bret, 163
Hathaway, Anne, 185
Hawthorne, Nathaniel, 68, 171, 175, 186, 195–6, 198, 203–4, 206, 214, 220–1; *quoted*, 197, 199–202, 205, 207–9, 212–13, 222
Hawthorne, Sophia, wife of Nathaniel Hawthorne, 201, 213; *quoted*, 209
Harden-Hickey, Anna H. Flagler, wife of James Aloysius Harden-Hickey, 40–1, 60
Harden-Hickey, James Aloysius (25–60): plans concerning Trinidad, 26–7; birth and childhood, 28–9; schooling abroad, 30; publishes as Saint-Patrice, 31–2; editor of *Le Triboulet*, 34–6; and Theosophy, 37–8; visits Trinidad, 39–40; marriage, 41; *Euthanasia* published, 42; claims Trinidad, 45–57; suicide, 58; *quoted*, 25–8, 30, 35, 37–8, 40, 43–6, 48–9, 51–3, 58, 60
Haussmann, Baron, 30
Hays, John, first husband of Mary Hays McCauley, 305
Hazlitt, author, 199
Hearn, Lafcadio, 93

Hecock, shopkeeper, 256
Heine, 12
Henry II, King, 28
Henry, Patrick, 248
Henry IV, 217
Henshaw, Sarah, *quoted*, 181
Henslowe, Philip, theater owner, 215
Hepworth, George, 269
Herndon House, Omaha hotel, 95–6
Heth, Joyce, 263
Hetzel, Pierre Jule, publisher, 63
Hickey, E. C., father of James Harden-Hickey, 28
Hickey, Mrs. E. C., mother of James Harden-Hickey, 60
Hill, Frank Ernest, author, *quoted*, 219
Hilton, Henry, judge, 124
History of New York, A, 267
History of Newburyport, 273
History of the World, The, 198
Hobson, Dr. Richard, *quoted*, 19
Hoffman, Calvin, author, 218
Hoffman House (headquarters for Woodhull, Claflin and Co.), 104
Holberg, Baron, 229
Hollow Globe, A, 240
Holmes, Oliver Wendell, *quoted*, 273–4
Holy Trinity Church (Stratford), 206
Homer, 170
Homer (Ohio), 107
Hooker, Isabella Beecher, 116–18, 130
Hooper, Madam, fortuneteller, 304
Horne, Charles F., *quoted*, 64
Howard, Elizabeth, barmaid, 29
Hugo, Victor, 28
Hull, Moses, 133
Humanitarian, The, 145–6
Humboldt, Baron Alexander von, 230
Huntress, The, 265–6
Hyde, Edward, governor of New York, 22

Illustrations of Masonry, 254
Independent, 125
Independent Democrats, 87
Ingersoll, Robert, 124
Innocents Abroad, 163
International Workingman's Association, 115
Ipswich jail, 295
Irving, Washington, 267

Jackson, Andrew, 238, 260, 262
Jackson, Holbrook, author, 268
Jackson, Jonathan, partner of Nathaniel Tracy, 283–4, 300–1, 312
Jaggard, William and Isaac, printers, 168–9
James I, of Trinidad, *see* Harden-Hickey, James Aloysius
James II, King, 28
Janssen, Gerard, 219
Jay, John, 302
Jefferson, Joseph, 265
Jefferson, Thomas, 249, 257, 281–2, 303, 312
Johnson, Richard M., congressman from Kentucky, 223–5, 231, 263
Jonson, Ben, 188, 194, 211, 217, 219; *quoted*, 193
Jordan, Maggie, mistress of William Sharkey, 94–5
Joshua Norton and Company, 152
Journey to the Center of the Earth, 240
Journey to the Earth's Interior, 241
Joyce, James, 271
Julius Cæsar, 188

Kahn, Dr. Eugen, professor of psychiatry, 11
Kant, 12
Kelley, Dr. E. G., 312
King, Rufus, 302
King Lear, 148, 211
Knapp, Samuel Lorenzo, author, 273, 279, 287, 290, 295; *quoted*, 280, 294, 300–2, 309
Knight, E. F., 39
Kyd, Thomas, 219

La Boissière, Count de, 27, 38, 41, 46–7, 49–51, 56; *quoted*, 53–5
Lafayette, 248, 265, 280
Lampre, M., 35
Lancaster, Lucy, 305
Lane, Allen Stanley, author, 161
Lawrence, Herbert, surgeon, *quoted*, 169, 171

Index

Lee, 162
Lefranc, Abel, professor, 218
Leicester, Earl of, 171, 185, 188, 197
Leslie, Sir John, mathematician, 229, 240
Letters from Alabama, 257
Letters from a Yank, 32
Life and Adventures of Common Sense: an Historical Allegory, The, 169
Life of George Washington, 267
Life of Timothy Dexter, 280
"Light Between The Spheres," 231
Liliuokalani, Queen of Hawaii, 57
Lincoln, 78–9, 82, 162
Lincoln (alleged telegram), 164
Lincoln-Douglas debates, 154
Lincoln Hall (Wash., D.C.), 118
Lind, Jenny, 263
Lindner, Dr. Robert, *quoted*, 21
London American, 78
Longfellow, Henry Wadsworth, 149
Looney, J. Thomas, teacher, 218
Lord, John, father-in-law of Timothy Dexter, 277
Louis XIV, 268
Louis XV, 29
Louis XVI, 303
Louisville Courier, 70
Louisville Courier-Journal, 138
L'Ouverture, Toussaint, 303
Love in Society, A, 31
Love in Vendée, A, 33
"Love's Martyr," 179
Love's Labour's Lost, 208
Lucy, Sir Thomas, 185
Ludlow Street Jail, 137, 139
Lundy's Lane, battle of, 227, 241
Lyceum of Self Culture, 161
Lyons, W. F., professor, 240
Lytton, Lord, *see* Bulwer-Lytton, Edward

McBride, James, 234; *quoted*, 235
McCauley, George, 305
McCauley, Mary Hays, seer, 304–5
McClellan, General, 90
McCormick, Cyrus H., 83
McCrea, Jane, 179
McGill, James, revolutionary leader in Australia, 72–3
McHenry, James, 76
McKay, Donald, shipbuilder, 68
McWhorter, Alexander, 181–5
Macy, William H., 83
Madison, Dolly, 258
Magellan, 8
Malden (Massachusetts), 274–5, 311
Maltby firm, 179
Manners, Roger, *see* Rutland, . . . 15th earl of
María Cristina of Spain, Queen, 75–6
Marie Antoinette, 29, 301
Markowe, Ralston J., Hawaiian Royalist, 57, 59
Marlowe, Christopher, 216–18
Marquand, J. P., *quoted*, 274
Martin, John Biddulph, husband of Victoria Woodhull, 143–5; *quoted*, 142
Martin, Victoria Claflin Woodhull, *see* Woodhull, Victoria Claflin
Martin, William, minister, 249
Marx, Karl, 62, 115
Mason, James, 80–1
Mathelá, 268
Mather, Cotton, 229
Maupassant, Guy de, 28
Mavrockadatis (ship), 81
Maximilian, Emperor of Mexico, 30, 161
Mechanic's Library (San Francisco), 160
Mehitabel (brig), 285
Melbourne, 13
Memphis Appeal, 136
Merchants' Magazine, 74
Meres, Francis, 219
Mesmer, Friedrich, 107
"Metzengerstein," 179
Milesius of Spain, King, 28
Mill, John Stuart, 24, 141, 212; *quoted*, 24
Miller, William, preacher, 22
Miller's Station, 247
Mills, Darius Ogden, 97
Milton, 170
Mitchel, Dr. S. L., 230
Monarch Of The Seas (clipper ship), 68
Monroe, 223, 244
Monroe Doctrine, 52
Montagu, Edward Wortley, 14–15, 20

Montagu, Lady Mary Wortley, 14
Montaigne, 198–9
Montgomery, Earl of, 168–9
Morgan, William, bricklayer, 254–7
Morgan, Lodge and Fisher, publishers, 234
Morison, Samuel Eliot, *quoted*, 282–3
Morse, Mrs. Nathan B., mother of Elizabeth Tilton, 127
Mozart, Wolfgang, 15
Mr. William Shakespeares Comedies, Histories, & Tragedies, 168
"Ms. Found in a Bottle," 239
Mulliken, partner of Timothy Dexter, 277
Murdock, Charles A., printer, 157
Must You Conform?, 21
My Life in Many States and in Foreign Lands, 97

Napoleon I, *see* Bonaparte, Napoleon
Napoleon III, *see* Bonaparte, Louis-Napoleon
"Narrative of A. Gordon Pym," 240
Nast, Thomas, 88
National Aegis, 273
National Woman's Suffrage Association, 116
Nebraskan, The, 85
Nelson, Horatio, 268, 303
Nesmyth, senator from Oregon, 82
New England Religious Weekly, The, 265
New York and Harlem Railroad, 105
New York by Gas Light, 109
New York Central Railroad, 103, 105
New York Herald, 32, 73, 81, 103–4, 106, 113
New England Historical and Genealogical Register, 274, 281
New York Observer, 125
New York Sun, 84, 91
New York Times, 46, 49, 54–5, 59, 88, 122, 138
New York Tribune, 25–7, 45–7, 49, 53–4, 59, 87, 121
New York World, 64, 92–3, 122–3
Newburyport (Massachusetts), 268, 270, 272, 276–80, 282–94, 297–8, 300, 302, 304, 306, 308, 310–11
Newburyport Impartial Herald, 273, 290, 297–8, 308
Newcastle (England), 288–90
Newport, William, father of Anne Royall, 246–7
Newton, Sir Isaac, 228
Norton, John, father of Joshua Norton, 150, 165
Norton, Joshua Abraham (148–167): 98–9; birth and childhood, 150; to California, 151–2; declared bankrupt, 154; proclaims himself Emperor, 155; issues Bonds of the Empire, 157; taxes business houses, 158; civic funeral, 166; *quoted*, 148, 155–7, 162–3
Norton, Sarah, mother of Joshua Norton, 150
Nothing, 268
Novum Organum, 189
Nye, senator, 82

Oakland Daily News, 162
Occidental Lodge F. & A. M., 158
O'Connor, William Douglas, 214
O'Conor, Charles, attorney, 87–8
Ohio and Mississippi Railroad, 76
Ohio Archaeological and Historical Quarterly, 235
Olcott, Henry, lawyer, 36–7
Olney, Richard, Secretary of State, 53
On Liberty, 24
Orations of Demosthenes, 101
Origin, Tendencies, and Principles of Government, 113
Osbourne, Lloyd, 163, 166
Owen, Orville W., Detroit physician, 217
Our Old Home, 222
Our Writers, 28
Oxford, Edward de Vere, 17th earl of, 187, 210, 216, 218, 220

Pacific Club (San Francisco), 154
Pacific Union Club, 166
Paganini, 12
Paget, Lord, 187, 210, 216
Paine, Thomas, 249, 274

Index

Palmer, Joseph, 22
Palmer, N. B., 238
Palmerston, Lord, 213
Pantarchy, 113
Parker, publisher, 204–6
Parnell, 166
Parson Pidgin: or, Holy Kissing, 312
Pascal, 12
Paul Pry, 260, 262, 265
Peabody, Elizabeth, sister-in-law of Nathaniel Hawthorne, 175, 195, 197
Peale, Charles Wilson, painter, 20
Peale, Raphael, Rembrandt, Rubens, and Titian, sons of Charles Peale, 20
Pearl, Cora, 29
Peary, 242
Peck, John W., *quoted*, 231–2, 239
Pedro II, Emperor of Brazil, 148–50
Pembroke, Countess of, 216
Pembroke, Earl of, 168
Pendleton, Captain B., 238
Pennsylvania, 257
Perrere, Emile and Isaac, financiers, 83
Perry, Oliver Hazard, 227
Perry, Commodore Matthew, 73
Petaluma (California), 164
Philadelphia Press, 107
Philadelphia Saturday Courier, 179
Philadelphia Times, 182
Philosophical Society (London) 170
Philosophy of The Plays of Shakspere Unfolded, The, 208, 212
Pickle for the Knowing Ones: or Plain Truths in a Homespun Dress, A, 268–71, 273–4, 285, 297, 308
Pickwick Papers, The, 262
Pierce, Franklin, 195, 244, 266
Pilgrim's Progress, 268
Pitcher, Molly, *see* McCauley, Mary Hays
Pitman, Isaac, 112, 268
Pitt, William, 303
Pius VII, Pope, 19
Plummer, Jonathan, poet, 305, 312; *quoted*, 306–8
Plymouth Church (Brooklyn), 124, 138
Poe, Edgar Allan, 12, 179, 239–40
Pope, Alexander, poet, 187
Port Elizabeth (South Africa), 150
Potter, Charles F., 42
Priestess of the Occult, 37
Prohibition Party, 87
Punch, 33
Putnam, Israel, 274
Putnam's Magazine, 175, 190
Putnam's Monthly, 192–5, 213

Raleigh, Sir Walter, 172, 175, 187–8, 194, 198, 210, 216
Randolph, John, 245, 274
Recollections of Seventy Years, 172
Retreat, The (Hartford, Connecticut), 221
Revolution, The, 127
Reymart, New York judge, 132
Reynolds, Jeremiah N., 238–9
Reynolds, John N., 239
Rice, David, *quoted*, 220
Richard III, 216
Ripley, Sophy, 194
Riverside (California), 58, 60
Roane, William R., attorney, 251
Robertson, partner of Joshua Norton, 152
Robertson, John Mackinnon, *quoted*, 218
Robinson, Henry Morton, *quoted*, 12–13
Romance of Yachting, The, 170
Romanozov, Count, 238
Romeo and Juliet, 17
Roosevelt, Theodore, 147
Rosetta stone, 270
Ross, Sir James, explorer, 7
Rousseau, Jean Jacques, 9, 268
Routledge, publisher, 198, 201
Royal Society of London, 229
Royal Statistical Society, 145
Royall, Anne Newport (243–266): 23; interview with John Quincy Adams, 243–4; birth and childhood, 246–8; marriage, 249; widowed, 250; begins travels, 251; publication of first book, 254; helped by Masons, 256; founds *Paul Pry*, 260; meets Barnum, 263;

Royall (*continued*)
founds *The Huntress*, 265; death, 266; *quoted*, 243–5, 248–9, 251–3, 257–8, 260–6
Royall, William, husband of Anne Newport Royall, 248–9, 251, 265; *quoted*, 250
Ruggles, Benjamin, Ohio senator, 225
Russel, Thomas, merchant, 280–2
Russell, Lillian, 96
Russell, William H., *quoted*, 79–80
Rutland, Roger Manners, 15th earl of, 218, 220

Sachs, Emanie, author, 139
Sade, Marquis de, 38
Sage, Russell, 12
St. Albans, 174, 190–1
St. Louis Times, 110
Saint-Patrice, *see* Harden-Hickey, James Aloysius
Saint Paul's Church (Newburyport), 292
Saint-Pery, Countess de, 31
Salamanca, José de, banker, 75–6
Sally, *see* Stack, Sarah
San Francisco Bay Bridge, 162
San Francisco Bulletin, 154, 156
San Francisco Chronicle, 166
San Francisco Herald, 99
San Jacinto (ship), 80
San Martin, General, liberator of Peru, 39
Saratoga Hotel boycott, 124
Saturday Evening Post, 214
Saturday Review, 49–50, 56–7
Sauvaitre, L., publisher, 37
Scott, Major General, 156
Seaborn, Captain Adam, pseudonym, 236
Second Presbyterian Society (Newburyport), 292
Seligman, Joseph, 124
Selwyn, George, 13
Seraph (brig), 238–9
Seven Shakespeares, 216
Seward, Secretary of State, 78, 81
Seymour, J., publisher, 236
Shakespeare, William, 17, 42, 168–75, 185–6, 188–90, 192–5, 197–204, 206–8, 210–13, 215–19, 221–2; *quoted*, 168 (alleged)
Shakespeare Problem Solved, The, 205
Shakespearean Society (England), 213
Sharkey, William J., 94–5
Shaw, George Bernard, 217
Shelley, Mary, 10; *quoted*, 10
Shepheardes Calender, The, 210
Sherman, 84
Shiloh House (Zion City), 5–6
Sidney, Sir Philip, 187, 210
Simon, Dr. Carlton, 99
Sitwell, Edith, 13; *quoted*, 13
Sketches of History, Life and Manners in the United States, by a Traveller, 254
Slater, Gilbert, author, 216
Slidell, John, 80–1
Smith, Mrs. E. Vail, author, 308; *quoted*, 273, 290, 297
Smith, Joseph, Mormon, 255
Smith, Sydney, minister, 10, 14; *quoted*, 3, 9–10
Smith, William Henry, author, 212, 216
Smithweeke, John, editor, 168
Social Contract, 268
Something New, 312
Soto, Benito de, pirate, 39
Southard, Samuel L., Secretary of the Navy, 238
Southern Tour, A, 257
Souvenirs of a Gommeux, 30
Spenser, Edmund, 172, 175, 187–8, 208, 210, 217–18
spiritualism, *see* Claflin, Tennessee, and Woodhull, Victoria
Spitzka, Dr. Edward C., alienist, 99
Spotted Tail, Indian chief, 133
Stack, Sarah, editorial assistant to Anne Royall, 261–2
Stanley, William, *see* Derby, . . . 6th earl of
Stanton, Elizabeth Cady, 116–17, 127, 130–1, 136
Stein, Gertrude, 271
Steinway Hall, 128–31
Stevens, Thaddeus, politician, 255

Stevenson, Robert Louis, 163, 166; *quoted*, 163
Stowe, Harriet Beecher, author, 135, 177
Stratford on Avon (England) 168, 174, 185, 192, 202–3, 206–7, 209, 220–21
Strauss, Johann, 75
Strong, Dr., minister, 310
Strong, governor, 303
Suffrage Association, 130, 132, 134
suicide, *see* Euthanasia Society
Sulgrave Manor (England), 146
Sutter, John A., 150, 164
Sutter Bill, 164
Sweet Springs Mountain, 248
Symmes, Americus Vespucius, son of John Cleves Symmes, 227, 240–1
Symmes, John, judge, 226
Symmes, John Cleves (223–242): 23; proposes expedition to center of earth to Congress, 223; birth and childhood, 226; Army career, 227; theory of concentric spheres, 229; death, 239; *quoted*, 223, 228, 230, 232–4
Symmes's Cavity, 231
Symmes's Hole, 231, 242
Symmes Theory of Concentric Spheres, Demonstrating that the Earth Is Hollow, Habitable Within, and Widely Open About the Poles, 240
Symmes' Theory of Concentric Spheres (by James McBride), 234
"Symmes Theory of the Earth, The," 235
Symzonia; a Voyage of Discovery, 236

Tacoma Evening Ledger, 93
Tales of the Puritans, 179
Tallmadge (Ohio), 176–7
Tammany Hall, 88
Taylor, Nathaniel W., minister, 182–3
Taylor, Zachary, 69
Tehama House (San Francisco), 154
Temps, Le, 63
Ten Lost Tribes of Israel, 241
Tennesseean, a Novel Founded on Facts, The, 254
Terrett, Mrs., 203, 206
Terrible Siren, The, 139
Theobald, Bertram G., author, 215–16
"Theory of Concentric Spheres," 231
Theosophical Society, 37
Theosophist, The, 38
Theosophy, 37–8
Thiers, Adolphe, 61
Thomas, Captain Thomas, pirate, 300
Thompson, J. M., 29
Thoreau, 12
Tichnor and Fields, publishers, 209
Tilton, Elizabeth Richards, wife of Theodore Tilton, 124–8, 136
Tilton, Paul, son of Elizabeth Tilton, 126
Tilton, Theodore, 123–5, 127–30, 135, 137–8; *quoted*, 108, 111, 126
Timberlake, Peggy O'Neale, *see* Eaton, Peggy O'Neale Timberlake
Times, London, 39, 79, 91, 144, 191
To Meet Will Shakespeare, 219
Todd, William C., 280, 290; *quoted*, 277, 281, 289
Tour du monde en quatre-vingts jours, Le, 65
Townsend, George H., scholar, 212
Tracy, Nathaniel, merchant, 283–4, 293, 300
Tracy house, 298
Train, Elsey, son of George Francis Train, 71
Train, Colonel Enoch, second cousin of George Francis Train, 67, 69–70
Train, George, son of George Francis Train, 71
Train, George Francis (61–99): 23; around the world, 62; Phileas Fogg, 63–5; birth and childhood, 66–7; in shipping business, 67–70; to Australia, 70–3; further travels, 73–6; promotes railroads in Great Britain, 76–8; promotes Union Pacific Railroad and Crédit Mobilier of America, 83–5; enters politics,

86–8; around the world, 89–92; death, 99, 147; *quoted,* 61, 65–9, 75, 78, 81–4, 88–93, 95–9
Train, Susan (later Gulager), daughter of George Francis Train, 71
Train, Wilhelmina Wilkinson Davis, wife of George Francis Train, 69, 82
Train and Company, shippers, 67–8
Train Ligne, The, 94
Train's Penny Magazine, 97
Trent (ship), 79–80, 82
Triboulet, Le, 34–6
Trinidad, 26–7, 39, 45, 48, 50–2
Trollope, Mrs., author, 257
Troppmann, 29
Truth Seeker Company, 42
Tucker, Benjamin R., student, *quoted,* 139–40
Turner, Bessie, 125; *quoted,* 126
Tussaud, Madame, 29
Twain, Mark, 160, 163; *quoted,* 163, 214–15
Tweed, William Marcy ("Boss"), 88

Uncle Tom's Cabin, 124, 135
Union Pacific Railroad, 83–5, 89
University of California (Berkeley), 148–9
"Unparalleled Adventure of One Hans Pfall, The," 239–40

Van Buren, Martin, 263–4
Vanderbilt, Commodore Cornelius, 83, 102, 104–6, 111–12, 114, 134–5, 141–2; *quoted,* 103
Vanderbilt, Cornelius, Jr., 141
Vanderbilt, Frank C., wife of Cornelius Vanderbilt, 106
Vanderbilt, William, son of Cornelius Vanderbilt, 141–2
Vathek, 15
Venetia, 170
Verne, Jules, 61–6, 89, 240
Victoria, Queen, 147, 164
Victoria League, 131
Voliva, Wilbur Glenn (3–9): Zion City, 3; birth and childhood, 6; conception of the earth as flat, 7–8, 22; *quoted,* 3, 7–8
Voltaire, 9, 249–50
Voyages Extraordinaires, 63

Walker, greengrocer, 191, 198
Walker, Mary, doctor, 25
Wallace, Alfred Russel, 37
Walpole, Horace, *quoted,* 15
Walton Hall, *see* Waterton, Charles
Washington, George, 146, 244, 248, 256–7, 263, 267–8, 270, 278, 281, 302–3, 312
Washington Capital, 88
Washington Star, 266
Washington Vita, 269
Waterton, Charles, 18–20
Watson, physician, 238
Watterson, Henry, librarian of Congress, 259
Wayne, Anthony, 305
Webster, Daniel, 68–9, 99, 280
Weems, Mason, 267
What Would Christ Do About Syphilis?, 42
Whatcom (Washington), 93–4
Whiston, author, 228
White, Richard Grant, scholar, 195
Whitman, Walter, 12, 193, 214, 273–4
Wilkes, Captain Charles, 80–1
William IV, of England, 165
William of Orange, 28
Williams, Mrs. Delia, 177–8
Williams, Gertrude Marvin, *quoted,* 37
Wilson, Joseph, artist, 302–3
Wilson, Woodrow, 146
Woodhull, Byron, son of Victoria Woodhull, 109
Woodhull, Dr. Canning, husband of Victoria Woodhull, 108–9, 111, 120–2
Woodhull, Victoria Claflin (100–147): 23, 87–8; leaves Pittsburgh, 100; to New York, 101; meets Vanderbilt, 102; opens brokerage house, 103–6; birth and childhood, 106–8; marriage to Woodhull, 108; meets Blood, 110; founds *Weekly,* 113; Beecher-Tilton case, 123–30; nomination for President, 133; Beecher-Tilton case, 135–9; marriage to Martin, 142; death in

Woodhull (*continued*)
England, 147; *quoted*, 94, 100, 106–7, 117, 119, 120–3, 129–30, 132–3, 136–7
Woodhull, Zulu Maud, daughter of Victoria Woodhull, 109, 146
Woodhull & Claflin's Weekly, 113–14, 121–2, 131, 134, 136, 141, 143
Woodhull, Claflin and Company, brokerage house, 103, 105
Woodward, Professor, 228
Wrecker, The, 163
Wyatt, James, architect, 16

yellow fever epidemic (New Orleans, 1833), 66
Yerba Buena, 163

Zion City (Illinois), 3–8
Zion's Herald, 66

Irving Wallace

was born in Chicago in 1916 and raised in Kenosha, Wisconsin. Since he sold his first article (he was fifteen), he has been a working writer, and he now always has several book projects in hand in addition to motion-picture and magazine work. He somehow manages also to find free time for his other interests, which include art, literature, sports, politics, and criminology. His enduring fascination with bizarre personalities in history led to his writing The Fabulous Originals, *his first—and immediately successful—book, as well as to the writing of* The Square Pegs. *Mr. Wallace lives in Hollywood, is married, and is the father of two children.*

A NOTE ON THE TYPE

The text of this book was set on the Linotype in JANSON, a recutting made direct from the type cast from matrices made by Anton Janson. Whether or not Janson was of Dutch ancestry is not known, but it is known that he purchased a foundry and was a practicing type-founder in Leipzig during the years 1660 to 1687. Janson's first specimen sheet was issued in 1675. His successor issued a specimen sheet showing all of the Janson types in 1689.

His type is an excellent example of the influential and sturdy Dutch types that prevailed in England prior to the development by William Caslon of his own incomparable designs, which he evolved from these Dutch faces. The Dutch in their turn had been influenced by Garamond in France. The general tone of Janson, however, is darker than Garamond and has a sturdiness and substance quite different from its predecessors. It is a highly legible type, and its individual letters have a pleasing variety of design. Its heavy and light strokes make it sharp and clear, and the full-page effect is characterful and harmonious.

This book was composed, printed, and bound by KINGSPORT PRESS, INC., Kingsport, Tenn. Paper made by P. H. GLATFELTER CO., Spring Grove, Pa. Typography and binding based on designs by WARREN CHAPPELL.